# JUVENILE VICTIMIZATION

The authors would like to acknowledge the following publishers for permitting them to publish certain materials found throughout this book:

D. C. Heath and Company, Lexington, Massachusetts, for permission to publish materials for Yitzhak Bakal's *Closing Correctional Institutions,* 1973.

Reproduced by special permission for The Adjective Checklist by Harrison G. Gough and Alfrid B. Heilbrun, Jr. Copyright 1965. Published by Consulting Psychologists Press, Inc.

Little Brown and Company, Boston, Massachusetts, for permission to publish materials from David J. Rothman's *The Discovery of the Asylum,* 1971.

Macmillan Publishing Company, Inc., New York, New York, for permission to publish materials from Oscar Newman's *Defensible Space,* 1973.

# Juvenile Victimization
## The Institutional Paradox

Clemens Bartollas

*Sangamon State University*

Stuart J. Miller

*Washington and Jefferson College*

Simon Dinitz

*The Ohio State University*

SAGE PUBLICATIONS

Halsted Press Division
JOHN WILEY & SONS
New York — London — Sydney — Toronto

Distributed by Halsted Press, a Division of
John Wiley & Sons, Inc., New York


Printed in the United States of America

**Library of Congress Cataloging in Publication Data**

Bartollas, Clemens.
    Juvenile victimization.

    Bibliography:  p. 275
    1. Juvenile corrections—United States.    2. Rehabil-
itation of juvenile delinquents—United States.
3. Prison psychology.    I. Miller, Stuart J., 1938-
joint author.    II. Dinitz, Simon, joint author.
III. Title
HV9104.B35      365.973      76-3476
ISBN 0-470-05490-5




FIRST PRINTING

# CONTENTS

# DEDICATION

To those who won't make it.

# ACKNOWLEDGEMENTS

The authors would like to acknowledge gratefully the Ohio Youth Commission Officials and Research Staff, the director of the institution studied, and all of those institutional staff members who were willing to give of their time in making this study a success. That these officials were willing to permit study of the sensitive issues and behaviors described in this book demonstrates the professionalism and dedication to research of the Ohio Youth Commission and its staff members. The contribution of three men in particular—James Roberts, Donald Jenifer, and Edward Redd—was unsurpassed. Without the help of these three men, the gathering of much of the data and many of the insights would have been impossible. Also of great help were the many youth leaders and social workers who assisted in giving psychological tests, filling out research schedules, and whose years of experience contributed to the writing of this book. These institutional staff and officials may disagree with the authors' interpretation of the processes involved in institutional living. The authors accept full responsibility for any errors. Certainly, only continued research of this nature will clarify the issues and problems raised and lead us to a greater understanding of institutional living.

We cannot, of course, identify the youths who responded to our questions, interviews, and measurement schedules, but the book is dedicated to these boys. We can only tell them that their tolerance was critical, and that we hope that others will be spared their experiences in the future.

The authors would also like to thank Washington and Jefferson College for its support of one of the authors on sabbatical and its assistance on various typing and xeroxing phases of the study.

Professor Franco Ferracuti of the University of Rome provided unique and invaluable assistance with his analysis and interpretation of certain psychological tests. Dr. Alvin Smith of St. Andrew's College also provided analyses of inestimable value on certain of the statistical tests involved. Mr. Richard Vella read the manuscript and made many useful stylistic, theoretical, and organizational suggestions.

Special appreciation is due the Ohio State University Research Foundation for its support of various phases of this project. Of special assistance was Dr. Harry Allen of the Program for Research in Crime and Delinquency of the Ohio State University for the financial assistance he rendered. Don Smelser of the Ohio State University School of Medicine ably and efficiently undertook responsibility for the many different computer programs necessary for this analysis.

Also of assistance were Margaret Lewis, Christopher Sieverdes, Richard Baum, and Jeffrey Muris who all made helpful comments on the manuscript. Billie Fay Evans and Brenda Bulloch were helpful in the library research phases of the project.

One of the most helpful and hardest working of those who assisted us was Donna Furda. Miss Furda transcribed tapes, worked up tables, typed many drafts, and performed other administrative tasks which enabled the authors to keep the manuscript moving without interruption.

Finally, and as every researcher and author knows, none of the work would have been possible without the forbearance of their wives. To JoAnn, Jean, and Mim, we again offer our thanks, appreciation, and love.

—C.B.
—S.J.M.
—S.D.

# PREFACE

This book reports upon juvenile victimization in a correctional setting. The juvenile correctional facility was originally designed to protect youths from a wicked society and as an attempt to simulate a normal family setting. The idea was to develop a rational and efficient social organization which would rehabilitate juveniles. Like schools, colleges, universities, hospitals, churches, prisons, welfare structures, business and voluntary organizations, a bureaucratic format emerged to help each specific organization achieve its goals.

Organizations are characterized by specific objectives, have names, describe the activities of those performing jobs, and have "charts, rules manuals, evaluation systems and a host of other procedures designed to plot every movement and provide every member with a clear prescription of his duties" (Hage and Aiken, 1970: 8). These characteristics are designed to guarantee that the organization reaches its avowed goals.

As the study of these social organizations intensifies, other properties are being discovered and analyzed. These properties include "the degree of complexity, centralization, formalization, stratification, production, efficiency and job satisfaction" (Hage and Aiken, 1970: 15). The results of these organizational features are discussed in this book, but their general relevance for the study of corrections must first be specified.

The complexity of an organization is related to the knowledge and skills of its members. Jobs are created which require that their participants undergo long and rigorous training. Generally, persons at the top of the bureaucratic structure have the greatest amount of knowledge and training whereas those at the bottom have the least.

This situation has considerable ramifications for the institution's governance. In highly centralized institutions, those at the top pass down directives which integrate participant performance with institutional goals. The decisions which reach the lower-level participants either emphasize that power is at the top, or, in prisons, charge the employees with making decisions which keep the inmates quiet.

The result is that life becomes highly formalized. The formal rules passed down from above combine with the informal methods used by often callous or inadequately trained staff and result in a repressive atmosphere. The rules and codes which evolve are numerous and, as Hage and Aiken point out, sometimes "lead to rigidity and neglect of the social and psychological needs of organizational participants" (1970: 21).

Such rigidity inevitably contributes to the prison's stratification problems. In correctional settings, the staff become the enforcers of minute and trivial rules and the inmates become the targets of staff scrutiny and pronouncements as to what is normative and right. The governed normally do not participate within this system of power and rules.

According to Hage and Aiken, justification for the existence of an organization comes from its ability to prove its successfulness to both outsiders and participants. But the very nature of correctional organizations limits prison success. Hardly anybody would argue that prisons rehabilitate; neither would they argue that they operate efficiently or effectively. None would argue that the staff-inmate ratio is close to ideal. And no one argues that keeping people in prison costs less than supervising them in effective organizations in community corrections.

Part of the problem is that, whereas most institutions try to keep morale and loyalty high, the prison does not and cannot. The prison is built upon coercion rather than upon either rewards or moral persuasion. Staff are urged to follow the rules and do their job, and inmates are told what they may and may not do. Nothing in its structure generates job satisfaction, high morale, or loyalty.

Etzioni suggests that prisons are unlikely to succeed; the principal variable he emphasizes is compliance.

*Compliance* refers both to a relation in which an actor behaves in accordance with a directive supported by another actor's power, and to the orientation of the subordinated actor to the power applied. . . .

*Coercive* power rests on the application, or the threat of application, of physical sanctions such as infliction of pain, deformity, or death; generation of frustration through restriction of movement; or controlling through force the satisfaction of needs such as those for food, sex, comfort, and the like [Etzioni, 1975: 5].

Using force in this manner creates alienation and diminishes the potential effectiveness of remunerative or normative power. The coerced individual is seldom positively oriented toward any institution; indeed, prisoners are, almost to a person, alienated. Prisons will probably *never* be able to get their participants to accept their confinement positively. Coercion and alienation, taken together, characterize the prison and stamp it as one of the most extreme of society's institutions (Etzioni, 1975: 8-12). It takes clients from their families, separates them from community institutions which provide roots and security, places them in feared and dangerous milieus, and forbids them to act as normal human beings. The inmates must wear identical clothes, share common haircuts, act deferentially toward staff, inhibit signs of personal growth, request permission to perform the most minute and trivial acts, accept body searches, follow trivial rules, restrain self-initiative and creativity, and keep quiet about everything that is happening. Even if the participants were only mildly alienated, the use of coercion would "affect adversely such matters as morale, recruitment, socialization and communication, and thus reduce effectiveness" (Etzioni, 1975: 13).

The major problem in any coercive organization is the lower-level participants—in prisons, the inmates—who receive very few privileges and no rewards. Even release is gained simply by remaining confined a legally constituted period of time; practically all else is illicit. The caste structure of the institution prevents inmates from participating in activities which benefit them (Etzioni, 1975: 16-19). Indeed, if one examines what is happening in prisons all over the country, one wonders why rehabilitation was ever postulated as even a potential outcome of coerced confinement.

The prison is considered a "total institution," and differs from other forms of social organization in its use of "locked doors, high walls, barbed wire, cliffs and water, open terrain, and so forth" (Goffman, 1967: 472). All of the prison's occupants are jammed into the same general place, are responsible to one single authority, are forced to do the same thing at the same time as others who are similarly defined, and must follow a tight, inflexible schedule (Goffman, 1967: 473). Add these features to the ongoing bureaucratic processes and one can assess the insuperable problems confronting our correctional system.

This volume suggests that no formal structure, no matter how coercive, can deny or prevent a counter culture and structure from emerging. What the institution denies in the way of self-respect, freedom, privileges, normative standards, and benefits, the inmates create for themselves on a surreptititious but nevertheless very effective, level. This volume shows that inmates both create and import values which they integrate into a set of codes of living; that everyday life is regulated as much by the inmates as by their keepers; that the benefits denied them by their confinement are achieved in devious and often contemptable ways; that the hierarchical structure of the institution is mirrored by an equally hierarchical structure of the inmates; and that the two worlds of the staff and the inmates are separate and unequal.

This book represents four years and countless manhours of research of every kind. It cannot address all of the questions which criminologists now raise—indeterminancy versus flat sentencing, incapacitation versus rehabilitation, justice versus punishment, treating serious juvenile offenders as adult criminals, the problem of the status offender in the juvenile setting, and the reorganization and even abolition of the juvenile institution as a correctional goal. Nor does this book present any evidence or claim that the juvenile setting is in all ways comparable to the adult prison except in its structure which Hage and Aiken, Etzioni, Goffman, Sykes, and others have specified. Even less should anyone presume that the structure and functioning of the juvenile institution reflects the female prison, either juvenile or adult. Indeed, we already know that the female juvenile offender tends to develop a family system in the correctional setting, mimicking the world of her free sisters on the outside.

By the same token, while we enter these caveats against generalizing from this particular institution to the six-hundred or more juvenile and adult correctional facilities around the country, we do not imply that the similarities deriving from centralization, formalization, stratification, production, efficiency, and job satisfaction characteristic of all social organizations do not generalize across all correctional institutions. Although this is an end-of-the-line institution we studied, we know it is no worse than other institutions in the various states with which we are familiar. Undoubtedly it is better than most because of its *relatively* small population, its high student-staff ratio, its proximity to medical, psychiatric, and social services, and its treatment orientation. The pain of punishment is probably just as acute for the juvenile as for the adult and for the male as for the female. Victimization may vary in its subtlety, but hardly in its occurrence or impact in the discredited organization we call the "total institution."

# PART I

# INTRODUCTION AND BACKGROUND

CHAPTER 1

TOWARD THE DISSOLUTION
OF TRAINING SCHOOLS

In the 1840s, America established institutions for delinquents. In the 1970s, America is talking about dismantling those very same institutions. Why, after almost 130 years, is the United States turning its back on what was once believed to be the savior of the nation's wayward youth?

Certainly, those who founded juvenile institutions had high ideals, but the intervening 130 years have demonstrated that even good intentions may have their idealistic base destroyed by disastrous results. This book examines a little of that history, but, more importantly, its major focus is upon what happens in juvenile institutions that makes people want to dismantle them. Specifically, we examine one institution, which we believe has its counterparts in almost every state in the union. What happens in some facilities is no doubt far worse than that described in this book; relations in other institutions are, no doubt, far better. Nevertheless, for any youth viewing the outside from within, the processes described here must strike a respondent chord.

## THE EARLY HANDLING OF DELINQUENTS

In *The Discovery of the Asylum*, David Rothman graphically portrays the avenues considered by communities in the late 1700s and early 1800s when juveniles transgressed the boundaries of community propriety. Youth in those days did not know the meaning of incarceration, nor, for that matter, did anyone else. About the only time the local jails were used was to hold an offender until it was decided what to do with him. Indeed, even punishment was not generally considered useful in rehabilitation, as the colonists "placed little faith in the possibility of reform. Prevailing Calvinist doctrines that stressed the natural depravity of man and the powers of the devil hardly allowed such optimism" (Rothman, 1971: 53). The sinfulness of man, then, was what led juveniles to transgress the law.

The colonists were not totally pessimistic about controlling vice, for they believed that appropriate community reorganization should prevent deviance. The family, the church, and the network of community relations were all conceived of as important weapons in the battle against sin and crime. If these bodies functioned well, towns would be spared the turbulence of crime and enjoy a high degree of order and stability. To these ends, "Families were to raise the children to respect law and authority, the church was to oversee not only family discipline but adult behavior, and the members of the community were to supervise one another, to correct and detect the first signs of deviancy" (Rothman, 1971: 16).

Between 1790 and 1830, many dramatic changes, such as the growth of towns and the settlement of the new territories, made the old techniques of social control ineffective. One of the problems created by the new social conditions was the disorganization of society. The unsettled environment, rather than the natural depravity of man, now became the cause of delinquency. Ways were sought by which order and predictability could be put back into the lives of juvenile offenders. The answer was the house of refuge, "the well-ordered asylum," an institution which used the family as its model of organization (Rothman, 1971: 206-236). Of some importance is the fact that not only juveniles, but also adult criminals, the aged, the mentally ill, vagrants, orphans, unwed mothers, the lame, and the poor were put in institutions which

tried to order their lives and thereby guarantee their clients successful participation in society. The principle was simple: Construct the asylum, with all its variations, so that any resident could
not help but be programmed into moral and right ways of living.

To accomplish this end, these houses of refuge were constructed
with the greatest of care. Thus, early administrators left no part of
institutional design or program open to chance; details as exact as
the placement of heating and ventilating ducts, the type of furniture, and especially, the overall design of the building were
carefully calculated to provide the milieu appropriate for the
inculcation of order:

> Boys and girls occupied separate buildings, each structure of bare brick
> and unvarying design. . . . The buildings were usually four stories high,
> windowless, with two long hallways running along either side of a row
> of cells. The rooms following one after another, were all five by eight
> feet wide, seven feet high, windowless, with an iron-lattice slab for a
> door and flues for ventilation near the ceiling. . . . In keeping with the
> external design, all inmates wore uniforms of coarse and solid-colored
> material. No sooner did they enter the institution than they were
> stripped, washed, their hair cut to a standard length, and put into
> common dress. Managers appropriately claimed that the refuge's main
> object, that of reformation, is never lost sight of, in any of its regula-
> tions, and in all its discipline. From the entrance of the child, he
> becomes subject to a routine of duties . . . order and method [Roth-
> man, 1971: 266; quote from Boston Asylum and Farm School, 11:
> 1845].

The regularity of the institution's physical design was expected to
influence juveniles and this, combined with the scheduling of the
daily routine, conditioned them to conform to societal norms.

The routines of these asylum-like juvenile institutions exem-
plified the ideals of righteous living and of leading a narrowly
proper existence. Bells were often used to waken the inmates and
to announce each programmed activity of the day. From one area
of the institution to another, residents were lined up for periodic
head counts, marched to all activities, and even went to pray in
ranks (Rothman, 1971: 225-226). If youths did misbehave,
punishment was certain to follow and involved deprivation of
privileges, bread and water diet, solitary confinement, ball and
chain, whip, or any combination deemed appropriate by the
keepers.

According to Rothman, these institutions not only programmed
youths on the inside, but also protected them from the disor-

ganizing effects of the community. Consequently, houses of refuge were given the mandate to take the juvenile offender and

> remove him from the family and community, placing him in an artificially created and, therefore, corruption-free environment. Here he could learn all the vital lessons that others had ignored, while protected from the temptations of vice. A model and small scale society could solve the immediate problem and point the way to broader reforms [Rothman, 1971: 71].

This institutional experience, then, was to isolate offenders from all that might harm them and, at the same time, provide a well-ordered existence which would instill all the virtues necessary for a law-biding life in the community.

## FROM 1850 TO THE PRESENT

By the 1850s, confidence had waned in the ability of these houses of refuge to teach their moral program, and institutional directors were beginning to argue that custody was all they had to offer. The treatment regimen was disappearing as regulated routine became difficult and then impossible to maintain. State legislatures in the pre-civil war era allocated their funds elsewhere, while towns and cities continued sending their hard-core juveniles to populate the houses of refuge and recently built reformatories. The overcrowded institutions, the inadequate numbers of staff, and the deteriorated buildings confined large masses of clients for whom no rehabilitation programs were developed. Further, a number of factors, including the mixing of different types of clients and a large influx of immigrants, made the task next to impossible.

The industrial or training school was the next innovation in the treatment of juvenile offenders. Utilizing the cottage system, which generally involved a series of small house-type structures within a compound, training schools were opened in the 1840s and 1850s and, by 1900, were found in thirty-six states (Task Force Report: Juvenile Delinquency, 1967: 3). It was hoped that cottage "parents" could create a home-like atmosphere in these training schools and that the asylum-like effect of the houses of refuge and reformatories could be overcome. Considerable emphasis was also placed on hard work; youths, for example, were expected to farm land and take care of live-stock.

In the past seventy years, only minor modifications have taken place in how society deals with institutionalized delinquents. As the number of juvenile offenders increased, the types of juvenile institutions multiplied to include forestry and honor camps (minimum security), educational and vocational training schools (medium security), and end-of-the-line training schools (maximum security). Therapeutic techniques, considerably more advanced, now attempt to deal with clients' psychological and behavioral problems by initiating individualized treatment. Juveniles are able to graduate from state-accredited high school programs while attending training schools, and some youths are permitted to work in the community during the day. Weekend home visits, too, are presently part of the treatment program in many institutions. Yet, little evidence exists that such programs are sophisticated enough to prevent recidivism (Robinson and Smith, 1969; Hood, 1967).

Unquestionably, juvenile facilities are designed to protect society from those considered dangerous. Barriers to the outside emphasize that the participants are limited to members of their own kind, and little emphasis is placed on helping inmates develop normal relationships. Most states continue to dwell upon institutionalizing their juvenile offenders because citizens remain dedicated to the concept of "locking them up and throwing away the key." In 1972, for instance, nearly 43,000 boys and girls were in residence at 384 training schools in this country (Carter et al., 1975).

A gradual movement toward deinstitutionalization, however, has taken place throughout this century. Certainly, probation has played a significant role in this movement, and many delinquents are now kept in the community under the supervision of a probation officer. As long as juveniles comply with their probational terms, they can avoid institutionalization. Foster homes and community treatment centers, in addition, have become important alternatives to incarceration. California, specifically, has been involved in a process of deinstitutionalization since the mid-1960s. Upon discovering that community resources are a great deal more economical and as successful, the California Youth Authority is placing more and more of its youths in community treatment programs (Warren, 1967).

## CLOSING OF TRAINING SCHOOLS IN MASSACHUSETTS

This movement toward deinstitutionalization was clearly stimulated by the shocking news that Massachusetts was closing all of its juvenile institutions. In August 1969, the governor of Massachusetts signed into law an act which was to lay the groundwork for this dissolution (Rutherford, 1974: 5). The reasons for dismantling the schools reflected an increasing awareness of the negative impact of juvenile institutions and was given impetus by scandals and disclosures made in Massachusetts since 1965.

In this state, the professional staff spent their time in writing reports rather than in contact with clients. The lack of preparation of other staff for their jobs meant that the reports would have little practical value in working with the youths even if utilized.

> The treatment of youths inside the institutions was at best custodial, and at worst, punitive and repressive. Marching, shaved heads, and enforced periods of long silences were regular occurrences. Punitive staff used force, made recalcitrant children drink water from toilets, or scrub floors on their hands and knees for hours on end. Solitary confinement was also used extensively and rationalized as a mode of treatment for those who needed it [Bakal, 1973: 154].

Other features of the system were also faulty. Autonomous institutions caused little genuine communication between the central authority and its institutional subdivisions. Officials went their own way, hired the staff they wanted, and initiated the procedures they felt most conducive for handling the age groups assigned them. Lack of funds prohibited the hiring of qualified staff, and those already in the system appeared unlikely to accept any new programs with either enthusiasm or commitment (Bakal, 1973: 154).

Not only were institutional programs and schooling lacking, but coordination among facilities and the probation and parole system was "disjointed and incoherent." The latter served more as a police force than as a champion for its clients. The result was identical to that caused by many similar institutions; youths were often more delinquent and bitter after their stay than before entrance into the system. Children who started their deviant careers merely as truant or incorrigible often ended up as hard-core offenders confined to adult penal facilities, an outcome clearly working both to their disadvantage and to society's.

By September 1970, one training school had been closed and, by 1971, the decision was made to close the rest of the Massachusetts schools. Almost a century and a half had elapsed since the first asylums for juveniles had opened their doors, and reformers had required all of that time to finally convince the public of the deleterious conditions that existed and of the harm which befell inmates.

Although the public has begun to awaken to the internal nature of its facilities, the dissolution of the Massachusetts schools remains unique in the annals of penal history. Prior to a series of scandals and exposés, the only people aware of the character of these training centers were professionals and a few parties interested in penal reform. The tight security, secrecy, and unwillingness of most correctional officials to open their doors to outside observers had prevented the public from knowing what life in them was like. Hidden still is the knowledge of how closely life in juvenile institutions parallels that found in adult institutions—a problem with which the public is more familiar. This book is written to help overcome that lack of information and is an examination of the types of relationships which transpire within walls of a juvenile institution.

## KEY ISSUES IN JUVENILE INSTITUTIONS

In this historical sketch of the hopeful beginnings and the partial dissolutions of juvenile institutions, the theoretical considerations have been kept separate. What, then, are the crucial theoretical issues which are pivotal in evaluating juvenile institutions?

### Organizational Goals and Client Compliance

One basic issue of juvenile corrections is that institutional goals do not reflect inmate goals. These goals, in fact, are often so far removed from providing viable alternatives to the subcultural goals of inmates, that the inmate world is pushed to ever greater cohesiveness. On the one hand, Lefton and Rosengren (1966: 802-810) suggest that today's institutions are beginning to substitute humanitarian values and an ethic of service for simple economic and bureaucratic efficiency. This trend toward service negates many of the old definitions of custody which are still extant in today's penal facilities. But, on the other hand, they acknowledge that most contemporary considerations of institutions ignore the clients they serve, focusing on formal bureaucratic structures, the relationship of the organization to the community, the relation of the organization as subsystem to other subsystems, and the view of organizations as systems of roles, identities, and symbols (Lefton and Rosengren, 1966: 804).

Studies are increasingly attempting to examine the nature of the relationship between goals and client behavior. Not surprisingly, because of their emphasis on organizational rules and lack of interest in clients, inmates in both adult and juvenile corrections have low conformity, low commitment, and a general lack of compliance to organizational goals (Clemmer, 1958; McCorkle and Korn, 1954; Sykes, 1958; Wheeler, 1961). Certainly, whether an institution is oriented toward custody or rehabilitation is reflected in the cooperation, acceptance, and harmonious relations found among staff and inmates (Street et al., 1966; Mouledous, 1963; Berk, 1966). Custodially oriented prisons, for instance, generate hostility, suspicion, and fearfulness among staff and inmates (McCorkle, 1956; Sykes, 1958; McCleery, 1961; Clemmer, 1940). Conversely, treatment-oriented juvenile training schools are observed to generate more trusting relationships with staff, less suspicion, and more cooperation among inmates (Street et al., 1966; Berk, 1966; Grusky, 1958-1959, 1959-1960; Street, 1965; Zald, 1960).

## Organizational Processing

To maintain control, staff believe that all facets of the inmates' lives providing them with a modicum of freedom must be regimented. Youths, thus, are stripped off anything providing a sense of security, identity, or independence. Further, authorities regulate all institutional activities by rules and plan them in order to allow the institution to reach its goals. The rules are looked upon as so necessary that the staff usually enforce them with a vigor seldom found elsewhere in society. Staff interpret adherence to these rules as a sign that inmates are showing progress and will eventually be fit for readmittance to the outside world. The signs of ingenuity, intelligence, or freedom of the will that distinguish the normal, thinking person are regarded as intransigence or sickness (Goffman, 1961).

Today, though censorship of mail usually is a thing of the past, physical movements are still restricted by the need for many permissions, and search lines are set up to determine whether contraband is being moved from one section of the training school to another. In some institutions, such movements must be done without comment, and the incarcerated are required to react to their peers as if they were automatons—faceless, humorless, and, indeed, without humanity. Talking in some training schools must be done in whispers. Even in more permissive settings, staff are suspicious of any deviation from normal behavior and use the slightest infraction as an excuse to prolong institutionalization. Through all this, the captive must exhibit appropriate demeanor and deference, aware that failure to do so may well result in punishment (Goffman, 1961).

## Mortification

Society's definition of juvenile offenders as deviants and of their acts as reprehensible is brought home again and again in the institutional milieu. Evidences of home-world identities, such as clothes, watches, money, and other personal items are stripped away and replaced by drab institutional clothing. All this, of course, has adverse impact on the self-esteem of juveniles. On top of the loss of personal identity items and the inability to respond to fellow inmates as human beings in free intercourse is the degrading manner in which juveniles are treated by staff. The barking of orders, the harsh tone of voice, and the deriding comment have long been found in juvenile institutions and contribute to the reason why staff tend to be looked upon as hostile, indifferent, condescending, and self-seeking (Bartollas et al., 1975[a]; Miller et al., 1975).

Juveniles' self-concepts are further challenged and devalued by relationships with fellow inmates. They are forced against their will to associate with those whom they may consider the dregs of society (Matza, 1964: 48-49). Not only do they find themselves in daily interaction with these dregs, but they are dependent upon them for status and well-being. The male newcomer, for instance, is quickly apprised of the fact that he must prove himself, for in his initial contacts with other inmates he is sized up and assigned a place in the inmate hierarchy (Polsky, 1962; Rose, 1959; Giallombardo, 1974; Barker and Adams, 1959; Fisher, 1961; Jesness, 1965). If tough enough, he may become an inmate leader; if weak, he will likely end up on or near the bottom of the peer hierarchy. Thus, inmates with status may recover some of their lost rights, while those with low status may lose everything.

The constant threat and occasional use of violence bring home vividly the terrifying nature of this social world. If physical strength is not one of his talents, the new inmate must either outsmart and outtalk those who attempt to exploit him, or he must feign bravery and toughness so convincingly that he is not challenged. Should his performance fail, he may be subject to the most devastating blow of all—he is sexually exploited. This traumatic event often destroys self-worth, compounding even further the problem of his reentry into the outside world.

## Boredom of Institutional Living

Beyond the problems inherent in living under institutional rules—that is, being mortified by the socialization process upon entry, having to prove oneself in order to gain an accepted position in the inmate hierarchy, and fighting to maintain possession of those small things granting some measure of self-esteem—youths must cope with the boredom and drudgery of institutional life. Since time is programmed from the moment of waking, days appear to be an endless succession of time schedules to be met and places to go for scheduled trivia. Free time means reading the same old magazines, playing cards with the same old group, playing softball, basketball, or watching television with the same old faces. This monotonous programming leads residents to dread the endless days and to look forward to their release with a passion understood only by fellow inmates. Little wonder that getting out becomes their primary goal and that they go to any length possible to persuade their keepers of their readiness to go home.

## Solidarity of the Inmate Society

One of the most interesting features of research in adult corrections over the past thirty years is the discovery and description of social roles. Functional for the inmate population, the argot roles indicate the interests and statuses of those found in institutions (Clemmer, 1958; Sykes, 1958; Schrag, 1944; Giallombardo, 1966; Ward and Kassebaum, 1965). The most well known of these argot roles are the "right guys," "square johns," "politicians," "merchants," "wolves," "punks," "gal boys," "queens," and "butches." Interaction among these different types results in the dynamics which give institutional life the form it takes. The patterns emerging from their interaction provide the basis for the inmate subculture into which newcomers are socialized.

Although little research focuses on the importance of social roles in juvenile institutions, enough exists to indicate that these roles are quite influential in the formation of the inmate subculture. Polsky, for instance, described the "bushboy" and "scapegoat" in analyzing the social struggle of Cottage Six (Polsky, 1962). Further, Rose portrayed the behavior of boys who occupied the status positions of leader, lieutenants, leader aspirants, followers, independents, and the rejected (Rose, 1959). In her study of three training schools for girls, Giallombardo (1974) identified these social roles: "finks," "snitchers," "squares," "straights," "sissies," "true butches," "true fems," "jive time butches," "jive time fems," "squealers," "studs," "pimps," "foxes," and "popcorns."

In addition to roles, the norms and symbols making up the inmate subculture constitute part of the world in which newcomers are immersed. While the inmate code has not been explicitly studied in jivenile institutions, it has received considerable attention in adult facilities. Some believe, for example, that the inmate code unites the inmate society against the staff world (Sykes and Messinger, 1960; Wellford, 1967; Tittle, 1972; Wilson and Snodgrass, 1969). Others, however, challenge the idea of this "solidary opposition" to staff, suggesting that inmates are actually splintered into many groups (Irwin and Cressey, 1962; Giallombardo, 1966; Ward and Kassebaum, 1965; Irwin, 1970). A further question is whether prison norms are the result of the institution's character (Heffernan, 1972; Thomas and Foster, 1973). Some argue, for example, that the prison is a microcosm of the outside world with its values and goals entering into and becoming a means of organizing inmates' values and style of life. Opposing this argument is that which describes the prison as a generating force of its own, producing a type of relationship peculiar to the institutional setting.

## Modes of Adaptation

How do institutionalized juveniles adapt to their incarceration? Over the past 130 years, juveniles, like adult felons and mental patients, have learned ways of coping with their confinement. They have learned, in particular, that rules must not be violated if an early release is to be attained, or, if they are, violated so that no one suspects the offender. The techniques for coping with institutionalization have been delineated by Goffman and comprise situational withdrawal, rebellion, colonization, conversion, and playing it cool (Goffman, 1961).

Withdrawal ranges from social isolation from all but a few friends to psychosis or suicide. Certainly, the assignment to a room, cell, or dormitory with others makes self-isolation and privacy difficult. Indeed, one gets up in front of others, dresses in front of others, defecates in front of others, and if the urge to relieve oneself sexually arises, this, too, must be done under circumstances where it is obvious that others know. In fact, privacy is sometimes only achieved by going to the library, to the chapel, or simply by sitting alone in a corner pretending to watch television. Apparently the need for some degree of social isolation to maintain self-respect not surprisingly forces some to choose extreme means of withdrawing.

Rebellion, on the other hand, consists of confronting the institution and its staff at every turn possible and involves a commitment to knowing the institution so well that staff control is reduced. Refusing to go along with rules or, if obeying orders, complying with such contempt that intentions cannot be mistaken indicates to others that the institution cannot achieve anything resembling total victory over the self. In the most extreme cases, of course, dissatisfaction is expressed by riot. While the chances of a successful riot are very small, this rebellion certainly reveals that the will and the sense of self are still intact.

Colonization is yet another way the best may be gleaned from the prison experience. Creature comfort requires that needs be met; for some, the benefits gained through incarceration outweigh those received in the community. Even though few would choose incarceration over life in the community, the fact remains that many inmates are able to accrue the necessities, if not the amenities, for life in confinement.

Conversion, which involves taking the staff line, is one of the most popular modes of adjustment. The task, of course, is to make staff feel that the inmate is inculcating their values. That is to say, the image must be presented that the institutional experience is beneficial and that benefits are received from the stay. Since fawning attitudes do work, inmates must consider adopting this ploy in demeanor and tone of voice, if staff are to be convinced of their sincerity. Although confronted by the reality that peers resent his "selling out," the inmate who chooses this adjustment knows also that staff will reward him when writing their reports and will expedite his parole.

Finally, those who wish to have little to do either with staff or fellow inmates find that a thin line may be walked between both, giving allegiance to neither the institution nor its clients. "Playing it cool" allows minimal commitment to both inmate and staff worlds, permitting its perpetrator to "do time" without paying homage to either. Minimal concessions are made to each world, so that neither challenges the lack of obedience. The inmate "bends with the wind" and pays lip service to the ideas and ideologies of those who wish to know whether he knows his part. He learns little from either world and passes from the institution only embittered by his experiences.

## Who Runs Juvenile Institutions?

One of the most intriguing aspects of prison life is the way informal power of the confined mitigates the formal authority of staff (Morris et al., 1961; McCleery, 1961; McCorkle, 1956; McCorkle and Korn, 1954; Sykes, 1958). Indeed, the legitimate authority of the staff often blends into and sometimes becomes subservient to that of prisoners. Strong inmates terrorize staff as effectively as they do other inmates. Staff find their orders laughed at, ignored, subverted, or in some manner refused.

Even though youths are younger, smaller, more dependent, and usually kept under closer surveillance than are adults, outside an institution, they resent the authority and control of staff inside and do everything possible to attenuate that control. Staff, faced with resistance, attempt to maintain control by any means possible. Highly desired jobs are given to the strong in exchange for keeping the institution quiet; new inmates are bartered to older ones for help in running the institution (Polsky, 1962).

Similar to staff in adult institutions, juvenile staff concerned about giving treatment or therapy find themselves under pressure from other staff not to do more than that for which they are paid. Staff must either accept the low pay and be co-opted into the normal operating procedures of the training school or find themselves frustrated and feel the need to "move on" (Bartollas, 1975a).

Efficacy of Institutionalization

The most important issue, of course, relates to the efficacy of institutionalization. Is the training school experience so punitive and destructive that no resident can benefit from an institutional stay? Or are those who argue that some juvenile offenders need confinement and isolation from society correct? What is the effectiveness of treatment within institutional settings? Are some training schools more therapeutic than others? While primarily impressionistic answers have been given to these questions, Hood concluded from his review of criminological research that lengthy institutional sentences are no more successful than shorter ones, that fines are more successful than probation or institutionalization with both first offenders and recidivists in all age groups, that open institutions seem to be at least as effective as closed ones for the "better type of offender," and that different treatment efforts made little or no difference in subsequent criminal behavior (Hood, 1967). Of importance also is the research finding of the Community Treatment Program in California that institutional experience did not lower the recidivism rate for seven of the eight I-level delinquent subtypes (Warren, 1967).

This book, in addition to describing the exploitative relationships which take place in a juvenile institution, discusses either explicitly or implicitly these theoretical and practical issues.

*CHAPTER 2*

## INSTITUTIONAL HISTORY AND SETTING

**The Ohio Youth Commission** is responsible for the institution under review. Therefore, before discussing the institutional setting of this study, some attention should be given the history and current emphasis of this commission.

The state of Ohio built its first institution for juveniles in 1857. The Boys' Industrial School (now the Fairfield School for Boys) was based on the "family model," and housed youths in cottages holding forty clients each. Eleven years later, the Ohio Legislature created the Industrial School for Girls (now Scioto Village). The Ohio Department of Public Welfare in 1921 was charged with administering the Boys' and Girls' Industrial Schools and, in 1949, established the Division of Juvenile Research, Classification and Training. Another change transpired in 1954 when this new division was placed under the Department of Mental Hygiene and Correction and renamed the Juvenile Diagnostic Center. From that point on, all youths judged delinquent were sent to this center for diagnosis before being assigned to state institutions. Then the Ohio Youth Commission was created as an autonomous department of state government in 1963. The governor was charged with appointing the executive director and two deputy directors and they, in turn, were confirmed by the State Senate—with one deputy director in charge of corrections and the other in charge of community services. Throughout the 1960s, the Ohio Youth Commission was kept busy constructing and staffing new facilities to house the increasing numbers of delinquents being sent to state facilities. By 1972, the OYC had grown to eleven institutions and its 1972-1973 biennium operating budget was $54,137,187 (see Appendix C).

These institutions hold close to 2,500 youths; of these, 79 percent are male and 21 percent female. The males range between ten and eighteen years of age (averaging 16) and the females between twelve and eighteen (averaging 15). Of the total population, 48.7 percent are white males, 32.4 percent nonwhite males, 11.5 percent white females, and 6.2 percent nonwhite females. Two-thirds of the youths come from broken homes, and the fathers of the majority of them are blue-collar and unskilled laborers.[1] The commission employs 660 youth leaders, of whom 60 percent are male and, of the total 660, 54 percent are black. They range in age between 19 and 67 years old (averaging 36.3); their average employment is 5.5 years. The job of these youth leaders, as well as that of social workers and other professional staff, is to implant the goals of the commission in their 2,500 charges.

The philosophy of the various institutions reflects a concern for rehabilitation. Here are several of their stated goals as taken from OYC descriptions:

> To create an environment in which each resident feels a sense of personal dignity and worth and to prepare him for return to his community as a responsible individual.

> To rehabilitate residents through a positive school experience and intensive treatment program so they can return to their communities and lead wholesome lives.

> To create and maintain an atmosphere of individual respect and dignity so that residents will learn to accept responsibility and realize that personal growth must ultimately come from within one's self.

The offender actually ends up in a training school only after being unable to adjust to the various community treatment programs offered by the Ohio Youth Commission. Several offenses are normally required before local judges and probation officers lose patience and decide to institutionalize the youth. Prior to institutionalization, for example, foster homes, special schooling, or professional counseling may be attempted, whatever is appropriate for the case. Needless to say, if these fail, the youth finds himself incarcerated. Beginning with minimum or medium security facilities, many progress to more secure institutions because of additional delinquent behavior in the community, running away, or behavioral problems created in their present institutions. At the time of this study, Riverview School for Girls and the institution studied in this book represented the end-of-the-line maximum security settings in the state.

## THE SETTING

To arrive at the subject of this study, one drives through the grounds of the state hospital for the mentally ill, a massive, imposing structure built in the 1800s and exemplifying an asylum of the highest order. About a half-mile beyond the asylum is the juvenile institution. Located on twenty-one acres, reflecting a pastoral scene (in the middle of Columbus), the institution is linked not only to the great asylums of the past, but to the isolated "total institution" of the twentieth century.

Built in 1961 at a basic cost of over two million dollars (the equipment was extra), and presently requiring $154,332.00 a year for maintenance and another $671,103 for staff salaries (per student cost is $6,000 per year), the building is a rambling, one-storey, red brick structure with wings angling away from the central admissions area. The land between and beyond the wings is enclosed with a high fence designed to provide the youths with a softball field, outdoor basketball courts, track and football fields— as well as keep the youths secure. Open areas around several sides of the institution permit easy surveillance for some distance, providing runaways with little opportunity for a head start.

The front section of the facility holds offices for 24 of the institution's 145 staff members, including a small library used for conferences and a room for institutional records. Before gaining entrance to the boys' side of the institution, the visitor signs in at the switchboard to obtain the necessary permission and escort before going any further. After the visitor leaves the switchboard, the switchboard operator pushes a buzzer which opens one of two heavy, reinforced glass doors allowing the visitor to enter a twenty-foot hallway at the end of which is a second door; upon ringing a buzzer, an ever-watchful secretary pushes a button admitting the visitor into the main part of the institution. Here, on the visitor's right and left are two long hallways containing offices for other supervisors and staff and a large desk in the center, which has another secretary behind it. Stretching out before the visitor is a long corridor with regularly spaced, small, screen-covered windows at head height. Twenty-five yards ahead is the junction of two more long corridors, each appropriately named for a popular street in Columbus. The corridor continuing from the central offices extends approximately another one hundred yards, and has several adjoining hallways which contain the chapel, the gymnasium, and the educational and vocational areas. The corridors going off to the visitor's right and left contain storage rooms, the nurse's office, and the canteen, and—most importantly—the eight cottages in which the youths live. This is a huge building—the cottages farthest from the front switchboard are a quarter of a mile away and some supervisory staff move around the institution in a small electric golf cart. As one publication noted, the long corridors facilitate good supervision of the inmates and protect them from inclement weather.

Although the institution houses 192 boys, with 24 in each cottage, many cottages were well below capacity at the time of this study. These cottages, too, have heavy screens over the windows in what is called the program area, and bars over the windows in the boys' rooms. A social worker and staff youth leaders have individual, small, glass-enclosed offices in the program area. When boys are in the dining and recreational areas, staff and youth are visible in all their movements and can keep each other under careful surveillance.

Each cottage has one social worker and six youth leaders. Two youth leaders supervise the cottage on the 7:00 a.m. to 3:00 p.m. and 3:00 to 11:00 p.m. shifts, and one leader supervises the cottage while inmates are in bed on the 11:00 p.m. to 7:00 a.m.

shift. Hence, boys are under supervision at all times of the day. Unless a boy is in the final stages of his stay and has pre-release status, a staff member must accompany him in all of his movements from one section of the institution to another. Additionally, even when in the cottages, boys must be either out on "program," in the dormitories, or in the process of getting dressed for the next routine of the day. If an inexperienced man is being trained, institutional officials attempt to keep one experienced leader on duty with him. This maneuver keeps the boys from disrupting the orderly flow of the day's events in any manner.

This cottage area is where the boys spend most of their time— eating, sleeping, getting ready to go to other areas of the institution, and playing either pool, pingpong, or cards, or watching television. Each cottage has sixteen single rooms, and two four-bed dormitories; the single rooms contain a bed, study table, chair, an "open closet" with shelves, and a place to hang clothes. The four-bed dormitories have the beds neatly arranged and, again, open wardrobe closets for clothes and other personal belongings. The rest of the cottage consists of a toilet and shower area and a small kitchen in one corner of the program area to which food is brought from nearby OYC facilities. The television section is separated from the rest of the program area by several well-used couches and hard-seated chairs; the tile floor is bare and bedsprings for those on maximum restriction are standing on end in one corner of the recreational area. Between the kitchen and the youth leaders' offices are six small, square tables used for eating, with the chairs often upside down on top when the boys are not eating. Hard-seated chairs and bare tables are scattered around this living, dining, and recreational area, and a few magazines are found near the television set. When no activities are scheduled, boys sit idly around talking in groups of two or three, watching TV, or playing one of the available games.

The school area, which is a five-minute walk from the farthest cottages, contains academic classrooms, vocational shops, the gymnasium, the swimming pool, and the auditorium. The six-year accredited high school runs for eleven months a year and is attended by most residents. If a boy decides not to attend, the social worker especially tries to persuade him of the school's benefits. Half the day is usually devoted to academic and half to vocational training, with the emphasis on the latter. Classes are small, generally containing ten or fewer students. Remedial mathematics and English are taught for the academically retarded, and approximately forty academic courses are taught by seventeen certified teachers. Also, one mathematical improvement lab and three communications labs are available for the students. Modern techniques are utilized, allowing each student to progress at the rate most satisfactory for him, and volunteer college students tutor those who need help.

The vocational program, on the other hand, offers automotive repair, welding, printing, woodworking, carpentry, barbering, machine shop, and food service programs. Boys practice some of what they learn by working in maintenance at another nearby facility and at the Ohio Youth Commission's food service center. Funds are available for eleven students to work full time at these jobs for a dollar a day. In addition to these compensatory jobs, the inmates perform a number of maintenance tasks around the institution. As one mimeographed commission publication puts it:

> It is felt that many boys can profit from engaging in necessary chores which must be done. We expect each boy to share in these tasks on a rotating basis. However some are assigned work details for a specific period of time. It is hoped in this way good work habits and skills may be offered on a 1/2 time daily basis, receiving school credits as occupational training courses. Some of these jobs include janitoring, painting, storeroom control, and general maintenance.

Further, a few students about to be released are allowed to work in the community. In their final two months of institutional stay, they leave for work in the morning and return after the completion of their work day.

The recreational program, too, is molded to the interests of the boys, and includes flag football, basketball, track, softball, boxing, volleyball, and swimming. Movies are shown at least once a week, and musical groups perform frequently. Dances are held with girls from other OYC facilities and the community. Also, there are arts and crafts, quiet games, an Explorer post, and the opportunity for pre-release boys to participate in the bowling and track programs of the Police Athletic League and other community-based programs. Volunteer groups help considerably by providing both institutional and off-grounds recreational activities.

Other programs include a medical program employing the services of one registered nurse who works from 7:00 a.m. to 3:00 p.m. five days a week and a community doctor who works at the institution one day a week. If anything serious happens, however, students are sent to nearby hospitals. Complementing the medical consultants are two part-time psychiatrists who counsel difficult cases and help train staff in treatment procedures. Too, the institution's eleven full-time social workers are in charge of coordinating treatment programs. Since the Ohio State University School of Social Work uses this institution as a training resource for its students, five to ten social work students are also available to provide services to the boys. A full program of religious services, education, and counseling is provided for Protestants and Catholics, with a full-time Protestant and a part-time Catholic chaplain. Religious services are held weekly and on special holidays; compulsory attendance of inmates is required for the weekly services.

The primary treatment program involves transactional analysis. A youth leader in each cottage is trained by a full-time group coordinator to run TA groups. In these groups, inmates learn the three ego states, four life positions, and their life scripts. Group leaders utilize this treatment modality to provide inmates with a chance to see how they affect the reactions of others. A second major treatment modality is reality therapy, which is more popular with older-line staff. Major assumptions of this modality involve taking responsibility for one's behavior, only dealing with problems occurring in the present, and reinforcing positive behavior. Both social workers and youth leaders use reality therapy in making contacts with boys, whereby inmates project both long- and short-range treatment goals. Milieu therapy is a third major treatment modality and consists of utilizing the impact of the cottage's total setting. In this modality, members of the cottage team—made up of youth leaders, the social worker, and two teacher representatives—interact to evaluate residents' progress, handle disciplinary decisions, and recommend pre-release status, release status, psychiatric clearances, and home visits.

The rehabilitation program, then, consists of cottage living experience, individual guidance, group counseling, educational and vocational instruction, recreation, and religion. Staff are expected to utilize all of their abilities in helping the boys develop the types of attitudes toward family, community, and society which foster self-control and positive community behavior. Subsequently, staff are expected to make every effort to understand the boys and provide for all needs which realistically may be fulfilled. By using all of these techniques, it is anticipated that a positive climate will develop throughout the institution and enable both boys and staff to deal adequately with their experiences there.

Since youths sent to this and other institutions vary considerably in behavior and characteristics, the best way to guarantee their efficient and effective rehabilitation is to classify them into homogeneous categories. These categories permit the staff to respond to their clients in the manner most suited to rehabilitation. At the time of this study, institutional officials were beginning to implement a classification technique known as "I-level," or Interpersonal Maturity Level Classification System, designed by Margurite Warren.[2] Before continuing, we will take a brief look at this classification system.

## The "I-Level"

The I-level (Interpersonal Maturity Level Classification System) is currently popular in juvenile institutions all across the United States. Developed in California in the early 1960s, the object of the system is to provide administrators with a reliable method of classifying offenders so that appropriate treatments may be used efficiently and effectively. As Margurite Warren (1967: 55) states, "The *goals* of correctional treatment with any offender should relate in some direct manner to the causes or meaning of the goals." The idea is to classify all offenders and put them in with others of the same type, thereby enabling staff to treat a homogeneous group of boys with the same techniques and preventing antisocial youths from negatively influencing those more prosocial.

The I-level system groups juveniles as well as adults on the basis of their social and emotional maturity. In a real sense, this classification system attempts to discover the world view of offenders, focusing in on their perception of self, others, and the world. According to Warren and others who were responsible for formulating this classification system, the I-level of a person is directly related to the client's ability to identify and be involved with others. For example, while an $I_1$ has the infant's total preoccupation of self, the $I_7$, which is the highest I-level possible, has the altruistic, self-negating response of a Christ figure. Delinquents are usually found in $I_2$s, $I_3$s, and $I_4$s, although occasionally an $I_5$ youth will be incarcerated. Research with delinquents also shows that those three levels are further subdivided so that there are a total of nine delinquent subtypes.

Generally, $I_2$ delinquents perceive living in the world as extremely difficult since they believe that they *are* the whole world and, therefore, feel that all desires must be immediately fulfilled without contributing anything themselves.[3] These youths have trouble distinguishing reality from unreality and are usually found either in mental hospitals or in fringe groups in the community as adults. This egocentric individual views the world as either taking or giving, and other people are evaluated purely on the basis of whether they satisfy his wants or whether they withhold desired goals. These youths believe in themselves so highly that they perceive their chances for success to be higher than they actually are. When unsuccessful, these boys feel that the world is against them and that they are the victims of unexplainable forces. Unable to ascribe any blame to themselves when something goes wrong and their desires are left unfulfilled, $I_2$s respond by blaming others. Further, these boys are unable to understand that their extreme dependency needs reflect their own problems rather than some "ill-meaning" person in their environment intentionally placing limitations on them. The net result is that relationships with adults deteriorate whenever others do not cater to their every whim. Thwarted in their desires, $I_2$s often blow up, reverting to infant-like behavior.

Treatment goals for $I_2$s are geared to help them develop some inner controls and some understanding of the relationship between their own needs and the behavior of others. The treatment agent, whether it be the family or the institutional staff, must exhibit extreme tolerance in order to help them attain that self-control. Staff are encouraged to reward any show of inner control without encouraging self-pity or dependency. If boys' tension levels begin to build, attempts should be made to reduce them; staff are advised also to make clear to inmates that limits placed on behavior are not punishments or some form of rejection. Finally, opportunities should be found for boys to help others and to be warmly rewarded for this positive behavior.

More sophisticated in their approach to the world, $I_3$s realize that people are more complex than simply being givers and takers.[4] Part of their problem is that they underestimate the extent to which others differ and believe that power is the way to gain wants. The $I_3$s, moreover, dichotomize the world and its inhabitants in a rigid, either/or fashion. Realizing that rules exist, these youths attempt to determine exactly what the rules and structures are. If no rules exist, these boys feel safe because they feel the danger of being controlled by others is diminished. Their subsequent behavior is based, then, not on internalized norms, but on the structure in the world around them; if the power structure changes, they change with it. The idea of self-change is uncomfortable, and any change is expected to come from others.

The $I_3$s tend to understand others only by the roles others play. Although they understand that their own behavior has something to do with whether they get what they want, they have difficulty understanding feelings, needs, and motives of those around them. They make an effort to manipulate their environment in order to bring about "giving" rather than "denying" responses. Failing to operate from an internalized value system, they seek external structure in terms of rules and formulas. They perceive the world on a power dimension. Similarly, these boys blame others for problems experienced in the past and minimize their own culpability. As a result of these features, they have an inability to predict accurately the responses of others.

Treatment goals consist of teaching $I_3$s that someone can control them. Structures are developed, and these youths receive punishment if they violate expected behaviors. At the same time, an agent who has the ability to empathize and communicate nonverbally, yet who can exert control, is the best therapist for this type of boy. Guided group interaction is appropriate and places these boys in situations where their emotions may be expressed. Basically, the idea is to persuade $I_3$s to admit that their ideas are not working and slowly to get them to try new ones which do.

$I_4$s perceive the world according to an internalized system of values which, if not fulfilled, leaves them feeling upset and guilty.[5] These boys see themselves as unique and better than others, and manifest these perceptions by trying to get ahead and by achieving recognition. They often model themselves after persons who are recognized as having accomplished important goals—even delinquent ones. Considerably advanced beyond the two types already discussed, $I_4$s are able to understand some of the forces impinging upon them from the outside. They understand to some extent why others act as they do, and also have some insights into the feelings and actions of others. Because they are achievers and oriented toward goals, they plan and worry about the future, aware that things may eventually change.

Their mode of responding to the world is also more complex than that of $I_2$s and $I_3$s, and include a greater ability to develop interpersonal relationships. Responsibility for self and others is evidenced even though they may be unable to carry through on what they and others expect of them; unlike the other two types, these boys are more able to delay their responses to stimuli presented them. Treatment centers around their inappropriate methods of achieving status, and treatment agents help $I_4$s perceive the world alternatively to enable them to respond in socially appropriate ways.

## INSTITUTIONAL STAFF

The institution has four different levels of youth leaders. The youth leader III works 11:00 p.m. to 7:00 a.m., has no contact with inmates, and merely sits in the youth leader's office when not making periodic checks of the rooms. The youth leader IV, on the other hand, is responsible for getting boys up in the morning and putting them to bed at night. Working two at a time, IVs take boys to school, keep problems from developing at mealtimes, and administer discipline when needed.

Two youth leader Vs are in each cottage—the senior youth leader and the group leader. The former works in the morning shift, supervising the morning youth leaders, whereas the latter works the evening shift and leads transactional analysis groups. Finally, the youth leader VI supervises all the youth leaders in his wing, which is made up of four cottages. Equipped with his golf cart, he moves from cottage to cottage—giving out medicines, checking whether inmates on home leave or outside jobs have returned, responding to the call of a youth leader concerning a recalcitrant youth, and checking the performance of the various youth leaders.

To be employed as a youth leader now requires a high school education, a clean police record (although several "ex-cons" have been previously employed as youth leaders), good physical health, (substantial physical size is almost a prerequisite), and passing an examination administered by institutional officials. As civil servants, youth leaders are on probational status until after a 180-day evaluation. Supervisors evaluate them several times their first year and annually thereafter. Youth leaders whose treatment of students is unacceptable—that is, those who employ brutality or are in some manner negligent—are either suspended for up to a month or are weeded out.

Social workers constitute the other staff members who work with the youths. In contrast to youth leaders, who are 97 percent black, social workers are generally 80 percent white, college-educated, and sometimes possess a M.S.W. degree. All eight social workers with offices in cottages are expected to coordinate treatment with the cottage team, interview and counsel boys, do the necessary paperwork, keep in contact with inmates' field counselors, work with boys' parents when necessary, help boys establish short- and long-range treatment goals, chair disciplinary reviews, represent boys before the administrative review, and place youths in the most appropriate programs. Social workers, too, are on probationary status for the first 180 days and receive annual evaluations. As professionals, however, they are not as vulnerable to suspension from work as are youth leaders.


## SOME GENERAL RULES

When boys arrive, institutional clothing is issued which must be worn at all times except during special events. Space is limited and restrictions are thus placed on the amounts of personal clothing boys may keep. The daily clothing is a military-type uniform consisting of grey, short-sleeved shirts, grey trousers, black tie, black socks, and black shoes.

Boys are encouraged by staff to write home often, but incoming and outgoing mail is censored to check for money and violations of security. Incoming packages are examined to guarantee that only appropriate books and magazines get through. Visitors are generally limited to family members and relatives, although girl-friends may come in with inmates' mothers. Visiting hours are liberal, daily visits permitted from 12:30 to 3:00 p.m. daily, and boys on release status may pay off-campus visits to their parents for the afternoons if staff feel they will return. Both release and pre-release boys are given the privileges of a monthly phone call home, can go home monthly for weekend visits which enables those near release to interview for jobs and register for school, take educational and vocational courses in the community, and be considered for off-campus jobs. In the case of a serious illness or death in the family, pre-release boys who have the permission of their field counselor may have an emergency home visit. Boys without pre-release in these circumstances must be escorted home and returned by a staff member.

Money may not be carried by youths even though they are allowed to spend up to four dollars a week at the canteen. Spending is controlled from the business office, and boys' purchases are charged to their accounts. Any money given to residents must be deposited in that account.

Normally, three stages are passed through before release—progress, pre-release, and release. Positive changes in behavior and attitude result in promotion to pre-release and then to release by a cottage evaluation committee consisting of the cottage social worker, two teachers from the academic-vocational area, six youth leaders, and the wing director. Excluding the wing director, who has no vote, all other members of the cottage team have one vote; the final decision is derived simply by counting the votes.

Pre-release status cannot be achieved before an inmate is confined for five months and has a suffix clearance, providing he has an "R" or "E" suffix. [6] In general, six or seven months are required to earn pre-release status, and another seven or eight months are required before release status is earned. Usually, release comes within four or five weeks after release status is earned.

Three different decision-making procedures are utilized before final release. First, the cottage review committee reviews the progress of the youth every three months. When the cottage review committee recommends release, the boy's case then goes to the institutional review committee. The social worker presents a boy's case before the deputy superintendant for treatment, the director of guidance, the wing directors, the school principal, and the chaplain. This group then reviews the cottage's recommendation and, if they pass favorably, the recommendation is passed on to the youth commission's classification and assignment division. Almost always, classification and assignment approves and aftercare plans are initiated. Then, unless problems in community placement are evident, the boy's field counselor usually sets a release date within a month.

The institution described here is one of the best Ohio has to offer. The facilities are modern, the staff is relatively well trained, treatment methods are up-to-date, inmates are well taken care of and are efficiently controlled by staff. Visitors come away with a feeling the youths here are going to come out better for their stay. Ohio has a number of other institutions, which, although they do not hold similarly aggressive and hostile inmates, are patterned in much the same way. Too, juvenile institutions very similar to the one described in this chapter exist all over the country. It is not difficult to see why the following statement expressing the philosophy of this institution excites the concerned citizen:

To promote positive attitudinal and behavioral change within an atmosphere of mutual respect and personal dignity; to provide a resident with opportunities to gain an increased understanding of himself, others, and his environment; and to learn to meet his needs in socially acceptable ways [Ohio Youth Commission, July 1974].

## NOTES

1. For a more detailed breakdown of the OYC population, see Appendix A.

2. The Ohio Youth Commission implemented the "I-level" at one of the girls' institutions in 1969 and the test was so successful that the decision was made to expand the program to all institutions. At the same time, the decision was made to phase out the Juvenile Diagnostic Center because of the costliness of sending youths there for up to twelve weeks for diagnosis by a fully trained, professional staff. The cost, time involved, and the fact that youngsters were in limbo there were the factors leading to this decision. The OYC now has fourteen I-level classification specialists in five areas around the state. These specialists make an on-the-scene evaluation of the youth and decide where to send him.

3. $I_2$s are divided into unsocialized, aggressives and unsocialized, passives. The reader is referred to the I-level manual for a fuller description of these as well as other subtypes in the I-level classification system.

4. Subdivisions of the $I_3$s include conformists, immature; conformists, cultural; and manipulators.

5. The $I_4$s are subdivided into neurotic, acting outs, neurotic, anxious; cultural identifiers; and situational emotional reactors.

6. An "R" suffix means that the youth is considered dangerous to himself or others, whereas an "E" suffix is assigned to those thought to be mentally disturbed.

CHAPTER 3

GETTING AT EXPLOITATION

The analysis of exploitative relationships is an elusive and difficult task. Part of the problem is that the researcher must catch the process occurring in the lives of those he or she is studying (Glaser and Strauss, 1967). These social processes often take place "backstage," where only participants are allowed (Goffman, 1961). Exploitation emerges from a dynamic process, constantly developing and being affected by previous occurrences. Hence, the outcome is produced from sequences of behavior created by the parties involved. Considerable resourcefulness and experience are required before a researcher becomes cognizant both of the sequences of interaction and how the outcome emerges from the interaction of the parts.

One important factor affecting the nature of exploitation is the normative system. Norms define and determine what is accepted as legitimate or illegitimate and govern the actions of participants (Sykes and Messinger, 1960: 5-9; Wellford, 1969: 197-203). Since the ability to exploit depends upon power, the parameters of power must also be determined. And if the institutional climate or milieu is as important as researchers suggest, the "character" of institutions must be delineated (Zald, 1960: 57-67; Grusky, 1959-1960; 59-67). Even though attempts to quantify these cultural and structural variables are improving, the complexity of the variables requires that a diversity of techniques be used in order to discover the nature of institutional life. (Moos, 1968: 174-188, 1970: 183-194).[1] Fortunately, present methodology permits the use of a variety of techniques which shed light on the problem of discovery, and many are already in use in the study of victimology.

Traditional victimology, for example, has long recognized that differential "risks" contribute to whether a person becomes either the criminal or the victim (Mendelsohn, 1963: 239-241; Von Hentig, 1948; Ellenberger, 1954; Fry, 1951; Schafer, 1968). The young, weak, aged, infirm, and strangers are all differentially involved in crime. Living in a particular nation, state, region, county, city, district, or ward also affects one's life chances for becoming a victim, just as one's sex, height, weight, and mental frame of mind help decide whether a person shows up on a police blotter or in the emergency ward of a hospital. Too, the nature of the relationship between the exploiter and the exploited very much depends on the interaction between the two.

In this study of the way juveniles who exploit in the community become victimized in an institution, a wide range of quantitative and qualitative methods are employed. Since the type of data affecting this victimization and the nature of the findings expected were largely unknown, this study is both explorative and descriptive. The exploration of those factors thought to be relevant to the quality of life in the institution largely dictated the type of techniques used. Needless to say, in order to explore victimization, research methods were required which allowed the researchers intimate access to all phases of institutional life. A phenomenological blend of methods was employed to gain the fullest possible understanding permitted by the data.

## THE NATURE OF VICTIMIZATION

Very few studies deal with victimization in juvenile institutions. Davis (1968) was one of the first to point out the extent to which juveniles were the victims of stronger inmates in the Philadelphia van system. There, inmates of all ages and every degree of criminality were stored together in vans awaiting disposition of their cases. Younger boys had no chance as older, predatory males took immediate advantage of their weakness by beating and homosexually raping them. Although Polsky (1962) mentioned that homosexuality was a concern in Cottage Six, he did not go into depth about either it or other forms of victimization. Halleck and Hersko, however, indicated that 69 percent of the girls in a training school were involved in homosexual behavior (1962). Huffman, in addition, studied the interpersonal problems created by homosexual involvements of youthful first offenders (1961). Giallombardo has further studied the importance of homosexuality in the social organization of incarcerated girls (1974). Finally, Toigo (1962) feels that line staff are aware of homosexuality in juvenile institutions, but feel helpless to protect the weak.

Fisher (1961) has made one of the greatest theoretical contributions to the understanding of victimization in juvenile institutions by portraying victimization and patronage as two of the major behaviors taking place. "Victimization is a predatory practice whereby inmates of superior strength and knowledge of inmate lore prey on weaker and less knowledgeable inmates" (1961: 89). Patronage involves boys building "protective and ingratiating relationships with others more advantageously situated on the prestige ladder" (1961:90). Fisher goes on to break victimization down into three further categories, physical attack, agitation, and exploitation (1961: 89). Physical attack consists of taking something by force; agitation is simply a form of verbal harrassing; and exploitation "is a process whereby an inmate will attempt to coerce another by means of threat and duress" (Fisher, 1961: 89).

Although we agree with much of Fisher's formulation, this study led to some modifications. First, the definition of victimization was expanded to involve a relationship in which one party loses material goods, or becomes involved in any interaction in which ego loses face to alter without receiving personally acceptable compensation or restitution. In these relationships, an imbalance exists in which one party is clearly the loser. Second, exploitation, agitation, and physical attack are seldom separate processes. The processes are interrelated, with agitation and physical attack generally being the prelude to exploitation and as a testing mechanism to determine where a boy should be placed in the inmate social hierarchy. Third, boys low on the social hierarchy were not the only ones to engage in patronage; even the leaders of the cottages engaged to some extent in "protective and ingratiating relationships" with those lower than themselves. This technique is used by leaders to maintain their position of power. Fourth, although patronage is pervasive throughout the facility, it is not a normatively supported behavior. That is, if boys want to "buy someone off," the decision is arrived at independently of any well-recognized, objectively known, or systematically supported value system. Fifth, we concluded that the terms exploitation and victimization are so close in meaning in their everyday usage that it becomes difficult, if not impossible, to discriminate conceptually between them.[2]

The few studies on victimization in juvenile institutions leave many questions unanswered. For example, does sexual exploitation constitute the major way in which victimization takes place? What forms of nonsexual exploitation occur? What is the extent of sexual/nonsexual exploitation? What are the characteristics of exploiters and victims? How do victims contribute to their victimization? What role does the staff play in the process of exploitation? And what is the relationship among organizational, structural, and personality variables? Our task was to seek the answer to these questions in a maximum security juvenile institution.


## INITIATING THE STUDY

The study was initiated by obtaining the customary permissions from the Ohio Youth Commission and the appropriate institutional officials. An institutional staff member who was working on his Ph.D. in sociology was approached and questioned about the feasibility of observing the institution's disciplinary hearings in order to understand victimization better. This staff member's response was that the incidence of exploitation far exceeded that represented by the occasional appearance of boys in disciplinary hearings. He said that such hearings involved only the most severe cases, and that instances of exploitation were handled informally in the cottages when they occurred. Thus, to really understand exploitation, a far more comprehensive plan should be developed— one which also did not alienate or frighten people because of the topic's sensitivity. This staff member agreed to approach other staff informally to discuss exploitation with them, and to get them used to the idea of having a study conducted on this very sensitive issue.

The first informal discussions with staff indicated that sex was only a small part of the overall picture of exploitation, for the taking of food, clothing, and cigarettes was a much more frequent occurrence. The staff also indicated that inmates could be ranked differentially—some youths were likely to exploit others, some were likely not to be exploited, some were exploited occasionally, and some often. For the first time, it became clear that the frequency of exploitation was perceived as constituting a continuum. The possibility was also raised that the boys could be fitted into a number of different exploitative categories.

Staff Questionnaire

Since the issue of exploitation continua and typologies was not discussed in the criminological literature, the decision was made to subject the staff's ideas to an empirical test. A schedule was constructed which included, by cottage, each boy's name, and which also had spaces for ranking each boy on the exploitation typology and the way he was victimized (see Appendix B). This schedule was given to all the institution's youth leaders and social workers and over two-thirds responded.

Of fifty-six staff members who worked directly with the boys (forty-eight youth leaders and eight social workers), thirty-six returned the questionnaires. Lack of staff response was attributed to the following reasons: the sensitivity of the topic; the fear of some staff that their ratings could result in lawsuits against them should the identity of sexually active boys become known; several staff who were noncooperative in all phases of institutional life refused; one staff member promised regularly to return the schedule but never did; and two were unavailable because they were on extended sick leave.

Exploitation was not found to be a "cut and dried" phenomenon. Staff agreement as to the status of many youths was apparent, but some staff saw boys exploited often and other staff, sometimes new or on alternate shifts, did not see them exploited at all. The problem was resolved by making a composite of how all the staff in each cottage rated the boys on the frequency of exploitation as well as the specific ways in which each boy was exploited.[3] Consequently, if one staff member observed cigarettes being taken from a particular youth, but another on a different shift did not observe any victimization, the matter was resolved by examining the composite of all staff observations, usually three or four per cottage. Thus, even though disagreement might exist, as it obviously did in that case, the ratings of the rest of the staff were also noted. If the staff's peers saw a boy victimized, no further follow-up of the case was undertaken. But if peers could not substantiate the observation, the boy was listed as a victim only if the original staff member could cite the specific nature of the victimization.[4]

One problem concerning the fourfold ranking system remained. Staff very often checked the first category "likely to exploit others," but then would also indicate that the youth was exploited to some degree. Thus, in contrast to previous anticipation that exploiters were not exploited, it became apparent that some not only exploited others but were exploited themselves. From this observation, a number of combinations of exploiter, non-exploiter, and exploited emerged from the staff's initial rating. At this time, the decision was made to treat the staff rankings as categories rather than elements along a continuum.

Obviously, the staff perceived exploitation as a vastly more complicated phenomenon than previously anticipated. Examination of the ratings showed that some of the emergent categories were logically consistent, and the decision was therefore made to combine logically consistent categories for ease of analysis.[5] This combination resulted in the fivefold typology shown in Table 3.1.

## Table 3.1

### GENERATED FIVEFOLD TYPOLOGY

1. Exploits others but is not exploited.
2. Exploits others and is exploited.
3. Does not exploit others and is not exploited.
4. Does not exploit, but is occasionally exploited.
5. Does not exploit others, but usually is exploited in all manner of ways.

NOTE: The boys in these five categories are referred to in the study, respectively, as the exploiters, the give and takes, the independents, the sometimes boys, and the pure victims.

The collapsed categories, then, were used as the basis of classifying all of the youths.[6]

Direct observation of exploitation of food, clothes, and cigarettes is relatively easy, and even though observations might not be quantifiable, a perceptive observer with a little practice can detect the inmate pecking order. But there is no question that sexual victimization is the most difficult form to analyze. Sexual exploits are normatively taboo from the staff's point of view; therefore, much effort is expended in making certain that boys are not exploited. Yet, sex does take place and is occasionally very widespread. Since the act is not directly observed by staff, knowledge of its occurrence comes through the inmate grapevine, rumors, and the names given to sexual scapegoats by the boys. In addition, the scapegoat is responded to differently by his peers than is the boy who is not victimized. But what makes the discovery of sexual exploitation so difficult is that only rarely will the victimized come forward and "rat." Staff reports, then, are based upon empirically unverifiable observations, and, indeed, some exploitation is never verified.

## Staff Member as Participant Observer

The value of having a participant in the institution's daily life on the research team became more and more apparent; consequently, the staff officer who was helping us was invited to become a team member. The goal of the research was "to catch the process as it occurs in the experience of those studied" (Bruyn, 1966: 13). Since the staff and boys were reluctant to talk to someone they did not know and trust, the addition of this institutional participant mitigated this problem. Of great importance were his extensive and intimate knowledge of institutional processes and personnel, his advice in selecting knowledgeable staff and inmates for intensive interviewing, and his consideration of his own experiences in conjunction with the findings of others. Nevertheless, some difficulties were created by his participation.

Exploiters were unwilling to discuss their activities with him because of his official position. Since this staff member was involved in the institution's everyday political life and in a supervisory capacity at that, certain staff were reluctant to confide in him. Indeed, a few exhibited open hostility by refusing to fill out the staff questionnaire. Further, being a participant-observer meant that this researcher had his own viewpoint, one not always shared by other institutional officers. Interestingly, as this team member moved from being a participant, to being a participant observer, and finally, to being an outside observer, his viewpoints were modified, elaborated upon, and eventually provided a qualitative richness the other researchers would have found impossible to achieve.[7]

One additional note on this researcher's role is interesting. This man had engaged in a confrontation type of therapy and the result was that the boys were afraid to talk to him. As his institutional and academic duties increased, he decided to change his approach to the boys, becoming more "fatherly" and more of a companion. The result was dramatic. The boys now began to confide in him, increasing his knowledge of their activities and permitting him to become more knowledgeable of institutional and inmate processes.

## Staff Interviews

Fortunately, having outsiders on the team permitted developing contacts and gathering information not obtainable by a participant (Junker, 1960). Only exploiters felt a threat from the outsiders.

Except for the staff who resented researchers, most were willing to discuss institutional processes in considerable detail. The advantage of these "experience surveys" (Selltiz et al., 1961: 55-59) with other staff was that they provided other perspectives and insights into the institution's operation. A description of the "interior life" of the cottages was desired and, to understand the boys from their own frame of reference to the greatest extent possible, the examination of both visible and sub rosa social interaction was needed. Next to the boys, experienced staff held the greatest knowledge of institutional life; so selected staff were interviewed to reach this understanding. Both formal and informal conversations and focused interviews were utilized to identify nonquantifiable social processes. Thus, the interviewer had the opportunity to pose "leading questions" where appropriate and to "pin down" responses (see Appendix D). Although some inmates and staff were interviewed only once, others were talked to repeatedly and, in one way or another, nearly every line staff member and inmate in the institution was interviewed.[8]

The respondents selected provided hour after hour of interview material, the content of which provided many new additions and insights to research already conducted and reported. Some interviews were taped, the microphone attracting the respondent's attention only during the first several minutes of the interview. Interviews lasted from twenty minutes to an hour and a half at a time and were conducted over a six-month period.

Inmate Interviews

Conducting interviews with the youths raised serious moral and ethical questions, since discussing an issue as sensitive as exploitation could create several serious problems. First, raising these issues could make inmates more sensitive to what was happening in the cottages and sharpen their ideas about exploiting others. The avoidance of value judgments in an interview could lead some youths to feel that exploitation was permissible. Of greater importance was the fact that inmates could be labeled or could label themselves as a result of the research inquiry. Also of concern was whether the type of questions utilized constituted an invasion of privacy and whether information gained could be forced from the researchers in a court of law.

Serious consideration was given to these issues, and the decision was made to interview a number of the inmates after taking all the precautions necessary to protect them. Anonymity was guaranteed and no names were kept. Tape recorded interviews were planned, and several boys were asked to participate. In spite of the ethical reservations of the researchers, inmates took the interviewing process right in stride. When a "sensitive area" was raised, inmates usually avoided the question. The boys obviously knew they could not be forced to answer; in fact, they knew they were doing us a favor just by talking with us. Hence, with the exception of testimony from several victimized youths, little information was gained through these inmate interviews.

Information was received quite serendipitiously, however, when one sexual victim approached the participant observer. He claimed that several staff were sexually exploiting boys and that he was scared. In addition, he mentioned names of several other youths whom he thought were being sexually exploited. When these youths were interviewed, they alleged that a homosexual ring was operating among several Ohio Youth Commission facilities; these youths accused several staff members of threatening to prolong their institutionalization unless they were willing to engage in sex. Dispositions were received as part of normal institutional investigative procedures. Those interviewed were especially willing to provide insights into the process of how staff exploited inmates.

Inmate Schedules

Psychological research over the past several decades has produced a number of tests theoretically capable of providing insights into the nature of personality. Since the inmate hierarchy consists of a number of different levels, as well as roles played by boys in those levels, the decision was made to test whether the boys differed psychologically.

The Gough Adjective Checklist (Gough and Heilbrun, 1965), and the Machover Draw-a-Figure Test (Machover, 1949) were administered to the entire student population in each cottage.[9] The

Jesness Personality Inventory (Jesness, 1965) was also administered, but at different times.

The Gough Adjective Checklist is a series of 24 scales consisting
of 300 adjectives and may be used to rank either oneself or others.
Although Gough and Heilbrun argue that the test may be given to
juvenile populations, the adjective checklist has several drawbacks.
Many adjectives were far too difficult for this inmate population
because many of the boys were functionally illiterate. Anticipating
that this cohort of youths might have some problems with the
words, a list of definitions was made up and read to the inmates
whenever requested (see Appendix E). With a few exceptions,
practically all adjective definitions had to be read. This reading,
however, resulted in an extended testing period which became
boring to the students.

Administration of tests of any type to juveniles is a difficult and
trying task, but these incarcerated boys were especially suscep-
tible to the boredom that accompanies such testing; many had
little schooling, and the tests had no relevance to their daily lives.
The boys were told the tests were for research only and would not
affect their release.

The boys broke the monotony every ten minutes or so by
making witty or sarcastic comments. This was, in part, simply a
status-gaining device by which some attempted to improve their
"rep" in the cottage or, in other cases, was simply the result of a
short attention span. On certain words, however, the "underlife"
of the cottage exuded as youths turned to the scapegoats and
suggested "that means you _____ ." Words such as "effemi-
nate" brought out these comments most frequently. The few boys
who refused to take the test consisted primarily of boys on
pre-release status who knew they had nothing to lose by refusing.
Still, almost 90 percent of the 149 inmates were tested on the
Gough Adjective Checklist. [10]

The Jesness Personality Inventory is designed to measure and
classify adolescents. The inventory consists of 155 true-false items
constructed to distinguish disturbed or delinquent children from
normals and also measures attitudes toward self and others. The
155 items are divided into eleven scales—including measures such as
maladjustment, immaturity, manifest aggression, and asociality—so
the scales theoretically, at least, should be of some value in

distinguishing among the various typological categories. A large proportion of the inmate population previously had been tested on the Jesness scales and, for this test, it was necessary only to go back into the population and find those who had not yet been tested. The testing of the remainder of the boys took place some time after the administration of the Goughs, but according to the research on the Jesness, this delay in the administration of the test should not have affected the results (Jesness, 1965). Because of the lateness of this test administration, the percentage of boys who were tested dropped to 81 percent of the population.

Finally, the Machover Draw-a-Figure test was given because it is a projective test designed to reveal hidden propensities. In this case, the boys were tested specifically for sexual identity, feelings of inferiority, aggression, maladjustment, and anxiety.[11] The latter four traits were quantified on a 1-5 dimension, and sexual identity was checked for "male," "female" or "undecided." Although the reliability of this instrument has been challenged, it had not been administered, to our knowledge, to a population of this nature. Therefore, the researchers felt that data received might be of additional help in understanding the personalities of exploiters and exploited.

The format of the Machover consists of asking respondents to draw a figure of any person. The respondent is allowed to finish the drawing and then is asked to put the number "one" on the top of the page. The respondent is then requested to draw a figure of a person of the opposite sex on a second blank sheet of paper. The administration of this test was quite interesting because boys resisted taking it much more than they did the other two.

Administrators pointed out that projective tests are feared by the boys since they cannot predict what it is that the researchers want. The intent of the Goughs and the Jesnesses often can be inferred from the adjectives and questions. Boys frequently are able to, or think they can, predict what is being examined and to answer accordingly. Because the intent of the Machovers could not be predicted, considerable resistance and comments resulted at its administration. The boys also perceived a further dilemma. If the tests turned out negative, the results might he held against them and endanger their release; if, on the other hand, they refused to take the tests, this too might be held against them and might also endanger their release. The usual precautions of assuring the youths no results would be held against them were taken, but there is no way of knowing the extent to which the researchers were believed. Since the participant observer was trusted (he had tested them before), most apparently did believe the tests would do them no harm and therefore agreed to be tested. Thus, 87 percent were tested on the Machovers. [12]

To those in penal research, the above experiences are, no doubt, quite familiar. It is very questionable whether someone unfamiliar with the boys, the cottages, and the staff in each cottage would have been as successful in achieving this high rate of return. Outside researchers, for example, have had whole cottages of boys refuse to take tests, and, in fact, one cottage was almost lost in our study. Of great value in the successful administration of these tests were the cottage youth leaders. These men knew their charges well, and were invaluable in helping the research team to administer the various tests.

## Criminal History, Demographic and Physical Characteristics

The next phase of the research was concerned with collecting data on youths' criminal history and demographic and physical characteristics through the use of institutional files. The use of files is, at best, a dubious procedure if one considers that ages, birthdates, height, weight, IQ, and other numbers have probably been transcribed numerous times, thereby leading to an increased probability of error. In addition, one is usually unaware of the conditions under which IQ and other psychological tests were given, the qualifications and standards of those administering the tests and making diagnostic decisions, the validity and reliability of the tests involved, and the adequacy of the information those compiling the files are able to find. Nevertheless, files often constitute the only information available and must be used. Fortunately, the data desired were missing in only a few cases.

## METHODOLOGICAL INTENT

The data were analyzed in a variety of ways. The interview data and the data collected as a result of participant observation have been sorted through and reconstructed in a meaningful fashion. Emphasis is placed primarily upon exploitation and related issues affecting the quality of institutional life. Other types of relationships exist, some of which are beneficial, but these are not developed so as not to detract from the present issues. For instance, only a few comments will be made about boys who apparently benefit from their experiences in the institution.

The demographic, criminal history, and physical data were statistically analyzed along with the Gough Adjective Checklist, Machover, and Jesness Personality Inventory. All data were factor analyzed against the exploitation typology as well as against other appropriate data. We have tried to make clear where one type of data as opposed to another had been used.

Although the large number of methodological techniques utilized provide a wide variety of data from which the analysis into exploitative relationships proceeds, this study is basically exploratory and descriptive: exploratory in that the new area of victimology in juvenile institutions is examined, and descriptive in that a wealth of data describing what actually happens among the participants in a juvenile institution is discussed. By combining the diverse sources of data, it is hoped that knowledge into the nature of relationships will be increased and provide further insights into exploitation generally.

We are concerned with both the objective and the subjective nature of victimization. By objective, we mean victimization as viewed and interpreted by the researchers. By subjective, we mean the degree and extent to which inmates feel they are being exploited. Clearly, the inmates' view of their situation may not always correspond to the views of the researchers. Some youths, for example, may not consider themselves exploited. The researchers, however, are assuming that if one person receives less than another in any but an altruistic relationship, regardless of how he feels about it, he is being victimized. It is our opinion also that victimization is intentional with most residents. We failed to perceive much of Matza's drift hypothesis—that boys drift in and out of delinquency (victimizing others) without being committed to it (Matza, 1964). Victimization is a way of life in this institution and facilitates survival for these youths. Wherever possible, the youth's feelings on these matters have been recorded.

Finally, we do not claim that all the behaviors observed are found in every juvenile institution (as certainly they are not), and we do not suggest that these findings are conclusive and final. We do suspect though that the relationships here observed *are* found in *most* juvenile facilities. Indeed, our observations must be examined carefully through more advanced research techniques and, where necessary, modifications in findings made. Only through a comparative analysis of many different types of institutions will insight be gained into the effect of different milieus on their population. Our purpose, then, is to stimulate this discussion.

## NOTES

1. A few of the factors involved are social variables, the character of the organization, personality variables affecting the nature of interaction, and the ecology of the organization.

2. Perhaps one way of usefully distinguishing between the two terms is to define exploitation as a culturally rationalized behavior pattern in which something is consistently taken from another, and to leave victimization to refer to the occasional, isolated, nonpatterned taking of valued objects of personal possessions. In this study, however, the two terms are used interchangeably.

3. See Appendix B.

4. The technique of having the staff rate each youth on the form of victimization helped resolve a number of issues of this nature. For example, staff would occasionally check on the typology that a boy was victimized but fail to note the form of victimization, which provided the clue to further verify the staff rating. Where questions such as this existed, they were answered simply by discussing directly with staff members whether victimization was observed. This technique was especially helpful in determining whether a boy was sexually victimized.

5. Construction of the typological categories was done in the following manner: The original four staff ratings, likely to exploit others, likely not to be exploited, likely to be exploited occasionally, and likely to be exploited often were each assigned the numbers 1, 2, 3, and 4 respectively. Then, the staff ratings of 135 boys were examined and the numbers 1 to 4, and all combinations thereof, were assigned to the staff rankings. All staff rankings for each boy were then combined. The ratings were then listed according to their logical complementarity, giving rise to the fivefold typology. Where a staff member believed a boy was not likely to be exploited, but facts proved otherwise, the corrected rating was used. Following are the emergent categories:

INITIAL RATING OF YOUTHS ON FOURFOLD TYPOLOGY

| TYPOLOGY | STAFF RATINGS | DESCRIPTION OF TYPOLOGY |
|----------|---------------|-------------------------|
| 1 | 1<br>1,2 | Likely to exploit others, not likely to be exploited (The Exploiter) |
| 2 | 1,3<br>1,4<br>1,3-4 | Exploits others and evidence of being exploited (Give and Takes) |
| 3 | 2 | Doesn't exploit others and no evidence of being exploited (Independents) |
| 4 | 2,3<br>2,4<br>2,3-4 | Doesn't exploit others and evidence of being exploited (Sometimes Boys) |
| 5 | 3<br>4<br>3,4 | Definitely exploited (Victims) |

6. Ambiguities still exist in how some of the boys are perceived, since "exploited occasionally" and "exploited often" are not clear-cut terms. As the phenomenon of victimization is more clearly defined through future research, better operationalization will no doubt evolve.

7. A basic problem, of course, is the validity and reliability of the observation of such a participant-observer. Fortunately, we were able to cross-validate the participant's observations with those of other staff and reconcile most staff-participant disagreements. A further problem, though, is that staff who are in close contact often reinforce and support each other's perceptions of reality. At present, we know of no totally satisfactory way of overcoming this source of possible bias.

8. One factor often overlooked by many sociologists is that researchers are looked upon not only as a nuisance to those interviewed, but as gatherers of other people's information as well. Staff are sensitive to the fact that sociologists take advantage of the staff's experience and receive all of the credit. In fact, the real observers are usually left only with the pain of sitting through long and arduous interviews. Thus, we have made an attempt to give staff credit for their ideas in both this book and published papers from this study. In addition, we have acknowledged staff co-authorship on several of these papers.

9. All boys were tested at one sitting whenever possible.

10. Earlier papers reporting preliminary findings of this study utilized 159 youths as the base for calculating certain percentages. In this book, however, 149 is used as the base. The reason for this is that a number of boys on the original institutional roster were released before later stages of the study began, thereby changing slightly the nature of the population.

11. We are deeply indebted to Professor Franco Ferracuti for both his suggestion to use the Machovers and his analysis of the data.

12. The high percentage tested also reflects the fact that the participant-observer was feared as well as respected and that the boys hesitated to incur his "wrath." In all fairness, it should be pointed out that he was feared because of his dynamic qualities and because his behavior could not be predicted: "He was wild, man."

# PART II

# INMATES VERSUS INMATES

*CHAPTER 4*

## INMATE PROCESSING OF INMATES

**To understand the life** and experiences of boys in this institution, three different levels of variables must be examined—pre-institutional variables, the interaction among peers, and the cultural life of the inmate population. Pre-institutional experiences and interaction with peers are principal determinants of how much respect a boy is given and, thus, influence the extent to which he is victimized. The pervasiveness of his victimization, in turn, affects his placement in the pecking order of the cottage. The cultural life of inmates refers to the rules and norms which help socialize new boys into the peer subculture. This "code" not only controls inmate behavior, but orients boys against the institution and its officials. Emerging in part from the conditions of imprisonment, the code provides a series of guidelines by which boys stabilize their lives.

### PRE-INSTITUTIONAL VARIABLES

Typical of other juvenile institutions, each youth arrives with a historical consciousness, which includes his race, social class, and values learned in the community. As this chapter will portray, the white in this black-dominated milieu has a much more difficult time escaping victimization than his black peers.

Too, boys vary widely in their abilities to defend themselves physically even though nearly all were troublemakers in their home communities. The youth who is "tough" in a middle-class section of town, for example, may be looked upon as a pansy in a ghetto; indeed, he may be frightened out of his wits by ghetto youths.

A boy's former institutionalization is also important, and the youths found here are generally of three different types. Some youths are transferred here directly after committing a violent crime in the community. More blacks than whites usually receive these direct transfers and, unless previously incarcerated, have had no experience with institutionalization. Another type includes those who have created problems in other youth facilities, are perceived as "troublemakers," and are transferred to more security-oriented institutions. Two-thirds of this group are black. Finally, runaways end up here simply because no other facility is secure enough to contain them. In contrast to the "troublemaker" category, runaways usually are two-thirds white.

The final factor concerns how boys react to the rumors circulating about the present facility. The importance of this variable may be gleaned from the following answers to the question, "What had you heard about this institution before you were sent here?"

> The same thing everybody else hears. That it is underground, people beat you all the time, and all that kind of stuff.

> I heard that all the staff were black, and that all the guys were big and tough and they messed with you. I also heard there was a lot of homosexuality up here. And that the institution wasn't together. It was more like a racial problem.

> I was scared, because when I was at [another institution], everyone was telling me[present institution] was supposed to be a bad place. Everybody was getting pushed around, jumped on all the time, fighting all the time, and all of this. Always being locked up, and they said [present institution] was under ground.

> I heard that when you first came that they took your handcuffs off, then hit you in the head, shaved your head, and beat you up before they put you in your cell in the ground.

That all the students would jump on you and try to get to you, and that all the staff members ever did was beat you up during the time you were here. And that you had to stay here three years.

Rumors that the training school is under ground, that staff beat boys, that inmates are huge and capable of victimizing anybody, and that if confined here, a long stay may be expected, are only a sample of the rumors heard. Other boys reported hearing that escape is nearly impossible, that staff use hoses on inmates, and that blanket parties sometimes occur (a blanket party is when a blanket is thrown over the head of an inmate and others sexually assault him).

## INTERACTION WITH INMATES

Initial Feelings

In over two years of interviewing boys on their first day, every youth was found to be fearful—not surprising considering the rumors. In fact, some were so frightened they tried to injure themselves upon hearing of their transfer. Their rationale was that if they could hurt themselves seriously enough, they would be transferred to a hospital where escape would be much easier. Although a few occasionally succeeded and were able to escape, most ended up at this training school.

Upon arrival, a youth first meets the intake cottage staff and then, escorted by a staff member, is taken to meet the superintendent, the chaplain, the nurse, and his social worker. Along with receiving his room assignment, customary haircut, and clothes allotment, a good portion of the first day is spent listening to various intake staff explain cottage and institutional rules. At this time, too, staff generally assign the newcomer to a work detail in the cottage. Throughout this indoctrination, however, the youth is usually so frightened that he only goes through the motion of listening to what is said.

Very much in a daze, the new boy attempts anxiously, almost desperately, to gain an understanding of his new social world— seeking to discover how he can best cope with it. He generally decides to stay by himself for the first few days and, unless he sees someone with whom he was friends in another institution, he is suspicious of peers. He knows that identifying with peers during past incarcerations only increased the length of his confinement. Since he wants to conceal his anxiety from fellow residents, he may brag about how "tough" he was in the community. If he has been sexually victimized elsewhere, he knows that this must be concealed at all costs; otherwise, he will receive relentless pressure from fellow inmates to engage in sex. Whites, especially, are concerned about being sexually exploited during these early days, even if they were able to escape being victimized in the past; blacks are more concerned about being "messed over" nonsexually by strong black peers.

The newcomer keeps his distance from the staff because he distrusts them. Because he has had difficulty in other institutions, he comes here with quite negative feelings. One boy expressed how new arrivals felt about staff and the institution by saying:

> Staff beat you a lot and stuff like that. If you mess up there isn't much hope for you. In other words, just a turnkey place where, you know, nobody cares about you. They just lock you up for a time.

Peer Reactions

In the meantime, cottage residents study the newcomer carefully. One strong white appraised how others size a new boy up:

> By the way you talk and the way you act, and when they talk to you they find out what you've done and they kind of put it all together in their own little way to determine whether you're bad or what. Whether you can fit in with them or not. If you just seem like some silly little kid off the street, then you're the scapegoat—like a few people are in this cottage. If you don't know how to handle yourself, then somebody is always picking on you.

This boy claimed that inmates are particularly able to spot the kid who is "putting on a big front." According to him, the anxiety behind the "big front" can be recognized by the following method:

> Watch him when he's alone, after he has been here in the institution an hour or two. Watch the cat sit down and smoke a cigarette, watch the way he sits and the way his eyes dart around. He's sizing everybody up.

He is looking out the corner of his eyes and quits looking when
somebody looks toward him.

In fact, most interactions are geared specifically to see how far a
neophyte can be pushed. When a boy walks into a cottage on his
first day, his peers have four basic questions, "How much does he
have?" "Will he defend himself?" "How is he holding himself?"
"Is he a punk?" These queries are concerned with what can be
exploited from him (food, clothes, cigarettes, and sex), whether he
will fight back, how fearful he is, and whether he has been
sexually exploited in the past.

When a white newcomer comes in, the answers to these questions begin to emerge when another white walks up and asks him
what his name is, where he is from, and why he is confined.
After feeling him out with these questions, this "new friend" will
probably ask him for a pack of cigarettes, promising to pay him
back in the near future. But more than exploiting a few cigarettes,
the purpose of this initial contact is to set the neophyte up for
later victimization and to see where he is going to fit in the cottage
pecking order. After watching this encounter, other whites get
together to talk with their white informant, as their initial efforts
to exploit will be largely contingent upon what was learned.
Regardless of the outcome of the interview, the new youth will
probably not receive any support from other whites in his struggle
to adjust.

The approach of black youths is quite different. Having to
engage in a politics of scarcity because of little or no money in
their canteen accounts, they have greater "need" to exploit
cigarettes and favorite foods. Consequently, they are more direct
and forceful than whites about extorting scarce items. Additionally, these youths will usually follow any possible avenue to
sexually victimize new boys.[1]

The white newcomer receives considerable harassment from
peers from other sections of the institution. Of major importance
is that "booty bandits" or sexual exploiters from other cottages
will try to exploit him, especially if he has a history of being
sexually exploited. Realizing that peers were becoming aware that
he had been sexually victimized in another setting, a white youth
ran to staff, hoping to receive protection. When questioned by

staff about his role in previous sexual encounters, he explained how he felt:

> It was like it wasn't my fault. I can just look back at it and say it was an experience that I had. And I look at it as an experience. Getting raped doesn't make a girl a whore, and any guy can get ripped off—I don't care who he is. If two or three guys decide to do it, they are going to do it, even to a staff member. So I don't feel bad about it anymore. I kinda accept it for what it was—just what the institution was like and I got myself into it so I had to abide by the rules and fight my problem.

To "booty bandits," this youth is a prime candidate for exploitation. Not surprisingly, he was approached in another cottage the very next day:

> Well, I went down to _____ Cottage and this black dude came in there and tried to approach me. I told him to get out of my face. I said you might as well go to someone else cause I ain't nothing of what you think I am. So he messed around a little. I got off the toilet stool and got ready to get into a fight and he left. But he came right back, and said "I'll give you a couple of packs if you do it." I said I'm not even interested in what you got to say. So I got pretty uptight because it brought back bad thoughts.

But unquestionably, the success of these "booty bandits" depends largely upon their exploitative abilities. The most successful ones are subtle, constantly harassing passive youths and waiting for a moment of weakness. The newcomer who demonstrates strength will eventually be left alone, but he must battle for some time with both sexual and nonsexual aggressors. One perceptive youth leader described the technique of the experienced exploiter:

> Well, actually, unless a kid is very passive, it's sort of a subtle type of exploitation. It may draw on or go on for several days or weeks before the guy really gets what he is after. If the experienced guys are exploiting, they take their time, they are patient, especially in the area of sexual exploitation.

If the new inmate is black, the response of residents is slightly different. Whites are afraid he might become an exploiter; therefore, they watch his associations with other blacks very carefully and, unless he bothers them, tend to let him alone. Very rarely will whites ever try to exploit a black. The only exception is the black youth who begins to associate with whites because he is not accepted by black peers. When they perceive his weakness, stronger whites may attempt to exploit cigarettes or food from him, but not sex.

To be expected, an aggressive black newcomer can threaten the reputation of black exploiters and may, in fact, interfere with ongoing exploitative relationships. Consequently, if a black neophyte disturbs an already established relationship, the established aggressor will usually try to intimidate him and put him in his place as soon as possible. For the new youth who emits cues of strength but is not trying to exploit peers, the chances are that exploiters will let him alone.

The victimized black youth, on the other hand, may see the new black as a potential exploiter and cultivate his friendship, hoping that this act will deter any aggressive ideas. Or he may attempt to turn the tables on the new black by beating him in a fight, thereby dropping the newcomer lower in the pecking order than he is. This latter ploy is used most frequently with middle-class blacks, chiefly because they have less skill in defending themselves and therefore are more likely to lose any fight.

To demonstrate how exploitation occurs, we will turn to the following common daily happenings in the life of a newcomer: He sits down for lunch or dinner and another boy walks over to him, picks up his dessert, and says, "You don't want your dessert, do you?" Unless he wants to fight, the new youth knows that his only possible answer is "No, take it." Or a peer walks up to a new boy and demands a cigarette: "Give me a square." Again, denying the request probably will mean a physical confrontation. When the weekly canteen is open, the prizes are even greater. As the boys bring their purchases back to the cottage, item after item disappears until the new or the weak lose all they have. If the new youth returns to the cottage loaded down with pop and candy brought by parents, he has his burden lifted as if by magic. Afraid of the consequences, he may find denying any request for food or desired goods difficult. Sometimes the exploitation takes more aggressive forms. For instance, a new boy may accidently bump another peer. The likely result is his being pushed and informed to "get out of my way, motherfucker." If he makes any attempt to defend himself, he is likely to receive a "sucker punch" (unexpected punch in the mouth or stomach).

Of more serious consequences is that the new youth may be confronted daily by his peers, "You're a punk, aren't you?" or "We heard what happened to you at Camp _____ . We all know you're a punk. You better give in, or we're going to hurt you." This type of harassment will occur especially if the new boy shows signs of weakness. Yet another means of sexual exploitation is to grab the "ass" of a new boy as he walks down the hall. The newcomer finds that he cannot really fight back or resist because he does not know exactly who grabbed him. New residents may experience these attacks several times during the first three or four weeks of their stay.

## REACTION TO THE POTENTIAL VICTIM

When the pressure of harassment begins to be felt, the target can pursue one of several courses of action. Obviously, he can resist and not give an inch. One white who was able to resist exploitation explained how he did it:

> On the first day I was in the cottage, this dude came up to me and said, "Give me a cigarette." I answered, you're asking me or telling me, man?' When he answered, "I'm telling you," I told him to get lost, and he left me alone. A couple of days later others came up and tried to get rough with me and things like that. It was basically the guys that had been there longer because the rest of them just fit in the same category with me. I'd say, "Get away from me, man, I'm not giving you anything, and if you think you're bad, take it." You just have to lay it out to them and show them, saying to them, "Maybe you can whip my ass, but we're going to fight, and if you want to take that chance, then we'll do it!" You've got to express that because if you just go in there and somebody says, "Give me this and give me that," and you give it up, then you're going to be giving for a long time and not getting anything back.

> The most important thing when you come into an institution is to show them that you're not scared of them. That's what I've had to do in all the institutions I've been in. When I was in another institution, I made a few mistakes by being a pushover. But I learned that it's those first few days that count.

If a new boy feels that standing up to the pressure alone is too difficult, he usually tries at first to form a friendship with one or two peers, hoping for protection. He soon discovers that peers are glad to "buddy" with him and include him in the cigarette pool (one boy each week keeps the cigarettes for one or two others), but they will not protect him from exploitative overtures. Upon discovering this, new residents typically say, "You can't trust nobody in here." Whites, especially, begin to feel more and more isolated from their fellow whites.

As pressure mounts and the uncertainty as to how to cope increases, the target may run to staff hoping for protection. Usually, he is informed that he has to be a man: "You can't let anyone push you around. If you give them an inch, they will end up screwing you." Having been reluctant to go to staff and now only receiving meaningless advice, the boy quickly decides that no help is available here either. Indeed, since reporting problems to staff means poor progress reviews, new residents learn quickly that problems should be kept to themselves.

Receiving no help from peers or staff, the new youth then generally approaches the inmate leader of the cottage and offers him cigarettes and food—hoping to gain protection. In spite of the fact that the inmate leader usually accepts the food and cigarettes, the youth soon discovers that the desired protection is not forthcoming because the inmate code decrees that the inmate leader or "heavy" may receive favors without reciprocating.

At this point, the new inmate usually decides that he will permit himself to be exploited. Typically, boys will give up only so much, but then fight if pushed any further. Thus, boys make a conscious decision that some exploitation will be permitted, but beyond that they will do everything possible to prevent it. A youth may be willing to give up his institutional food and canteen "treats" for example, but he will not give up his cigarettes. Another youth may be willing to yield all his material possessions, but fight viciously to prevent sexual exploitation. A third may permit occasional anal sodomy, but will absolutely refuse to commit oral sodomy or masturbation of others. This, of course, suggests that a ranking is given all the valued commodities, and this will be explored in later chapters.

Unfortunately, in three weeks or so, the new resident must start over again in another living unit, repeating the same testing as experienced in the intake cottage. Certainly, if he demonstrated weakness or permitted himself to be victimized in the intake cottage, his past will go with him and will determine the nature of relations with his new companions. But even if he was strong and aggressive, he must still demonstrate his prowess in the new cottage.

## CULTURE OF THE INSTITUTION

Whites are clearly the most seriously exploited inmates. Of sixteen sexually exploited boys, for example, thirteen were white; and, in every cottage, whites usually occupied the lowly positions in the pecking order.[2] In fact, outside of one white youth who became a "heavy," all other inmate leaders and lieutenants were black (Bartollas et al., 1976a).

Deeply resenting the fact that this institution is black-dominated, whites expressed some of their feelings in the following three representative statements:

> Blacks have more control in the jails than the whites do. They call it the revolution, and they kind of press down on it, too. They turn the whites into punks. You don't see any black punks around.

> Blacks are in control in here because of the black-dominated community. All blacks here try to be bad and stuff and show their masculinity. They always use the cop-out that they come from the ghetto and that they are better with their hands. I've only seen a very few blacks in the whole institution take whites for what they are and give them respect. They won't smoke after us; why should we smoke after them? The blacks want to bring slavery back to us now. They want to run everything. They always have to be first in line. They always have to be first to get their food. This ain't no good. They always try to take the white guys' goods they get from visitors. It just ain't no good.

> Blacks feel that they can exploit whites without being exploited because they use the old thing that they were slaves and the white dudes always picked on them. Like, in the detention home and any place I ever went, a black dude would get up and sucker punch a white dude and when the boss comes down, they'd say, "Man, he was messing with me because I'm black; he called me a 'nigger' and things like that."

One youth leader ascribed this black domination to their greater aggressiveness and greater group cohesion. He noted that "blacks are just naturally more aggressive because most of the black kids we get here are from the ghetto," and he further felt that the willingness of blacks to stick together made whites fearful of retaliation if they contested black power. He finally expressed the opinion that victimization and injustices suffered by blacks in the community motivated them to retaliate against whites; and they used this opportunity to gain revenge.

The ruling position of blacks results not only in the exploiting of cigarettes, food, clothing, and sex, but the socializing of whites into a black subculture. Through their prevailing position, blacks control the music played, the television programs watched, the kinds of food eaten, the style of clothing worn, and the language employed. If a white places an unacceptable record on the stereo in the program area, for example, a black usually just walks over and changes the record.[3] Boys also refrain from playing anything but "soul music" in the dormitory unless all four are white.[4] Blacks choose the television programs, and whites must either watch these programs or do something else. Blacks particularly want to watch television programs which feature black entertainers.

Food is an even better barometer of the influence and pervasiveness of the black culture. While "soul foods" (greens, ham stocks, ribs) are always acceptable, certain foods are eaten but not necessarily liked, and other foods are simply ignored. Only a few whites feel secure and strong enough to eat what they want. Yet another indicator of black power is clothing; although the drab daily clothing hides black influence, whites imitate blacks' modish dress at dances and other special occasions.[5] Language, too, reflects white impotence; blacks may say what they want to whites, but whites watch what is said to blacks. Additionally, even though the language of a ghetto black and the white who lives near the ghetto is similar, the black's distinctive dialect is generally adopted by whites soon after exposure to it. Finally, blacks control certain territories in the cottage, such as the pool table, the ping-pong table, and around the card table, and only the stronger whites dare invade this territory. At that, even the stronger whites are quite limited in the time they are permitted to spend in these areas.

Reflection upon these aspects of cottage life points out the extent to which this institution has its internal dynamics regulated by rules understood by the participants. Food, clothes, cigarettes,

music, and language are not the only features of the cottage life
that are regulated. Close examination of the interactions of boys
and staff indicates that practically every behavior has a cor-
responding rule stating the appropriate actions to be taken. What
emerges, then, is a normative code—one which all newcomers hear
as they struggle to find out how to survive. In many instances, this
code is made up of a series of general tenets for living. These are
statements passed on from one youth to another and inform each
how to get along with his neighbors (Bartollas et al., 1975b).

## CONTENTS OF THE INMATE INFORMAL CODE

"Exploit Whomever You Can"

The conduct norms suggest that the powerless may be victimized in any conceivable way. If, for example, a boy runs out of
"squares" (cigarettes), then extortion of "squares" is quite permissible. In addition, "booty bandits" have few qualms about
coercing weaker whites into submitting to their sexual advances.[6]
This norm explains how a new inmate can be compelled to
commit oral sodomy on several boys waiting in line. Talking with
the aggressors the day after an attack, one finds a total lack of
sense of wrongdoing or feeling for the victim.[7] Nevertheless, the
exploitation of others is justified because inmates feel they have
been victimized all their lives; therefore, they have the right to
take whatever is wanted from weaker inmates.

"Don't Kiss Ass"

Urging boys to stand on their own two feet, this tenet warns
them not to be dependent on staff and to treat youth leaders,
social workers, and schoolteachers with distrust and suspicion.
Initially, new inmates closely adhere to this norm and talk very
little with staff. They soon discover that special privileges and
progress toward release will not be forthcoming until cottage staff
are approached; consequently, after being confined for three or

four months, more friendliness is exhibited toward staff members simply to expedite release. When interactions are efforts to manipulate staff, then this is not considered as a violation of a reference group norm. If this friendliness is considered sincere by peers, the youth is punished and warned against the dangers of becoming too involved with staff.

## "Don't Rat on Your Peers"

Similar to the situation found in adult prisons, to betray a peer is to break one of the most inflexible of the informal norms. Boys attempt to keep the "interior life" of the cottages hidden from staff as much as possible. "Backstage" happenings, nevertheless, are occasionally exposed when a youth steps forward to tell the staff of his or someone else's exploitation, of a planned escape, or of hacksaw blades smuggled into the cottage. "Ratting on your peers" is considered a serious violation and results at least in isolation from the group (i.e., putting the offender on "chunk"). Surprisingly, the only inmate capable of violating this norm consistently without punishment is the inmate leader or "heavy." He usually informs the staff of events which jeopardize cottage control, principally because his special privileges and rapid release depend upon the staff maintaining tight restraints (Miller et al., 1974).

## "Don't Give up Your Ass"

Complementing the first maxim, "exploit whomever you can," is the tenet telling boys to avoid becoming sexual victims. Since a boy who is sexually exploited often runs the risk of becoming the cottage scapegoat, youths usually fight rather than submit to the pressure.

## "Be Cool"

This tenet informs boys not to "whine" when things are not going well (i.e., turned down at review, denied a home visit, or not sent to a dance), and the code advises, "be a man" and "don't act like a baby." Especially sensitive to the expression of weakness to staff, the code advocates "doing time like a man" and keeping away from staff. "Being cool" also means not running from fights or aggression from peers. In other words, no one should be permitted to push them around physically or mentally. When someone becomes aggressive, the admonition is clear—put him in his place.

## "Don't Get Involved in Another Inmate's Affairs"

This maxim promotes granting as much social distance as self-contained cottage living permits. Hence, if visitors arrive from home, the fortunate one should not be approached, regardless of how pretty his sister is. Or, if a youth hears that a physical or sexual assault on someone is imminent, he must not get involved. Even if a boy threatens to cut his own wrist, interference with his decision by interceding or "ratting" to the staff is a code violation.

## "Don't Steal 'Squares' "

Although cigarettes or "squares" are not the only medium of exchange, they are probably the institution's most valued commodity. Interestingly, the "squares" tenet admonishes "honor among thieves." But in almost every cottage thieves steal cigarettes from unlocked rooms. If caught stealing, these violators are often seriously assaulted by code enforcers.

## "Don't Buy the Mind-Fucking"

The final general maxim of the code concerns boys' responses to institutional treatment efforts. Throughout the boys' time with the youth commission, repeated attempts are made by staff to modify boys' behavior and values. Guarding against these techniques, which are geared to change the inmate into a more acceptable person, this reference group norm reminds boys not to accept the keepers' version of reality. Boys, of course, may pretend outwardly to accept staff viewpoints to gain release, but any sign of genuine acceptance is condemned.

The above maxims are accepted by nearly all of the boys; even victims, early in their stay, tend to adhere to these norms. There are, in addition, four maxims which seem to apply to blacks only and two more which apply only to whites.

## NORMS FOR BLACKS ONLY

### "Exploit Whites"

The animosity held against whites motivates blacks to pursue retribution for exploitation occurring before incarceration. Isolated by their lack of group cohesiveness, whites make ready targets for aggression. This norm is considered so important that blacks who do not exploit whites are regarded as deviant and are consequently verbally harassed by their black peers.

### "No Forcing Sex on Blacks"

Black cohesiveness also encourages blacks to develop a group norm prohibiting sexual victimization of other blacks. Realizing the effect of sexual exploitation on the victim and how difficult it is to expunge oneself of this stigma, blacks do not want to see their own "brothers" made into sexual victims. The only exceptions are the "booty bandits" and the black youth who wants to become involved in sexual activity because of homosexual desires. In the latter case, sexual exploiters are usually more than willing to oblige. Also, two or three black inmates usually can be found who want to be a reciprocating partner in sexual relations. If these boys are in the same cottage or can arrange a secret rendezvous, they "trade off"–a "trade off," of course, is not regarded as exploitation.

### "Defend Your Brother"

Closely related to the above norm is the prescription to defend fellow blacks, a norm which becomes particularly important when a black youth has been physically manhandled by a white. The responsibility of fellow blacks, according to the code, is to retaliate for the loss of their soul brother's dignity. Sometimes it is necessary to gang up on powerful whites in order to accomplish this task and to keep them in their place.

## "Staff Favor Whites"

Even though the line staff is 97 percent black, this group norm warns that white boys are favored over blacks and frequently leads to some staff being referred to as "Uncle Toms."[8] This contention is correct for at least two reasons. First, the majority of line staff are extremely sensitive to exploitation and spot it immediately. Knowing that whites need to be protected, staff not only watch blacks more closely than whites, but punish them more severely for the same offenses. Second, in order to avoid the charge of favoritism toward blacks, staff members tend to make stricter demands of black inmates than they do of whites. Black youths, for example, average a longer stay in the institution, take longer to receive institutional privileges, and receive fewer home visits than whites (Bartollas, 1973).[9] Blacks certainly resent both the preferred treatment of whites and being controlled so tightly by their "keepers."

## NORMS FOR WHITES ONLY

### "Don't Trust Anyone"

Whites, in contrast to blacks, feel alienated from each other. While they may share cigarettes, they are very hesitant to reveal their true feelings even to those considered friends. They believe that other whites will never support them, and that other whites will even make deals with blacks which result in their sexual exploitation.

### "Everybody for Himself"

A corollary of the first norm for whites is that everyone is on his own. Especially vulnerable white youths, then, must either flee the institution, accept exploitation, withdraw from normal social interaction, or try to escape through suicide. Consequently, two out of every three runaways the past three years were white. Some exploited whites suffered significant weight loss and became withdrawn psychologically during their stay. Furthermore, not only were the two suicides in the twelve-year history of the institution white, but another fifty to sixty suicide attempts by whites were thwarted by the quick intervention of staff.[10]

## STAGES OF THE INMATE CAREER
## AND HIS RESPONSE TO THE CODE

Inmates' responses to the code depend both upon their position in the inmate power structure and the stage of their institutional career. Not surprisingly, boys undergo a change in attitude and orientation toward the institution during different periods of their stay.

All new arrivals are initially fearful but begin to relax within a few weeks. Older and more experienced boys are quick to socialize new youths into the tenets of the inmate code. New inmates are reluctant to do anything contrary to the norms of the other inmates, since they are very concerned about maintaining good relationships with their peers. The first stage, then, is one in which nearly all youths accept these conduct norms in toto.

During the middle period of their stay, boys become concerned about attaining release. They realize that approaching the institutional program positively means not only a shorter stay, but also immediate institutional privileges.[11] Boys also become aware that staff members grant privileges to those who fulfill staff expectations—which means they must talk with the staff, do their chores, stay out of trouble, refrain from exploitation, keep their rooms clean, and appear interested in their rehabilitation. This, of course, places considerable strain on inmates, for the code demands one thing and the formal criteria for release dictate something else.

The response of whites to these contradictory pressures is somewhat different from that of blacks. Whites who have already begun to experience exploitation are more willing to forsake the inmate code. Certainly, part of their willingness to ignore the code results from their lack of commitment to the dominant black culture. Blacks, on the other hand, find the abandonment of the code much more difficult than whites. Some stick with their conduct norms, in spite of the way their incarceration is pro- longed. But, in general, the average black decides after a review or two that he must adapt to staff expectations, regardless of the code. Still, he attempts to maintain the tenets of the code on a sub rosa level.

In the final stage, which consists of the last three of four months of confinement, there is little acceptance of the inmate code. Being youthful—some boys are as young as fifteen years old—they find incarceration very painful; thus, they are willing to do almost anything to be released. For instance, inmate leaders become more compliant, "booty bandits" tend to turn away from sexual exploitation, and even scapegoats begin to struggle with more aggressive peers to show staff that they are ready to be released.

Importation versus Deprivation

Some controversy exists as to whether these relations and values are found in prisons because of being imported from the outside or because they emerged from the deprived conditions under which prisoners must live. Examination of many of the norms regulating inmate behavior suggests them to be reflections of norms found in society in general. "Don't kiss ass," "don't rat on your peers," "be cool," "don't steal," "defend your brother," "don't get involved in another's affairs," "don't trust anyone," and "everyone for himself" all have their counterparts in the outside world. Few, if any, of these norms could be called unique to institutional settings.

On the other hand, conduct norms such as "exploit whomever you can," "don't give up your ass," "don't buy the mind- fucking," "staff favor whites," "exploit whites," and "no forcing sex on blacks" reflect chiefly the adverse and deprived environ- ment in which inmates find themselves. Two of these norms— "exploit whomever you can" and "exploit whites"—do represent outside and, particularly, ghetto society. The deprivation model gains double importance for blacks who come from the ghetto only to experience even greater deprivation in the institution.

Considering all of the tenets, the importation and deprivation models appear equally important in the origin of the inmate code.

These conduct norms receive a differential response for each stage of inmate institutionalization. In general, the longer a boy remains incarcerated, the less obedient he is to the code. This code, in addition, receives a more positive response from black youths than from whites. The reason is that the code supports the powerful inmates, and blacks have the majority of the power. Thus, the code ends up facilitating the victimization of passive white and black boys.

Beyond the issue of their origin and acceptance, these norms are unquestionably functional for aggressive inmates. Postulating what the ideal inmate should be, the code enables those who "live up to it" to maintain some sense of dignity, self-esteem, and confidence in their achievements. The code also places the stamp of approval on victimization of passive inmates. Living up to these conduct norms further protects the strong from being forced to accept the "people-changing" techniques of their keepers.

By legitimizing and encouraging the exploitation of others, the code makes the life of victims much more difficult. Compliance to the code prevents those low in the pecking order from protecting themselves by going to staff except as a last resort. Those inmates who cannot live up to the code's tenets are looked upon as "losers" and are alienated more from peers. Therefore, the code clearly works to the disadvantage of the weak by increasing both their exploitation by peers and their isolation from staff.

## NOTES

1. No overt sexual exploiters were in the intake cottage at the time of this study.

2. Staff indentified thirteen whites and three blacks as sexual victims. Later interviewing indicated that the blacks were, indeed, participating in sex, but that their participation was very likely consensual. Some staff felt the boys were coerced initially, but others disagreed. For purposes of this study, the boys were considered victims, although the possible consensual nature of their participation must be granted. This subject is discussed in greater depth in later chapters.

3. Cottage staff permit only one record player in the recreational area.

4. Each cottage has two of these four-bed dormitories.

5. Although the argument may be made that whites imitate blacks simply because of the modishness of dress, the milieu of the institution suggests otherwise. Whites, fearing victimization, feel that the only way to be accepted is to imitate those above them.

6. Occasionally a white "booty bandit" is found who sexually exploits whites, but there were no white "booty bandits" in the institution at the time of this study.

7. "Booty bandits" exhibit no feeling for their victims, but occasionally they become involved with boys playing feminine sexual roles.

8. Many cottages seem to end up with one older, experienced staff member who protects whites, and a younger, inexperienced staff member who actually takes out some of his frustrations on them.

9. Exceptions to this are emotionally disturbed whites and cottage scapegoats. These boys receive the longest stays of all.

10. Until the admission of emotionally disturbed blacks several years ago, very few blacks attempted suicide. Since their admission, however, the number of attempted suicides has gone up. Staff feel this is primarily an attention-seeking device.

11. It may be remembered that boys on pre-release status may have home visits, one telephone call a month home, and unsupervised access to certain areas of the institution.

CHAPTER 5

# THE EXPLOITATION MATRIX AND STIMULUS QUALITIES

**All boys eventually** get a position in the social hierarchy, first in the intake and then in their permanent cottage. The object of many is to attain as high a position as possible and then to improve their position during their confinement. As indicated in Chapter 4, certain variables influence a youth's ultimate place in the pecking order. Race is one of the most important simply because blacks have higher social status than whites. Other important variables include seriousness of criminal offenses in the community, ability to handle oneself physically, fearlessness, receptivity toward the inmate code, and interpersonal skills.

Not surprisingly, these variables are related to whether boys exploit or are exploited and this, in turn, influences their position in the pecking order. But a difference still exists between the exploitation matrix and the social hierarchy. This is reflected most clearly in the youths who neither exploit nor are they exploited. Even though they are independent of the exploitation matrix, they still have high status. At other times, hidden exploitation may not affect one's social standing, although suspected exploitation may very much lower a boy's prestige. The social hierarchy and exploitation matrix are closely related and usually overlap, but still are not identical.

As defined in Chapter 3, victimization involves a relationship in which one party loses material goods, becomes involved involuntarily in homosexuality, or is involved in any interaction which causes loss of face without personally satisfying compensation or restitution. In these relationships, an imbalance exists in which one party is clearly the loser. As a matter of fact, most boys deeply involve themselves in every scheme imaginable to fleece their peers and staff of desired items and to gain the maximum freedom possible.

To understand the dynamics behind the formation of the exploitation matrix, a number of factors must be considered. Of special importance are stimulus qualities. These are characteristics which indicate to others, consciously or unconsciously, the type of person a youth is and the likelihood of his being exploited. Also important are the social processes of exploitation, where different types of victimization take place in the pecking order, the way the matrix is organized, and how different social types respond to the possibilities of exploitation.

## THE EXPLOITATION MATRIX

The exploitation matrix typically consists of four groups, and the form of exploitation found in each is fairly clear cut.[1] At the top normally is a black inmate leader called a "heavy." He is followed closely by three or four black lieutenants. The third group, a mixture of eight to sixteen black and white youths, do the bidding of those at the top. This group is divided into a top half of mostly blacks, known as "alright guys," with the bottom half comprised primarily of whites, designated as "chumps." One or two white scapegoats make up the fourth group in each cottage. These scapegoats become the sexual victims of the first three groups.

Varieties of Homosexual Behavior

Probably the most striking feature of the matrix is the extent to which its formation depends upon youths' willingness to be sexually exploited. Material goods are taken frequently and regularly and result in feelings of frustration and poor self-esteem on the part of the victims. But the boys' actual ranking on the matrix ultimately depends on how far they are from being sexually exploited. If sexual victimization is out of the question, then only material goods remain.

In addition, only victims are labeled as homosexuals. Little distinction is made among boys oriented toward homosexuality as a life style, those forced to participate against their will, or those who have ulterior motives for participating (Bartollas et al., 1976a).

The first type is made up of boys who willingly had homosexual encounters in other training schools, but came here hoping to escape their past. When peers become aware that they were "punks" in other institutions, great pressure is placed on them to continue this life. Few youths with a history of sexual encounters are able to resist the persistent pressures received from the sexually deprived. Finally submitting to the continued harassment, these youths sometimes become committed to homosexuality as a life style before leaving the institution.

The second type is the boy who gives up sex in exchange for something else. A resident out of cigarettes, for example, occasionally masturbates another for a pack or two of cigarettes. Some whites buy protection from strong black peers by granting sexual privileges. The objective, of course, is to receive protection from everyone else.[2]

The third type of labeled homosexual is the passive and dependent boy who submits strictly out of fear. Afraid of being physically attacked and mentally fatigued from abuse received from aggressive peers, these youths are simply overwhelmed by their environment. Generally middle-class whites, they feel alienated and bewildered—very much in a state of anomie. Certain psychological tests indicate that these youths have some need of self-abasement and humiliation (see Chapter 8).

Made up of lower-class boys, the fourth group comes into the institution with reputations as "tough guys." But either in an encounter with an extremely aggressive black or in gang rapes, they are sexually victimized. These residents sometimes experience a drastic change in personality following this event. In one incident, an aggressive lower-class white who had pushed others around experienced a dramatic change after a gang rape. Becoming quite passive, he tried to withdraw from everyone but was eventually coerced into becoming the cottage's scapegoat.

The fifth type is made up of white and black residents who "trade-off" with another white or black because they like and feel close to each other. Intraracial in nature, most of these sexual affairs are characterized by the exchange of friendship, rather than the coercion of exploitation. Since the behavior is voluntary, these relationships come very close to what is considered to be true homosexuality. Even here, however, the relationship appears to be temporary and a function of institutional living.

The final type consists of "queens." These boys play the role of women, both in dress and mannerisms; in contrast with scapegoats who are usually white, these inmates are almost always black. These residents clearly come into the institution committed to the "gay" life and take great joy in teasing peers.

## Ranking of Exploitation

Compared to community living, institutional life represents deprivation. Subsequently, the politics of scarcity becomes a way of life, and every item has a value out of proportion to its value in the community. Even though material possessions are ranked a little differently in each cottage, inmates are still very much aware of the rank ordering of items. This information helps them to decide what to give up if harassed. As indicated in Chapter 4, boys decide where to draw the line, permitting themselves to be exploited up to a point, but vigorously resisting further victimization. Certainly, this point may change over the period of a boy's stay. Too, a boy may find himself in situations where a compromise is necessary. He later reverts back to what is acceptable in his own way of thinking as the situation changes (Bartollas et al., 1976a). Table 5.1 shows the rank ordering of the various items and sexual acts, and is set up so that items of least value are listed first.[3]

The first item refers to cake and other desserts served for lunch and supper. Boys do not mind giving up institutional dessert very

## Table 5.1

## RANKING OF MATERIAL AND SEXUAL EXPLOITATION

| Institutional Dessert | Institutional Favorite Foods | Canteen Pop and Candy | Parents' Pop and Candy | Institutional Clothing |
|---|---|---|---|---|
| 1 | 2 | 3 | 4 | 5 |
| Toilet Articles | Cigarettes | Personal Clothing | Radios | Physical Beating |
| 6 | 7 | 8 | 9 | 10 |
| Anal Sodomy | Masturbation of Others | Oral Sodomy | | |
| 11 | 12 | 13 | | |

much at all. The next has a little more value because foods such as "ribs" are highly desired and boys resist giving them up. The third refers to pop and candy brought from the canteen on Saturday morning. Because these items are purchased by their money, pop and candy have more status than even the best institutional foods. Not surprisingly, the next item has an even greater value because "mom" brought it from home. Since staff harass boys who do not have clean clothing for school, the fifth involves not only losing respect from peers for giving up a clean shirt, but being hassled by staff for wearing dirty clothes.

The next item is again concerned with personal property; in fact, in this impersonal and sterile setting, soap and lotion are highly esteemed. Cigarettes, too, are a valued commodity and are used for trading, gambling, and buying sexual favors. Nearly all of the boys smoke, and the familiar white and green "Kool" pack is a status symbol. Personal clothing used for home visits, dances, and other off-campus trips have even higher value than cigarettes, principally because boys have few nice clothes and, once extorted, clothes are gone for good. Loss of the ninth item connotes even greater loss of status due to the expense of a radio and the fact that it was usually brought by "mom" from home; in general, boys feel that anyone who gives up a radio will give up anything.

The next involves permitting oneself to be physically beaten by other boys, and certainly involves greater social degradation than the first nine items. The eleventh item, anal sodomy, is looked down upon so much that being a passive participant will place a boy on the bottom of the exploitation matrix. The last two items are considered so undesirable that the victim is considered a social misfit and excluded from all cottage interaction.


## STIMULUS QUALITIES

### Impression Management

Impression management is the major key to success in escaping pressures from residents. The tools of impression management include tone of voice, facial expression and posture, and confidence in interpersonal relations. Social characteristics are also important and will be delineated in the next two sections. Through impression management, boys project either the image of strength (ability to take care of self) or of weakness (amenability to victimization). If strong images are projected, positions of leadership are often attained. Weak images may result in extensive exploitation. When newcomers become aware of the importance of these interpersonal clues, they sometimes consciously attempt to adopt the mask or "front" they want others to accept.

The impression management of "heavies" and lieutenants consists of looking others directly in the eye when answering questions, stating the location of their home matter-of-factly, discussing the seriousness of crimes they committed, holding their "ground" during an argument, and reminding others how tough they are. No indication of being afraid of anything or anyone is given, and these characteristics drive home the point they are not to be "messed with." One boy, when asked what he thought kept him from being victimized said:

> People respect me because of the charge [bank robbery] and they feel that I'm a lot rougher than what I let on. I have wrestled an awful lot of guys and I'm not that big, you know. There's a lot of power here that people just can't understand where it comes from. There will be a

boy about twice my size and when we go down to the gym, we'll pull the mats off the wall and we'll wrestle for a while. Maybe I'll flip the dude or slam him and he says hey, I underestimated your little ass. You know, they don't mess with me and all the other guys see me do it once or twice and that keeps them off right away.

When asked how a potential leader would act upon coming to the cottage, this boy said:

It would be a guy who came in with a small touch. He'd come in cool, quiet, and like sit around and size everything up. Ask a few questions here and there and then learn how to manipulate. . . . Don't be real forward, don't go showing off a lot. [He] stays silent and learns pretty much what's going on, eaves-dropping a lot, finds out where so and so's head is and how to get along around here.

On the third level of the matrix, inmates do not project the appropriate images so well. Their impression management is less convincing; they have less direct eye contact, back off slightly when talking, are incarcerated for less serious crimes, and are less able to "use their hands." They, of course, are not accorded the same status as those at the top of the matrix. Although not devoid of strength, they possess it to a lesser degree than the "heavy" and the lieutenants. The impression management of the "alright guys" is, in fact, reasonably good, while the "chumps" project the types of stimulus qualities which alert peers to their amenability to victimization.

Finally, other boys come into the cottage with obvious fear. Soon on the threshold of victimization, these youths walk with their heads hung low, nervously shift from one foot to the other, back up when talking with others, do not hold eye contact, answer questions with a weak projection of voice and in a hesitating, unconvincing manner. These youths clearly appear too anxious to develop normal relationships with peers. A youth describes one of these boys:

He is a younger, scared dude. He's the one that people take his cigarettes, candy, anything he's got. If there's going to be any sexual exploitation at all, this is the cat. They push him around a lot too, because he is so chicken. He is so unwary [sic] of what goes on around him. They even give him stuff left and right. Then they come with the old approach, you owe me something, right. Now, come on. That's the type of person who gets exploited.

These boys are so frightened they volunteer the information that they "give out hand jobs," that they were a "punk" in another institution, or that they might engage in sex. Terrified because of what happened to them during previous confinements (where they were forced into sexual activity), they do anything to escape the pressure to "give in." The easiest way out is to volunteer the information that they will participate in sex immediately upon walking into the cottage. Through the use of this ploy, the testing that other newcomers must go through is escaped.

Race as Stimulus Quality

With 97 percent of the line staff and 51 percent of the inmates black, race becomes a stimulus quality. With black staff in charge of the cottages and black residents at the top of the exploitation matrix, power is identified with blackness. Whites coming from middle-class suburbs and rural areas find their minority relationship confusing and threatening.

Although black staff attempt to be fair, as attested to by the fact that black inmates accuse them of letting whites off too easily, some white boys feel that black staff are prejudiced against them. White youths tend to single out one staff member in each cottage for this charge. Representative of this feeling against black staff members is the following statement from a white youth:

> I tell you this. The white dudes need a white man. Those black leaders eat our food. The suck asses in the kitchen give them the best food. _____ is the worst one. He always took our food. He is a real fuck up; he will burn you.

> He was the one that caused me to go AWOL. When I returned from trade school the night before, I lit a cigarette and _____ was all over me. He called me a white bastard. I decided then that I was not going to school the next day, that I was not coming back to the institution. He would not even let me go back to my room to take a shower.

Of importance also, as suggested in Chapter 4, blacks are much more cohesive than whites. Blacks identify with fellow black residents whether a confrontation is with staff or whites. In their interactions with whites, blacks are especially careful to support "the brother"—particularly when a white youth is intimidating a black. But if a black is threatened with serious punishment from staff unless he informs on "troublemakers," the youth will generally protect himself rather than his black peers. This is particularly true during the latter stages of incarceration.

Whites, meanwhile, lack social cohesion and find themselves involved in an anomic condition. Accustomed to looking down on blacks, whites find themselves in a strange world, in which they become the impotent and victimized. Why, then, do they fail to unify and use group pressure to mitigate their victimization? A group consciousness and identity could vastly improve their position of power. But whites seem to be bewildered by their minority status and are unable to escape the resulting confusion. Whites are also aware that greater group solidarity risks violent reactions from blacks who are unwilling to lose their power to whites. Confrontation is a prospect that most whites want to avoid. There is also conflict between lower- and middle-class whites who appear to have little in common and have difficulty uniting even when both are being victimized. Finally, the white usually has a shorter stay than the average black; he focuses on being released and blocks out the present world as much as he can.[4]

Empirical data demonstrate that whites are exploited more than blacks. Table 5.2 shows that, on the average, staff check blacks as "likely to exploit others" more than twice as often as they check whites on the same category. Staff also check more blacks than whites as "likely not to be exploited." Whites, too, are more apt to be "occasionally exploited" and "exploited often" than blacks. Although some blacks are obviously heavily exploited, they are exploited by fellow blacks. Likewise, some whites are exploiters, but qualitative data indicate that whites seldom or never exploit blacks.

Social Class as Stimulus Quality

Four basic social classes are included in the institution's population: the lower-class ghetto black, the middle-class black, the lower-class white, and the middle-class white.[5] Divided into the "haves" and "have-nots," the "have-nots" (lower-class blacks) are in control of the "haves" (middle-class blacks and whites). These social and economic characteristics also help set the stage for those who become victims.

Table 5.2

## MEAN EXPLOITATION RATINGS OF BLACKS
## AND WHITE ON INITIAL TYPOLOGY

| Exploitation Category | Whites (n = 73) | Blacks (n = 76) |
|---|---|---|
| Likely to exploit others | 0.669 | 1.382 |
| Likely not to be exploited | 1.192 | 1.579 |
| Likely to be exploited occasionally | 1.534 | 1.303 |
| Likely to be exploited often | 0.438 | 0.105 |

NOTE: This table gives only a rough idea of what happens in terms of race and victimization. Staff were asked to rate all 149 boys on the four categories. Then the total number of checks for all blacks and all whites were calculated for each typological rating, and the average number of checks for each was determined. This table does not, however, take into consideration who the targets or aggressors were. As the reader saw from the construction of the fivefold typology in Chapter 3, each boy may have checks on more than one category. For the way other data relate to the mean number of exploitation checks, see Appendix L. For the way race relates to other data, see Appendix N.

A lower-class white, for instance, is not as easy to victimize as the middle-class white because of his physical and mental toughness. Perceiving himself as capable of taking care of himself, he may, in fact, be looking for a good fight in order to move up the status hierarchy. His exploitation is made even more difficult by the fact that he never had much to begin with. He is, therefore, extremely reluctant to give up items such as the food and cigarettes brought by parents and friends.

In contrast, the middle-class white youth seldom has any "savvy" on how to survive in this environment. Even though a troublemaker in his own community, he usually does not know how to defend himself physically. His fear of bodily harm makes an aggressive peer seem particularly threatening. Thus, the enormous amounts of food brought by his parents—usually far more than one person needs—are either forcefully taken from him or are given up in order to buy protection.

No one points to a newcomer and says, "Here comes a middle-class punk, let's get him," nor do they say, "That kid comes from the ghetto and looks tough, we'd better stay away from him."

Living in the middle- or lower-class milieu simply provides each youth with behavioral patterns, manners, access to material goods, and a philosophy which makes him different from his neighbors. To a strong, aggressive kid from the ghetto, the middle-class "virtues" are signs of weakness. To the "well-mannered," reticent boy from a white- and blue-collar area, the "strengths" of the ghetto youth come across as vulgarities and animal-like conduct. Social class background, then, sets the stage for who becomes the victim and who becomes the aggressor.

## THE SEXUAL EXPLOITERS

It was thought originally that other factors would have a significant effect on victimization. However, no significant differences appeared between the sexual and nonsexual exploiters on the factors of age, weight, height, IQ, number of previous commitments, or number of previous offenses. Examination of Table 5.3

Table 5.3

### SEXUAL AND NON-SEXUAL EXPLOITERS BY CRIMINAL HISTORY AND PHYSICAL CHARACTERISTICS

| Does the Boy Exploit Sexually | N | Age at Admission | Weight | Height | IQ | No. of Previous Commitments | No. of Previous Offenses |
|---|---|---|---|---|---|---|---|
| NO | 124 | 16.91 | 153.53 | 68.10 | 90.61 | 1.45 | 4.54 |
| YES | 25 | 16.88 | 147.28 | 67.80 | 89.92 | 1.56 | 5.00 |
| MEAN | | 16.91 | 152.48 | 68.04 | 89.99 | 1.47 | 4.62 |
| F Scores | | 0.0303 | 0.7585 | 0.3654 | 1.8516 | 0.1378 | 0.5201 |

Between degrees of freedom    1       Analysis of variance indicated none of these
Within degrees of freedom    147      measures to be significantly significant.

NOTE: For how the Gough Adjective Checklist relates to whether the boy exploits sexually, see Appendix K.

shows that sexual exploiters, as normally would be expected, did average more prior offenses than the rest of the boys and had slightly more previous commitments than nonsexual exploiters. The sexual exploiters, in addition, were 0.3 inches shorter, weighed six pounds less, were a little less intelligent, and were almost exactly the same age as their peers. The lack of significance of these factors suggests that some of the variables previously thought to be important in exploitation were not as influential as expected.

In analyzing the data in terms of "how the boy was leaned on," moreover, a significant difference was found only on the variable "number of commitments to other institutions," (see Table 5.4).

The youths who were not leaned on at all (28 percent of the sample) had more previous commitments than those in other categories. They were also slightly older than the others and were actually lighter in weight than the sexually exploited. What they

Table 5.4

## HOW LEANED ON BY CRIMINAL HISTORY
## AND PHYSICAL CHARACTERISTICS

| How Leaned On | N | % | Age at Admission | Number of Previous Commitments | IQ | Weight | Height | Number of Previous Offenses |
|---|---|---|---|---|---|---|---|---|
| Not at all | 42 | 28.2 | 17.05 | 1.91 | 90.64 | 156.43 | 68.43 | 4.14 |
| Items | 91 | 61.6 | 16.87 | 1.32 | 89.14 | 148.93 | 67.99 | 4.96 |
| Sex | 16 | 10.7 | 16.76 | 1.19 | 93.13 | 162.31 | 67.31 | 3.94 |
| Mean | | | 16.91 | 1.47 | 89.99 | 152.48 | 68.04 | 4.62 |
| F | | | 0.7622 | 3.3019* | 0.7781 | 1.5757 | 1.1565 | 1.6331 |

Between degrees of freedom    2
Within degrees of freedom    146          *F = .05

NOTE: For the youths' Adjective Checklist scores on "how they were leaned on," see Appendix K.

lacked in weight was made up for by the fact that they were somewhat taller than the other boys. The youths who escaped victimization also had fewer previous offenses than those exploited on material items only. The sexually exploited were slightly younger, heavier, shorter, had fewer previous commitments and offenses than their stronger and generally more aggressive peers. Those exploited on material items only were somewhat between the other two age groups on age at admission, number of previous commitments, and height, but weighed less and had more previous offenses than any of the others. Surprisingly, of all these variables, only the number of previous commitments was statistically significant.

It would appear, then, that various stimulus qualities separated the boys in the different levels of the exploitation matrix. Impression management, race, social class, and the number of previous commitments to institutions were the most important of these stimulus qualities. Through these qualities, boys projected to others the image of either strength or weakness.

## NOTES

1. Boys are also ranked within each group. Further, the constant shifting of power and the resulting flexibility of the matrix means that, as youths shift positions in the matrix, the extent and types of exploitation change. Labelling is also important in this process of victimization (see Chapter 6).

2. The buying of protection appears to be common in adult prisons but is infrequent here; when it does take place, serious conflicts are created among aggressive inmates who are attempting to both protect and victimize a youth.

3. In our initial scale, "how the boys were victimized," we did not ask staff about each of the items separately, but simply about food, clothing, cigarettes, and the various forms of sexual exploitation. We were not, therefore, able to demonstrate the present ranking empirically, but have done so on the basis of our experience with institution life.

4. Obviously, not all whites are successful in blocking the effects of victimization. As future chapters will indicate, some are devastated emotionally by its impact.

5. The reader may remember that both middle- and lower-middle-class boys are being referred to as middle class. First, adequate data on social class were unavailable. Second, qualitative data indicated that a few youths in this category come from white-collar homes, but most are from blue-collar homes.

## CHAPTER 6

## DOUBLE AND TRIPLE STIGMA: THE
## MULTIPLE VICTIMIZATION OF LABELLING

**Many illegal acts** are performed by presumably "law-abiding" citizens who would be incarcerated if the acts were reported and prosecuted (Wallerstein and Wyle, 1947: 197-112).[1] Crucial is an awareness of the act and the willingness of someone to make an issue of the infraction. If community proprieties are transgressed and sufficient evidence is available, the offender may be publicly labelled as "deviant." Most students of the labelling perspective stop here, content to concern themselves with the consequences of labelling by community norms or public agencies charged with the responsibility of social control. Less well recognized is the fact that the labelling process has really just begun, and that, once an offender is incarcerated, more labels are assigned.[2] The wayward youth is officially judged a "juvenile delinquent" and perhaps "emotionally disturbed," but additional labels such as "punk," "weak-minded," "pain freak," "mess-up," and "crazy" are assigned. A look into the labelling process reveals its potentially serious consequences.

The labelling perspective was given impetus by Edwin Lemert in

1951, and, since then, the perspective has gained in prominence. It is now recognized as a major theme in the study of deviancy. The labelling perspective focuses upon the idea that deviance is the result of definitions by others. Central to this perspective is the deemphasizing of the importance of the act committed by the perpetrator, and the emphasizing of the idea that deviance is a "consequence of the application by others of rules and sanctions to an 'offender' " (Becker, 1963: 9).

While these themes hold a poignant relevance for the confined, also important are the ideas of "mortification" and "status degradation ceremonies." Mortification describes what happens to clients of "total" institutions. Basically, the person's "home world" identity is stripped away, leaving no personal effects or identity which may be comfortably relied on. This technique results in the mortified individual succumbing to official requests passively, with only a shred of the personal integrity brought to the institution (Goffman, 1961).

Status degradation ceremonies are processes by which labels are assigned to those believed to be deviant. According to Garfinkel, a number of processes are involved—beginning with a "presentation of self" which others define as "out of the ordinary." The performance and the performer must be identified as having qualities which others expect to find only in "that kind of person." Personal characteristics are ignored to justify the impression that the actor is just like the others who also perform deviant acts. This legitimates any actions taken against him or her. Denouncers must not appear to be speaking for themselves, but for the community as a whole. Every effort is made to demonstrate that ultimate values rather than personal experiences or prejudices provide the basis for castigating the offender. During these processes, the total cast—the denouncer, witnesses, and the offender—find the social distances among them increasing, until, finally, the offender is defined as standing diametrically opposed to everything considered "right" (Garfinkel, 1956: 420-424). At this time, the target is considered an "outsider," and a label is assigned.

These ideas primarily are applied to offenders against community normative systems, and reflect the fact that officials and others have the power to label them. If the community and its agencies are successful in their denunciation, a label is assigned which gives the offender clues as to how to act, generating a self-fulfilling prophecy. The labelled observe the impressions and reactions toward them, wonder whether they are really the type of person the labels claim, look for the label features within their behavior and feelings and, finding them, accept the definitions as real. The process is complete once the individual takes on, believes, and acts out the expectations of others.

For the delinquents we studied, labelling began some time before their present confinement. The boys, simply by being caught and prosecuted, became known to home community and institution officials as antisocial and dangerous.[3] In the present setting, both the institution and its inhabitants continue to assign labels. At each level of the exploitation matrix, labels reflect the positions of inmates.

Assigned on the basis of the characteristics of the holder, the labels portray certain types of role behavior. They are sometimes used as part of the "status assignment process" in which the position of the boys in the inmate status system is determined. One or more labels may then contribute to the actual "status degradation ceremony." At this point, boys are forced to "give in" and adopt certain social roles. At other times, labels keep youths imprisoned in roles; consequently, the continuous use of certain labels attenuates the possibility of role abandonment. At still other times, labels serve a constructive function by helping boys escape lowly social positions. Determining the effect of labels is a complex process and depends on a number of factors, both in the behavior and characteristics of the recipient and in the perceptions of others.

## ORGANIZATIONAL PROCESSING LABELS

Organizational labels are functional both for treatment purposes and as a means by which youths are stereotyped by staff and peers. But even if assigned for treatment purposes, a label identifies a youth as a certain kind of person and pressures him to conform to others' expectations. Labels help some to escape facing the consequences of prior antisocial behavior. For others, victimization is speeded up; a "fortunate" few find their treatment process facilitated. In view of these considerations, the formal institutional labels are discussed below.

## Institutional Records

Institutional records are one of the first and most general ways these youths are labelled. A case history is compiled and drawn from materials gathered by the courts and others concerned with each boy's development. School records, pre-sentence reports, early court appearances, records of intake interviews, and psychological testing are all found in the case folders. Unfortunately, the amount of information available on each boy varies. Of greater concern is the adequacy of the information.

Some of the reports are statements from school officials, social workers, pre-sentence investigators, and others. This variety of backgrounds contributes to an equally diverse quality of the information received. Not surprisingly, inaccuracies, misinformation, and irrelevancies often are utilized in making judgments. The youth is reminded constantly of past mistakes, which should be of no current concern. One boy who committed bestiality under the influence of alcohol at the age of ten still has this held against him at the age of seventeen. Obviously, he is a much different boy than when he committed the act. Another misuse of records is that occasionally boys steal them from the social worker's office. If residents read the records of peers, they can use this information against them. Or, upon reading their own records, boys become extremely angry with the institution and society for passing on misinformation and critical statements. Although relevant and accurate information *may* lead to genuine therapeutic intervention, misinformation, irrelevancies, and nontypical incidents keep coming back to haunt the boys.

## Cottage Assignments

Another form of labelling which results in victimization is cottage assignment, as each cottage gains a reputation for working with certain types of boys. Prior to 1972, boys were assigned to cottages on the basis of past behavior. Those involved in violent crimes against the person were placed together, as were boys involved in minor property crimes or considered incorrigible. As a result, all eight cottages gained a reputation for containing boys who had certain behavioral characteristics. In some cases, staff refused to be assigned to certain cottages because of the aggressiveness of their inmates. One youth leader said quite emphatically, "You can ship my ass out of here, but I'm not going to work in Washington cottage. They're a bunch of animals down there."

Since the winter of 1972, youths have been assigned to cottages on the basis of "I-level." Therefore, cottages are known as $I_4$s (emotionally disturbed), $I_3$s (manipulators), or $I_2$s (aggressives).[4] Once in them, inmates are expected to perform according to their "I-level" classification or world view.

When assigned to a living unit, boys often take over the characteristics imputed to those living in the cottage. Those assigned to cottages for the emotionally disturbed often become quite upset at finding out the nature of their assignment. But, at least early in their stay, most consistently fulfill the "sick" behavior expected of them. Tranquillizers are prescribed for many who convince the institution's medical personnel that they need the medication to "make it." "I'm so nervous, man, that I can't do anything. I need something to calm myself down." One cottage reserved for the most aggressive, "acting out" inmates, did, indeed, have boys who consistently "acted out" more than their peers.[5] In this cottage, for instance, peers were more likely to jump staff, rape peers, break out the windows, and escape. Whether the appellation of a particular cottage is deserved is discussed in the following section on psychiatric labels.[6]

Psychiatric Labels

The "Rs" and "Es" discussed in Chapter 2 are the means by which the youth commission identifies emotionally disturbed or dangerous boys. A psychiatrist at the diagnostic center, or psychiatrists at other youth commission institutions, recommend these labels. The Classification and Assignment Division then attaches them to the suffix of boys' institutional identification numbers.[7] They are assigned either because behavior in the community was such that the label was believed to be deserved, or because these youths "acted out" in an institution. In some cases, no labels were assigned, and in other cases, "Rs" and "Es" both were assigned. Institutional officials, of course, believed the labels to be justified, but evidence exists that the labels should never have been attached.

One line of evidence concerns the exploitation typology—the development of which was discussed in Chapter 3.[8] One would expect, if the labels were justified, to find the "Rs" and "Es" concentrated in certain of the categories more than in others. For instance, "Rs" should be heavily concentrated in the exploiter category and lightly in the victim category; similarly, few "Es" should be found in the nonexploited or the exploiter category.

Examination of Table 6.1, however, shows this is not the case. The four special designation categories showed almost random distribution among the five typological categories. The only exception was the underrepresentation of "Es" among the "exploiters" and their overrepresentation in the "give and takes" category. While the expected directionality is present, chi-square analysis did not show the difference between categories to be significant.

On the basis of this analysis, the labels appear to have little to

Table 6.1

**CROSS TABULATION OF SPECIAL DESIGNATION AND TYPOLOGY**

| Special Designation | Exploiters | Give & Takes | Independents | Sometimes Boys | Victims | N | % |
|---|---|---|---|---|---|---|---|
| R | 15 | 22 | 8 | 16 | 14 | 75 | 50.3 |
| E | 1 | 12 | 2 | 4 | 4 | 23 | 15.4 |
| NONE | 11 | 13 | 5 | 9 | 7 | 45 | 30.2 |
| BOTH | 1 | 3 | 0 | 2 | 0 | 6 | 4.0 |
| | 28 | 50 | 15 | 31 | 25 | 149 | 100.0 |

DF = 12          $X^2 = 9.48$          P = NS

do with inmates' positions in the exploitation matrix. The reason may be found in the fact that nearly all these boys were exploiters in the community (i.e., stealing items, forcibly taking things from others, or physically intimidating weaker youths); "Rs" were given only to youths who actually committed violent harm. Upon arriving at this institution, the "Rs" discovered that boys with less "acting out" in the community were sometimes actually more aggressive than they. One other reason for giving the label is that the boys "acted out" in the institution—a behavior which, as any good therapist knows, often reflects improvement in the boys' mental state.[9]

## SPECIAL DESIGNATIONS

Yet another means of analysis was to compare the boys in the "R," "E," "none," and "both" categories on their physical characteristics and criminal history (see Table 6.2). Analysis of variance indicated that only one variable, age, was statistically significant. This difference did not appear to be logically connected to the

Table 6.2

### SPECIAL DESIGNATION BY CRIMINAL HISTORY AND PHYSICAL CHARACTERISTICS

| Special Designation | Age | No. Previous Commitments | Weight | Height | No. Previous Offenses |
|---|---|---|---|---|---|
| R | 16.78 | 1.32 | 100.59 | 68.15 | 4.35 |
| E | 17.13 | 1.17 | 146.83 | 67.87 | 4.52 |
| NONE | 17.11 | 1.91 | 159.18 | 68.16 | 5.02 |
| BOTH | 16.17 | 1.67 | 147.67 | 66.50 | 5.33 |
| MEAN | 16.91 | 1.47 | 152.48 | 68.04 | 4.62 |
| F | 2.9711 | 2.5350 | 0.9844 | 0.8471 | 0.6344 |

Between degrees of freedom    3          N = 149          F = 2.68 = .05
Within degrees of freedom    145                          F = 3.94 = .01

labels in the manner expected. One would expect, for example, "R" to be assigned to the oldest boys simply because they had more time to become involved in violent activity. But the oldest boys were the emotionally disturbed. This group had the greatest difficulty in gaining release from the institution. The "Rs," on the other hand, were next to the youngest group, and on none of the other variables analyzed—number of previous commitments, weight, height, or number of previous offenses—did these boys rank highest.

Another possible explanation for the lack of labelling of older boys is that older boys are the more institution-wise and have curbed their aggressiveness in order to gain an early release. If this is the case, clinical staff apparently assigned many of the labels on the basis of factors traditionally thought to be related to institutional adjustment but, in reality, having little to do with the boys' actual adjustment.

The special designation categories ("Rs," "Es," etc.) were factor analyzed according to scores on the Gough Adjective Checklist. Only four scales—achievement, dominance, endurance, and order—were significantly differentiated at a .05 level (see Table 6.3). The personal adjustment and nurturance scales were also ranked in the same order, but were not statistically significant (see Appendix I for the rank ordering). Six other scales were patterned, but not statistically significant, and included defensiveness. self-confidence, self-control, affiliation, intraception, and heterosexuality. On these scales, the boys with both "R" and "E" had the highest scores, followed by boys with an "E" suffix only, then by "Rs" and nones. In fact, the boys with some of the ostensibly most serious problems scored highest on many scales.

As Chapter 8 suggests, the Gough Adjective Checklist is a personality instrument which can be used to measure the psychological stability and health of youths.[10] Therefore, it is extremely interesting that boys with "both R and E" labels ranked highest on eleven of the twenty-one scales and second on another seven. This suggests that boys whom this personality instrument indicates are the healthiest emotionally are doubly stigmatized by institutional staff. Additionally, on the four scales which were statistically significant, the "Es" scored highest, followed by boys with

Table 6.3

## GOUGH ADJECTIVE CHECKLIST BY SPECIAL DESIGNATION*

| Number of Adjectives Checked | R | E | None | Both | F | |
|---|---|---|---|---|---|---|
| Defensiveness | 23.26 | 27.05 | 22.71 | 30.40 | 1.0625 | NS |
| Self-confidence | 36.20 | 40.05 | 34.98 | 41.40 | 1.9772 | NS |
| Self-control | 30.35 | 33.70 | 28.44 | 33.80 | 1.3098 | NS |
| Lability | 37.46 | 38.90 | 38.98 | 44.00 | 0.6303 | NS |
| Personal Adjustment | 19.47 | 25.35 | 18.12 | 21.00 | 1.9093 | NS |
| Achievement | 21.77 | 26.95 | 19.54 | 23.60 | 3.0819 | .05 |
| Dominance | 19.92 | 24.70 | 18.51 | 22.40 | 2.6907 | .05 |
| Endurance | 27.39 | 31.55 | 23.49 | 28.40 | 3.7217 | .05 |
| Order | 30.12 | 35.05 | 26.71 | 30.20 | 2.8560 | .05 |
| Intraception | 13.07 | 16.90 | 10.98 | 17.60 | 0.9028 | NS |
| Nurturance | 11.55 | 13.30 | 10.29 | 13.00 | 0.2455 | NS |
| Affiliation | 20.04 | 25.35 | 19.59 | 29.00 | 1.3315 | NS |
| Heterosexuality | 23.48 | 23.60 | 22.20 | 27.40 | 0.3549 | NS |
| Exhibition | 50.58 | 49.00 | 51.32 | 51.00 | 0.5105 | NS |
| Autonomy | 59.07 | 58.75 | 60.24 | 54.40 | 0.5483 | NS |
| Aggression | 70.42 | 67.30 | 70.76 | 66.00 | 0.6802 | NS |
| Change | 36.33 | 35.20 | 35.90 | 42.20 | 1.2259 | NS |
| Succorance | 71.67 | 67.75 | 71.54 | 72.00 | 1.6880 | NS |
| Abasement | 60.58 | 58.05 | 60.37 | 62.20 | 0.9126 | NS |
| Deference | 35.41 | 37.50 | 34.66 | 38.40 | 0.5244 | NS |
| Counsel. Readiness | 70.97 | 68.60 | 71.93 | 65.00 | 2.2071 | NS |

Between degrees of freedom    3
Within degrees of freedom    131

*For a rank ordering of the above scales see Appendix I.

both "R and E" suffixes. To challenge this label assignment even further, the boys with no labels assigned to them consistently had the lowest scores, indicating they were the most disturbed.

The lack of significance on all but four scales certainly does not warrant drawing final conclusions about the differences among those who were labelled and those who were not. It is impossible from these data to determine whether the differences existed before labelling or developed as a result of labelling. The best way to determine the reality of this situation would be to test all boys before entering the institution and again when they are ready to be released.

Other evidence exists that assignment of the "R" is not justified. A prior study in this institution indicated that "Rs," when compared with boys who were reincarcerated varying numbers of times, had a lower rate of reinstitutionalization than their peers (Miller, 1971: 107). The "Rs" had the highest degree of success, 63 percent, at the time of their release from parole supervision, approximately eight months after release from the institution.[11] An average of 4.7 years after the last boys were released, the "Rs" again were the most successful (Miller, 1971: 119-120). Thus, youths perceived as the most hostile and aggressive in this unrelated study actually were the best risks for release. At the time of that study, it was suggested that "acting out" reflected positive self-improvement on the part of inmates and that staff were punishing the boys for improvement by assigning them labels.

The findings of both the Gough Adjective Checklist and Miller's study suggest that labelling serves no useful purpose to staff or institution. Boys assigned the "E" suffix find the label disturbing and distasteful. Residents also become anxious about having their labels cleared, and some run away when the psychiatrist refuses to clear them (see Chapter 10).

Informal Staff Labelling

In addition to the formal labels applied by the institution, staff and boys also assign labels to inmates. These informal labels are neither sanctioned nor always recognized for their importance in institutional life. Each carries with it either stigmatizing or positive stereotypes, depending upon the set of values by which the recipient is judged. Certain labels are employed by staff as a means of orienting themselves to their charges. Some of these labels are not assigned to definite positions in the status hierarchy, but do stereotype particular types of boys. The boys who receive these labels are generally found in the middle levels of the hierarchy, but their position is not as important as their characteristics.[12]  Included in these staff labels are "pain freak," "the you'll never make it" label, "punk," "pussy," "sickie," "bogarter," "booty bandit," and "manipulator."

"Pain freak" and "sickie" describe emotionally disturbed youths. "Pain freak" is reserved for youths who employ masochistic, self-defeating behavior. In contrast, "sickie" is a label used when boys demonstrate bizarre or excessive behavior and is discussed in detail in the chapter on emotional disturbance. Staff handle youths with these labels by telling them they will not be released until they cease this negative and self-defeating behavior. Since release is everyone's paramount goal, the youths feel pressure to change their behavior, at least temporarily. How long the change lasts and whether the "pain freak" and "sickie" orientation continue to be suppressed are open to speculation. One can theorize that a lack of acceptance of the label eventually results in the boy shifting his behavior to a more positive and constructive mode—unless this behavioral pattern is too deeply ingrained.

Another popular staff label is "you'll never make it." Shortly before a boy's release, staff tend to speculate about his chances in the community. Usually, someone on the cottage team will apply this label to an inmate and, at times, the entire cottage team makes this prediction to a boy. In fact, a favorite staff pastime in some cottages is to bet on the community adjustment of inmates. One staff member will say, "I bet he doesn't last six months." A second quickly responds, "I'll take a pint of ice cream on that." A third joins in, "Count me in on that, too." Often the betting takes place before the youth who, in turn, makes his contribution to his prognosis. "Man, there ain't no way I'm going to get into trouble.

I've had enough of these places." Not uncommonly, inmates announce to each other how "the money" is resting on them.

This label receives a differential response from the boys. For some, the fact that a staff member tells them that they "cannot make it" serves only to make some resolve to be successful. One released boy, for example, returned to the institution, walked into a staff member's office, put his feet on the desk, and informed all present that he had just graduated from barber's school and that all had been wrong about him. The assignment of the label in this case may have enhanced the boy's chance for success. On the other hand, some boys internalize the label and thereby reduce the possibility of a successful community placement. In this latter case, a self-fulfilling prophecy tends to guarantee that the label's recipient will get into trouble, sometimes very soon after release.

In addition to those labels, two for aggressive inmates are "bogarter" and "booty bandit." The "bogarter" is one who pushes others around and is always trying to intimidate his weaker peers. In an autobiography, a youth described his interaction with another whom staff accused of being a "bogarter." He stated:

> The first person to say something to me was a black dude named _____. He looked at me, and calmly stated, 'another mother-fucking pecker-wood,' which is another name for 'whitey.' I developed a disliking towards him right then and there.

This aggressive youth was disliked for his verbal abuse and for constantly trying to intimidate peers physically. As a result, he participated in more fights than any other youth in the institution, certainly earning the "bogarting" label. In fact, he was so aggressive that the cottage staff attempted to get him transferred to the adult reformatory.

The "booty bandit" is a sexual exploiter who plays an important role in the exploitation matrix. Staff use this label on boys whom they feel are sexually exploiting their peers. Until staff actually confirm their suspicions, usually by the victim's testimony, they accuse the aggressive youth half in jest: "Hey, man, are you a 'booty bandit'?" "No," responds the youth, "I don't do things like that." From the inmates' viewpoints, these staff labels give the recipients greater prestige in the inmate hierarchy. They reinforce the idea that the strength and aggressiveness of these youths is sufficient to allow them to take what they want from weaker boys. These labels do have some positive effect because "booty bandits" know that if they do not stop exploiting, their length of stay will be increased and institutional privileges reduced.

A passive inmate who has difficulty protecting himself is known as a "punk," "pussy," or "weak." The "weak" inmate has difficulty making decisions about himself and seems to be always vacillating, uncertain of what he wants. Staff feel that these boys bring on their victimization by refusing to stand up for themselves. Permitting oneself to be pushed around at all in this setting results in extensive exploitation; staff, knowing this, coach "weak" boys to strike out in self-defense. Boys who are labelled "pussy" seem to be helpless in warding off aggressive acts. While the "weak" boys want to protect themselves and avoid exploitation, the "pussy" has given up, at least in the eyes of staff. Definitely seriously stigmatized, these boys experience some secondary deviance and are often forced into sexual acts. The "punk" is a youth whom staff feel has been or can be sexually victimized, and often brings the "punk" label with him from other institutions. Knowing the ominous consequences of a boy's being a scapegoat, staff generally make an extended effort to persuade boys with the "punk" label to walk away from sexual exploitation.

Significantly, almost every inmate who brings a sexual label from another institution continues being a sexual victim here, partly because staff sometimes pass this information on to his peers. Although the staff may do this intentionally, it is more likely that peers will overhear a staff member saying to a boy, "You're not going to be a punk again, are you?" Since few inmates sexually labelled are able to escape the consequences of the social definitions given to them, the close relationship between labelling and victimization is demonstrated. But also demonstrated is the importance of social interaction in the creation of deviant behavior. Sexual victims said in interviews that they did not want to continue this "stuff" but were unable to turn aside peer expectations.

Finally, staff refer to some boys as "manipulators." This label is reserved for those skillful in getting what they want. Quite willing to make requests to staff, the manipulator "puts his best foot forward." Usually intelligent and with some prestige in the peer hierarchy, this youth knows when and how to ask for things. In fact, part of the reason he does so well with staff is that he has some strength in the cottage. One very effective "manipulator" had the respect of both peers and staff. He would approach staff with two requests, expecting that the first would be turned down; but as soon as the first was turned down, he would then present the second, more reasonable request, and never failed to have it received affirmatively. Staff joke about these youths, but still respect their abilities. Although earning the youth respect from peers, this label does not appear to have any adverse effect on inmates.

Some of the above staff labels are occasionally passed on to the youths and provide clues or signals as to what type of boy a youth is. These clues or signals indicate what kinds of pressures may be put on him to result in certain behaviors. In some instances, defining by staff is done so subtly that staff do not recognize they are giving off clues. In other cases, the labels they give are the same or close to those used by the boys. Once the boys realize that staff disapprove of a boy's behavior, they know that he may be victimized without staff intervention.

Labels assigned to inmates do in some instances benefit the boys, reflecting the fact that not all labels carry a negative stigma. Those who are called "pain freak" and "sickie" must terminate this type of behavior in order to be released. The "you'll never make it" label, as previously noted, sometimes motivates certain inmates more toward success. Aggressive labels tend to protect victimized boys, principally because the boy being watched for sexual exploitation will either terminate or cut down his sexual exploitation. The "bogarting" youth has to be a little more careful when he pushes his peers around or subjects them to physical exploitation. Even the labels referring to weak inmates—"weak," "pussy," and "punk"—may motivate them to defend themselves more and be less victimized. Utilizing labels, staff warn these latter boys of the serious implications of sexual exploitation.

## INMATE LABELLING OF INMATES

Similar to staff, inmates use many labels to refer to fellow residents. The most popular are "weak-minded," "chump," "ass-kisser," "punk," crazy," "bad dude," and "alright guy." Since many of these labels are closely related to those used by staff, it is obvious that they have influenced each other, but which came first is impossible to determine.

Confronted by behavior which far exceeds that expected from peers, boys tend to label the performers as "crazy." Not surprisingly, the "crazy" label is closely related to the "sickie" label used by staff. Fellow residents feel that the "crazy" youth is not only "sick," but also dangerous to be around. He is totally unpredictable and may without provocation pick up a pool stick and strike a nearby boy in the head. Being so unpredictable, he makes peers very uncomfortable. Since they do not know what to expect, they are afraid to put any pressure on him because of what he may do either to himself or to them. Two illustrations may be helpful. In the first, a boy lost control of himself, picked up a knife in the kitchen, and went running around attempting to stab anyone in the vicinity. Needless to say, his shocked peers never trusted him again. In another incident, a boy set his room on fire shortly after the death of another boy. This fire spread and nearly burned the entire living area, as well as several boys who had to be pulled from their rooms. This action resulted in his being assigned the "crazy" label by his peers. A number even requested a transfer out of the cottage because they did not trust him. The use of this label does not seem to generate any positive improvement in the recipient. He becomes permanently stigmatized by his occasional bizarre behavior.

In contrast to staff, boys do not use the "pain freak" label. Boys tend rather to blame their problems on institutional staff and officials "messing over them." Therefore, staff's "unfairness" makes a boy repeatedly lose his pre-release badge. When a release is postponed, the real reason is that "staff are playing games with him and do not want him to go home."[13]

The "bad dude" is a label for aggressive inmates who can take care of themselves. From day one in the institution, the "bad dude" is an aggressor. He comes in pushing inmates around, trying to impress all as to how "tough" he is. He is the same youth whom staff will label a "bogarter" and also the same boy who will challenge new and fearful staff. Both of these labels reinforce the boy's behavior, making him feel better about himself. The self-concept of these boys, therefore, profits from this particular label.

Again, boys avoid using the staff's "booty bandit" label. The apparent reason is related to their trenchant refusal to reveal the "interior life" or "backstage happenings." If certain boys are labelled sexual exploiters, staff attention will be called to the aggressors and their victims and will achieve more power over them.

Inmates have several labels for the passive and easily exploited boy. The most popular are "weak-minded," "chump," "punk," and "ass-kisser." The "weak-minded" is very similar in meaning to the staff's label "weak." The "weak-minded" boy, according to his peers, has trouble making decisions, is indecisive about defending himself, and at times will permit himself to be walked over. Although he has difficulty standing up for himself, he, like the "weak" youth, resists exploitation, particularly if he feels peers want too much. Instead of trying to stand up to his peers, the youth who is given the "ass-kissing" label continually runs to staff for protection. Completely abandoning the inmate code, this youth places all his hopes on staff protection. After the "ass-kisser" has yelled for the staff a few times, staff become impatient with his "bellyaching" and tell him to fight his own battles. Stripped of staff's protection, these youths are especially vulnerable to victimization.

"Earning" the "chump" label are those who are new to the institution and who are particularly amenable to material exploitation. Instead of giving up, as does the youth with the "pussy" label, this youth is confused by his new, strange environment and does not know how he can survive. He usually gives up his material things, but makes an attempt to avoid sexual exploitation and physical intimidation.

Consistent with staff, inmates use the "punk" label to refer to a boy who has been or appears to be in the process of being sexually victimized. A common question of a new youth is "Are you a punk?" The translation is, "Have you been or can you be sexually exploited?" Especially in the academic area, a new inmate is confronted with, "I bet you're a punk. How about getting down for me?" Significantly, inmates classify different "punks" into different categories. "Undercover punks" are boys interested in sexual relationships with others on a sub rosa basis. Some punks "trade off" with other punks. Others like to flaunt themselves before their peers, saying in effect "I'm available for somebody." Still other punks can be coerced by someone using the right approach into becoming a sexual victim.

Finally, there are the punks whose victimization is such that they are the social outcasts in the cottage. Definitely seriously stigmatized, boys with all of these labels are placed under considerable pressure. Once they permit themselves to be sexually exploited, they may become a "vegetable" in the eyes of their peers—becoming a prime candidate for the sexual satisfaction of all interested sexual exploiters.


## STIGMA

Once the boys are confined to the institution and embedded in the matrix, their quality of life centers around the labels assigned by the institution, its staff, and their own peers. In view of the extensiveness of the boy's immersion in this subculture and the closeness of their contact with peers and staff, escape from the consequences of the labels is next to impossible. Living twenty-four hours a day in the close company of the others, who do the defining, means that unless the boys have and use particular strengths, the labels stick. Indeed, the stigmas require the boys to react defensively in order to protect themselves from the increasing cycle of damage. They have almost no opportunity to challenge the effects of the labels.

Thus, boys must concern themselves with "Rs," "Es," "both Rs and Es," and other labels, such as "you'll never make it," "punk," "chump," "weak-minded," and "ass-kisser." Of greatest concern is that youths receive a number of these labels at the same time. The labels assume a weight of deadly proportions in terms of the boys' self-concepts. The cumulative effect of these multiple labels is enhanced by the fact that the boys and staff use them, so that regardless of the direction in which a youth turns, he is faced with a consistent definition of self reinforced by all in the cottage.

In addition to the fact that labelling is usually the result of victimization and has an effect on the personality structure of the recipients, the boys are forced into a "career" during their stay. In many instances, the careers are carried over into life in the community. Unfortunately, this aspect of institutional life has not been well studied and much further research must be undertaken before the effects of labelling upon community success will be known.

Of importance is the relationship between labels and social roles. As developed in the next chapter, social roles are institutionalized behavior expected of these youths and are ranked from the most highly to the most lowly esteemed. In this milieu, labels and roles are associated in several different ways. First, one label is influential in a boy adopting one social role. An example of this is the youth accused of being a "booty bandit" who then takes on the social role. Second, several labels combine in pushing the youth toward a social role. In his early stay, an inmate may receive the "ass-kisser," "weak," "weak-minded," "pussy," and "punk" labels from staff and peers, and he eventually ends up adopting the scapegoat social role. Third, one label is influential in a boy adopting a social role, and he, in turn, is eventually given a new label because of his assigned social role. This is illustrated by the "alright guy" later adopting the role of the politician which later results in staff labelling him as a "manipulator." Fourth, the label emerging from a social role sometimes provides an incentive to walk away from that role. For instance, the "status degradation ceremony" of the scapegoat, in which he is labelled as an "outcast" and "dirty," is the motivation some boys need to "get off the bottom" of the cottage social hierarchy.

Since knowledge of how different boys respond to labels is unknown, the best that may be said is that although a few may be helped by some of the labels, most, in fact, are hurt. An instance of a boy who was helped is the youth mentioned earlier, who, after being informed by staff that "you'll never make it," drove halfway across the state sometime after his release to inform all present that they had been wrong—that he had just graduated from barbering school. Over forty percent, however, are returned to correctional facilities, suggesting that the impact of the institution is not what was predicted by its builders. One of the major problems faced by researchers is determining the effects of labels and, possibly, if institutions of this type are to survive, learning how to diminish those effects. Until the response of youths to labels is known, reliance upon any type of name-calling by staff should be strictly prohibited and staff educated as to the possible effects on their charges.

## NOTES

1. See also "The Challenge of Crime in a Free Society," 1967, pp. 20-22.

2. With several exceptions, the labels discussed in this chapter are primarily the more negative labels found in use in the institution. Several labels with positive connotations are discussed to demonstrate the paradox of labelling and victimization—that is, that even labels with a positive connotation result in negative outcomes.

3. This institution has a reputation throughout the state as being one where only the worst boys are incarcerated. A graduate of this institution, then, commands respect in many quarters.

4. See Chapter 2 for a discussion of I-level and Chapter 15 for a discussion of how I-level affects the ecological structure of the institution.

5. The definition of "acting out" which is used by the Ohio Youth Commission is as follows: "This is a general institutional term for unacceptable [overt behavior]. It usually takes the form of aggressive behavior directed toward other students or institutional staff. The term does not usually include a child's self-directed aggression, such as body mutilation and suicide." This definition, of course, allows staff to interpret behavior in any way they want.

6. Medical labels, too, may have their negative consequences by leading the boys to make use of them in escaping legitimate institutional programs.

7. It is important to note that the Classification and Assignment Division almost never ignores the recommendation of a psychiatrist concerning a suffix for a youth.

8. It may be remembered that five categories were developed: exploiters; give and takes; independents; sometimes boys; and victims.

9. The labels assigned, on the other hand, do impute stigma to the extent staff feel they are deserved. More work is generated for psychiatrists as a result, and boys are placed under the additional stress of worrying about whether the labels will be cleared. Thus, even though the labels do not connote extreme deviance, clearing them does create a hardship for residents, and the damage is done.

10. In Chapter 8 on the exploitation typology, it is suggested that the boys with the highest scores were apparently reflecting more of what is considered to be a "middle-class" orientation than the rest.

11. No evidence existed that "Rs" were treated any differently than were those with whom they were being compared.

12. With the exception of the "booty bandit," the labels described here do not stand for particularly important social roles. A discussion of the major and minor roles of the exploitation matrix, including that of the "booty bandit," are found in the next chapter.

13. Staff do, of course, refuse home visits for legitimate reasons. These reasons are not, however, accepted by the boys.

*CHAPTER 7*

## SOCIAL ROLES AND EXPLOITATION

**As reflected in the labels** discussed in the preceding chapter, the inmate social structure in each cottage contains several major and several minor social roles. These roles integrate, as well as differentiate, the focal issues of exploitation. At the top of the social order are highly esteemed roles and at the bottom are the more unacceptable roles. From top to bottom are the "heavy," the lieutenant, the "slick," the "boys who profit," the "booty bandit," the peddler, the "messup," the thief, the queen, and the scapegoat. The "heavy," the lieutenant, the "booty bandit," and the scapegoat are major social roles, while the others tend to be minor. Nevertheless, even the minor roles are nearly all represented in the daily life and activities of each cottage. Excluding the "heavy" (top) and scapegoat (bottom) roles, the others tend to blend into each other.

The majority of the roles are recognized by both staff and inmates and are part of the institution's argot. These roles eventually become a major component of the residents' personality structure, pushing them to perform certain kinds of behavior. For example, boys who exhibit aggressiveness and make "dominance gestures" take over highly esteemed roles; in contrast, those who are passive and make "submissive gestures" adopt the more unacceptable roles (Mazur, 1973). The occupants of certain roles then, gain priorities to food, extra privileges, and sexual partners, and others find themselves the victims of material and sexual exploitation.

## HEAVY

The most highly valued role is that of the "heavy." As stated in Chapter 5, there are two types of heavies. The first is an intellectual or cooperative type who does not overtly exploit his peers and who is respected and liked by all. In return for giving staff what they want—i.e., keeping other inmates under control—the boys receive power, extra privileges, and esteemed prerogatives. The second type, the aggressive "heavy," exploits others, remains less cooperative and even hostile to staff, and freely uses lieutenants to carry out his wishes. The aggressive "heavy," in addition, will sometimes utilize an intelligent inmate as a type of "co-heavy," seeking his assistance in making important decisions (Miller et al., 1974).

The social role of the intellectual or cooperative "heavy" calls for a youth who is bright, mature for his age, has a good self-concept, relates well to other boys, is a good manipulator, has some desire for this social position, and is willing to undergo some personal changes in order to achieve his desires. Usually labelled as an "alright guy" upon admission, this youth avoids being exploited. He quickly is accepted by the boys, often becoming a leader on the cottage football or basketball team. Although physical intimidation is the norm here, this cooperative youth frequently has never had a fight during confinement. Fellow inmates simply assume that these youths can handle themselves.

Before the first stage of his institutionalization is over, this youth is normally promoted to one of the existing heavy's lieutenants. Along with one or two others, he then carries out the wishes of the inmate leader. However, a "heavy's" release initiates a power struggle among those eligible for this social role. The criteria for eligibility include being in the right social stratum (lieutenant) and the right race (black), having sufficient popularity with peers and staff, and exhibiting the necessary personal characteristics to be a leader.

At the time of a "heavy's" release, two or three boys are usually present who are approximately equal in status and have the right credentials. Since fighting is not the way to become a cooperative "heavy," only verbal confrontations take place among the potential successors.[1] The end result is that a new leader is chosen.[2]

Once a new "heavy" emerges, lieutenants are faced with several dilemmas. They wish to remain on the "heavy's" good side, but they also would like to take his place. Because the "heavy" is there by tacit agreement of his peers, the boy who confronts or challenges him risks jeopardizing his own position if he loses. In view of the "heavy's" support, it is unlikely that inmates will recognize the legitimacy of a challenger's claim to the position. To be safe, the insurgent must get his own backing within the cottage before a power bid will be successful; but this rarely happens. Thus, when a boy becomes a "heavy," he generally has little serious opposition until release.

From the time he is chosen until release, the "heavy," nevertheless, must maintain his support among his peers, especially those with power. He pals around with certain peers because he needs them to maintain his social role; they, in turn, need his attention to boost their own egos and improve their standing in the hierarchy. Realizing that the strength of his leadership depends upon this relationship, the "heavy" communicates covertly that he enjoys being around these youths even though he also tries to communicate that his leadership does not depend upon them.

Inmates desire a cooperative "heavy" because he brings stability to the cottage.[3] They are aware that honest and fair leadership creates harmony, especially when the "heavy" operates as a go between for both staff and peers. A boy becomes a "heavy" with his peers' permission, and these same youths may also remove him from power.

Staff, in turn, play an important part in the creation of the cooperative "heavy." Since the cooperative "heavy" can be used to control other inmates, it is not surprising that staff actually want such a boy in their cottage. Their jobs are made easier, and the possibility of serious and dangerous confrontation with older, aggressive delinquents is reduced. The "heavy" also keeps staff informed about potential runaways, racial incidents, fights, homosexual behavior, and mass assaults.

To motivate the desired types to attain power, staff give them every possible privilege. Special favors or responsibilities are granted, including running errands, helping staff do certain jobs, placing boys in the kitchen to serve meals, calling them into the office frequently for conversation, playing cards or shooting pool with them more often than with other boys, sometimes allowing them to carry their own matches, permitting them to put their feet on the desk in the youth leader's office, occasionally asking them to unlock the other boys' doors with staff's keys, awarding pre-release status at their second review (the earliest possible time it could be received), and seeing to it that they have the shortest stay of any youth in the cottage. Seeing these boys favored by the staff leads other youths to look up to them as well.

On the other hand, the aggressive "heavy" is a youth who is strong and forceful, physically large, good with his hands, able to intimidate both staff and inmates, and has a "don't care" attitude. Usually labelled as a "bad dude" upon first entering the institution, this youth easily avoids being exploited. In contrast to the acceptance of the cooperative leader, the aggressive "heavy" is feared by his peers, usually because of his strength. He is quick to fight and, in fact, goes around with a "chip on his shoulder," ready to attack anyone who appears hostile. Taking advantage of the fearfulness of peers, this aggressive youth exploits both sexually and nonsexually. A history of conflict with staff sometimes leads him to physical altercations with other staff, especially new youth leaders who are unsure whether they can handle him.

Before his first period of institutionalization is over, this youth generally becomes a lieutenant. Surprisingly, he does not challenge the existing leadership, but waits until the "heavy" is released. Needless to say, upon the release of the leader, the aggressive youth moves in and simply intimidates all heirs apparent. Lacking other challengers, he then becomes the cottage's "heavy."

Upon taking over the cottage's leadership, he attracts other aggressive youths as his lieutenants. Not especially caring about how other inmates feel, he and his lieutenants generate a much more aggressive and exploitative milieu than is found in cottages with cooperative "heavies." While usually refraining from sexually exploiting blacks, the aggressive "heavy" and his lieutenants vastly increase the material exploitation of blacks. They are also much more likely to "hit on," "push around," and verbally attack their black "brothers" than are any of the other youths.

Although the majority of the aggressive "heavies" do not want to share their power, some (generally because they have some reservations about their mental acumen) seek out an intelligent black for assistance and guidance. As a result of this sharing of power, the "heavy" becomes less physically exploitative of cottage peers. Significantly, his lieutenants have less power and control over other inmates when an intellectual is the co-leader.

Instead of creating a smooth operating social order, the aggressive "heavy" and lieutenants generate conflict. Utilizing power and force, they bring instability and change to the cottage. Therefore, although both blacks and whites would like to overthrow them, a coup is practically impossible, chiefly because the boys are afraid of repercussions from those in power.

Staff, on the other hand, are able to place considerable pressure on the aggressive "heavy" by threatening to prolong his institutionalization, by threatening to transfer him to an adult reformatory, or by promising to give him institutional privileges. Knowing the ultimate power of staff, nearly all of these "heavies" become less aggressive and exploitative. In fact, these combative leaders' role performance tends to become similar to that of cooperative "heavies" during the final state of their confinement.

But not all boys are willing to give up their aggressive postures; with these boys, staff do everything possible to dampen their negativistic leadership. A custodially oriented youth leader said quite emphatically:

> I'm the boss here and that's final. The aggressive bogarting heavy is no better than anybody else. We have to bring him back to his own size.

To illustrate how far staff will go, nearly every boy transferred from this training school to the adult reformatory during the past four years was an exploitative heavy. Good reason exists to feel that staff were partly responsible for "setting him up" for the event which precipitated his transfer.

The case of one of these aggressive "heavies" demonstrates the staff's role in the demise of the combative boy. Before the social worker came to his office one day, several staff members informed this youth that the social worker did not feel he should receive pre-release status. Knowing that the youth detested the social worker and that the social worker was arrogant toward inmates, staff continued to provoke the heavy. Upon entering the social worker's office, the boy angrily demanded why the social worker did not want to grant him pre-release status. Without being aware of the youth's feelings, the social worker quickly answered, "Because you don't deserve it." "What do you mean, I don't deserve it?" asked the youth. The social worker made another remark without thinking and the youth exploded, rushing toward the desk and turning it over. Finding himself trapped, the social worker began to scream. The youth stood there making accusations and indicating what he should do to the social worker. At that time, the other staff suddenly appeared, came into the office, and dragged the boy back to his room. The youth barricaded his door, claiming that he would kill anyone who entered. Several days later, the boy was escorted in a straitjacket to the adult reformatory. Staff later admitted that they expected the boy to act the way he did.

In describing the cooperative and aggressive leaders, we have been speaking of the boys who are at the top of the inmate hierarchy and who exercise control over the remainder of the cottage. But what about the cliques which exist in all institutions? Are there not leaders of these groups, too, i.e., someone who, once approached, can bring members of the clique in line and thus add to cottage control? Although these leaders do exist, they are definitely subordinate to the top "heavy" and are not in the ranks immediately below the "heavy." Whites, for example, often have a "mini-heavy" for their leader. This youth is normally granted little esteem by the blacks. He is, in other words, a "heavy" for that group only—someone who operates as a spokesman and exercises limited control. Of especial value in times of racial conflict, the white "mini-heavy" is often approached by the black "heavy," and the differences between the two groups are ironed out.

A final note about this social role is that an institutional intelligence network exists through which "heavies" in various cottages become aware of each other and sometimes work together. This is especially evident when the entire student body is assembled for church or a special event in the auditorium, for "heavies" sit in the front row of each cottage and on the end seat. Sitting across from each other, they occasionally lean over and discuss things. This is striking, as other members of the cottage rarely engage in conversations with peers from other cottages. A staff member made the following observations:

> During church services, the kids have a special way of sitting. Whites always sit in back of blacks. The first row is made up of the heavy and his lieutenants. The heavies also sit on the end seat so that they can talk with a heavy from another cottage.

## LIEUTENANTS

The "heavy's" social role is fairly distinct. But immediately subordinate to him in the inmate hierarchy are his assistants, the lieutenants. Three different types of boys occupy this role. The first is the boy who eventually becomes the cooperative or the intellectual "heavy." In case an aggressive "heavy" already controls the cottage, this youth can become the intellectual "co-heavy." The second type of lieutenant is the aggressive youth who assists the cooperative "heavy" until this leader is released. Both of these types were described in the section on the "heavy." The final type is the boy who has many of the characteristics of the cooperative or aggressive "heavy" but is never chosen to be the cottage leader. Sometimes he is content to remain in a subordinate position until release; at other times, he tries to challenge the youth who is becoming or has become the "heavy," loses, and drops to a lower position in the social order. Or he may be "passed over" by his peers because he sexually exploited others.

## SLICK

The "slick" and the "inmate who profits" are highly esteemed positions, even though boys occupying these positions are not struggling for power and leadership. These roles blend into each other and have much in common. In outward appearances, the boys who occupy them are much the same.

In general, the role of the "slick" calls for a mature youth who has a good self-concept, is able to stay out of trouble, relates well to other boys, is strong enough so that others do not bother him, and is knowledgeable about institutional life. The strongest prerequisite for this role is the ability to manipulate staff. Usually labelled as either a "bad dude" or an "alright guy" upon arrival, the "slick" (especially if he is black) frequently becomes involved in the exploitation matrix early in his stay. The "slick" quickly discovers that immersion in the inmate subculture will prolong his stay; therefore, he divorces himself from the inmate culture and its exploitation matrix.[4]

From that point on, the "slick" realizes that the most effective way to beat the system is to stay out of difficulty. "Playing it cool," the one or two slicks in each cottage focus entirely upon avoiding trouble. Their purpose is to convince staff that they have become more pro-social in their attitudes. In a real sense, "slicks" merely "do time." They spend most of their free time watching television or loafing around with other "slicks." "Slicks" consistently maintain social distance from staff throughout their first two stages of institutionalization, both because they do not want to be labelled "ass kissers," and because they find close association with the "man with the keys" extremely distasteful. "Slicks" are also reluctant to become very friendly with peers. If they become too close to peers, "slicks" are afraid that they will be asked to stick their necks out and get into difficulties with either staff or other peers.

Interestingly enough, the slick becomes slightly more involved with staff during his last two or three months, apparently to ensure his early release. At this time, he receives much positive reinforcement from staff, who see maturity and strength in him.

But there is little evidence that the "slick" discloses anything of himself during this time; he is still simply presenting a "front."[5]

## BOYS WHO PROFIT

Over the past four years, at least twelve inmates have remained outside the exploitation matrix. Unlike the "slick," however, the "boys who profit," are surprisingly positive about their institutional experiences. Almost always black, their most salient characteristics are that they come from ghetto areas, have extensive contacts with the juvenile court (usually for serious crimes), are generally in their second or third commitment to the Ohio Youth Commission, are physically well developed, and are a year or so older than their peers. Not unexpectedly, these inmates score very high on the asocial index of the Jesness Personality Inventory.[6]

Soon after their arrival they seek out a staff member whom they respect and spend much of their free time with him. Tending to have a "right guy" background with a "square John" posture, these boys ponder continually how they can make something of their lives (Schrag, 1954). This contemplation of the future not only leads staff to consider them more mature than other inmates, but also encourages staff to spend more time with them. Involved in a "search for identity," these residents look upon their "new-found friend" as a guru.[7]

Throughout their first stage of institutionalization, then, they refuse to become involved in the cottage social structure. Nevertheless, they still are accepted by the inmate leader and his lieutenants; in fact, fellow inmates never try to exploit them. "Boys who profit" also are able to violate certain tenets of the inmate code without being negatively sanctioned. An example is their occasional fraternizing with the cottage scapegoat—a social outcast.

The middle of their stay generally consists of the fourth through the sixth or seventh month. By this time, their relationship with the youth leader is well developed and a relationship with a treatment staff member (group leader or social worker) is also likely to have been initiated. If a relationship with a treatment person is developing, they usually become interested in the treatment modality advocated by the treatment agent. For example, one youth established a good relationship with a group leader interested in transactional analysis. Before he left the institution he had developed so much expertise that he was able to lead TA groups in the community.

Beginning to see themselves as potential leaders, "boys who profit" talk about the importance of dedicating themselves to some principle greater than self. At this time, they may begin to write poetry or prose to describe themselves and the slavery of their people. Quite unexpectedly, these boys, who are becoming committed to racial justice and equality, now begin to help exploited whites. Several white scapegoats were able to "get off the bottom," largely because of the assistance and support of "boys who profit." At the same time, the "boy who profits" extends himself more to black inmates.

During the final stage of institutionalization, these boys begin to demonstrate extreme anxiety about making it in the community. They know that a return to the old environment will be accompanied by the same temptations. Friends, for example, will come around every two or three days and say, "Let's hit the store tonight. It's an easy job." At this point, the youth fully expects to say, "Get out of my face," but he knows that refusing will become increasingly difficult if he cannot find work. Beginning to search for reasons why they will not make it, these youths typically spend much of their time talking with supportive staff. During this final stage, they become more argumentative with peers and, at the same time, begin to dissociate from them. This preoccupation with community adjustment seems mostly related to their history of failure and the awareness that the next step is the adult reformatory. Moody, insecure, but still determined, they make their way toward the day of release and the long bus ride home.

## BOOTY BANDIT

In this institution, youths committed to the sexual exploitation of other inmates occupy the social role of the "booty bandit."

Lacking the prestige of "slicks" and "boys who profit," this role occupant is still considered one of the stronger youths. His sphere of behavior is involved almost entirely with sexual exploitation; improving himself is not a primary concern. Eighteen or nineteen years old, "booty bandits" are generally black and are both older and more mature than the average inmate. As a rule, they come from ghettos and fatherless homes, were involved in crime against the person, and have spent several years in institutional settings. Upon adjudication to the Ohio Youth Commission, they are often assigned "R" suffixes, indicating that they are considered dangerous to themselves or others (Bartollas et al., 1975c).

Staff rated twenty-five youths as sexual exploiters. Of these, fifteen boys adopted the sexual exploitation of weaker residents as a primary role.[8] Labelled as "bad dudes" during their initial stay, they are taught the techniques of sexual exploitation by already established "booty bandits." Compared to other black youths, "booty bandits" seem to be more indignant about victimization received from whites on the streets. Therefore, driven by racial animosity and utilizing techniques learned from other "booty bandits," they begin the exploitation of weaker, white inmates during the second stage. Some "booty bandits," in opposition to the inmates' normative code, will even sexually exploit compliant blacks.[9] Lacking emotional involvement with their victims, "booty bandits" like to "work alone" or sub rosa, usually concealing their activities form other sexual exploiters.

There were two basic types of "booty bandits." One consisted of six boys involved in the peer hierarchy, generally as lieutenants. Struggling for peer recognition and approval, they found themselves exploited by the "heavy," particularly for cigarettes. Yet, they seldom became the cottage "heavy" because of their sexual exploitation of others. The second type was represented by nine inmates; these were boys who considered themselves outside the cottage's social organization. This type was merely "doing time" and did not want to get involved in "kid stuff." Interestingly, although this latter type refused to honor the informal inmate code, they still maintained greater social distance from staff members than other youths. In contrast to the first type, the latter was not exploited by anyone, including the "heavy."

This latter type of youth is described by a white victim in an autobiography. He wrote:

> The first Saturday we had to go outside for P.E. (physical education). I was in my gym shorts and _____ came over and grabbed my leg. I politely got up and walked away. What I should have did was knock him on his ass. Everything went well for the first couple of months. But my fourth month here I was placed in a dorm with _____, _____, _____ and _____. I got along fairly well until one night _____ [same youth who had grabbed his leg earlier] had some narcotics which he took. He became sort of violent and forced me to commit an unnatural sex act. This took place after everyone was asleep. He forced me several times after this also.

In talking about being exploited, he admitted that after the first incident, he said to the aggressor, "Let's rap," but the "booty bandit" merely replied, "Mother-fucker, let me alone," and rolled over and went to sleep.

Before long, the staff discover the chronic nature of the "booty bandit's" predatory activity. Staff begin to apply negative sanctions by bringing up these activities at reviews and turning the boys down for release. Becoming aware of the consequences of their acts, "booty bandits" usually either terminate their exploitation or "lay low" for a while, later resuming it on a smaller scale. During the final stage of their career, they generally avoid sexual exploitation as they may try to prove that this activity no longer interests them. As one "booty bandit" said, "Man, I don't do that anymore."

## PEDDLER

Generally one inmate in each cottage—more often black than white—trades goods from one cottage to another. Because the goods are either stolen, illegal, or exploited, they must be concealed from staff. Similar to the merchant in adult prisons, this social type works sub rosa because institutional rules and procedures are being violated. Although role occupants are not the strongest boys in the cottage, they still are able to extort goods from weaker peers and yet stand up for the "legitimacy" of their trading.

In the first stage of their institutionalization, white boys who later occupy this role are frequently labelled as "chumps" and "weak-minded," while blacks are usually known as "alright guys." Whites, particularly, may be extensively exploited by their stronger peers; but before very long, they begin to stand up for themselves and the exploitation tapers off. In fact, they may begin to command considerable power among whites. Evident at this point is a strong desire for upward mobility and greater prestige.

These boys adopt the peddler's role by the second stage of their institutionalization. Generated by the "politics of scarcity," a great need for this social role exists in each cottage. Higher-status boys, nevertheless, do not want the role, and lower-status boys are not respected enough to be considered for it.[10]

A common transaction is for a peddler to pay so many "squares" (cigarettes) for a coat or other stolen items. He then finds a "buyer" somewhere in the institution who will guarantee him a profit, usually of several packages of cigarettes. Or a boy may "borrow" a radio from one of the weaker youths, and the peddler will then trade the radio for merchandise from another cottage and give some of the merchandise to the original thief. Especially aggressive peddlers sometimes coerce weaker inmates to buy something like cigarettes for a ridiculous price, even though they may already have cigarettes. Other peddlers serve as the middle men between the youth who wants to "sell butt" for a couple of packs of cigarettes and the youth interested in buying the offered commodity.

Yet another role performed is the passing of contraband into and out of a cottage. Suppose, for example, an inmate is planning an escape and needs a little money. The peddler gets a five dollar bill from someone—perhaps even his own parents—and passes it on to the potential escapee.[11] Or another youth wants some pornography; the peddler persuades a staff member or his own parents to bring him the desired material. Another inmate wants some dope, and the peddler does his best to get him grass or pills.[12] When someone on maximum restriction needs hacksaw blades to saw through his windows, the peddler may do what he can to get them, expecially if he owes the boy a favor or feels coerced. Extremely serious requests involving potential danger are denied, especially if a staff "bust" will jeopardize his own release.[13]

One of the most interesting peddlers in recent years was a youth who always wore a coat. When he was finally stopped and searched, the staff discovered that his pockets were full of contraband. This youth was so good that stripping the coat from him did not stop his peddling. He was, in fact, such a "pro" that staff would stop him and say they needed something. Somehow the peddler would come up with the requested items. One staff member related how he approached this skillful youth about needing some wax tor the cottage floor and the next day the peddler brought him a full can.

As with the "booty bandit" the peddler does most of his work in the middle stage of his stay. If discovered, he "wises up" and stops his peddling to protect himself from a long confinement. Being true manipulators, many peddlers become so friendly with staff during their final stage that they are labeled "ass-kissers."

## MESSUP

The next three social roles—"messup," thief, and queen—all receive deprecation from both staff and inmates. The "messup" creates feelings ranging from bewilderment to mild irritation and pity; the "thief" creates anger; and the "queen" generates feelings of disgust. These social roles—the first two occupied primarily by whites and the final one by blacks—are occupied by boys who find institutional survival difficult. Another characteristic in common is that they bring conflict to the cottages, disturbing their stability and harmony.

The "messup" generally needs considerable attention from staff. Labeled quickly as "pain freak" and "messup" by staff and "weak-minded" by peers, this youth has problems on several fronts. On the one hand, he appears to be compelled to create trouble in order to attract staff's attention. Besides making mistakes, violating institutional rules, and creating conflicts with peers, this youth has a remarkable penchant for doing and saying the wrong thing. Needless to say, his problem-creating behavior results in punishment and greater rejection from staff. Too, this youth, who is generally a lower middle-class white, is generally poorly equipped to defend himself against stronger peers; consequently, he is extensively exploited, sometimes sexually. To make matters worse, his inability to make an adequate institutional adjustment results in a lengthened stay. Usually one boy in every cottage continues this type of behavior throughout his confinement. Staff are sometimes able to persuade him to terminate this attention-getting but self-defeating behavior in order to expedite his release.

An illustration of the "messup" is a boy who was incarcerated for over three years. Although he was not sexually exploited, he was in constant conflict with peers and engaged in fight after fight—most of which he lost. Indeed, he had an affinity for challenging those whom he did not have a chance of beating. Since fighting results in seven days' maximum restriction, this youth spent much of his time "on the floor." He also went out of his way to irritate staff. If a staff member came into the cottage moody or irritable, this youth always took the opportunity to bother him; the other boys had enough sense to let alone staff who were having a bad day.[14] Another way of irritating staff was to ask question after question, most of which had been answered before. In this and other ways, he had a remarkable facility for generating anger in other people. Staff who were usually calm and controlled sometimes reacted with violence to his antics.

Saddest of all was the fact that this youth always destroyed upcoming good events by "acting out." For instance, he lost his pre-release badge three times shortly after receiving it. Long-awaited home visits were cancelled because of negativistic behavior only a day or two before the event. Making sexual advances to a female teacher cancelled his release date once, and picking a fight with a staff member cancelled it a second time. Then he would wail and scream because his home visit was cancelled or his release day put off. Staff were finally able to release this resident by setting his release date without informing him when it was.

## THIEF

In spite of his lowly status, the thief is found in nearly every cottage. Like the "messup," the thief seems to want to get caught and punished.[15] But even deeper than these common characteristics is the possibility that both stealing and constant trouble-making are attention-seeking devices. One leader analyzed this social role by commenting, "There are two types of thieves. One is a compulsive thief; the other steals for need." The leader went on to say that a compulsive thief "is a boy who comes into the staff's office for a pencil and leaves with your gloves."

Even though strong inmates extort material goods from weaker boys, the inmate code does not permit residents to steal items from rooms. Of importance also is the attempt of inmates to retain privacy of personal goods in their rooms. Consequently, usually labeled "chump" or "weak-minded" in the first stage of institutionalization, the thief has conflict with peers as a result of his stealing. Sometimes this conflict precedes the stealing, but at other times arises from it.

Throughout his stay, the occupant of this social role has problems with both staff and peers. Some thieves operate solely because of the truncated supply of goods and steal simply because they want something. Others steal items possessed in abundance and do so in such a way that apprehension is almost certain. Still others steal in an effort to get back at someone who exploited them. Thieves may steal cigarettes, hair spray, toilet articles, class rings, pictures, magazines, and food from inmates' rooms. But, whatever the reason for stealing, they continue this unpopular activity throughout their institutionalization. Predictably, the pattern of their stealing guarantees that they are "busted" very soon after they start. From that point on, both staff and inmates are extremely alert to their "sticky fingers." Strong sanctions and cruel physical abuse are meted out by peers who frequently violently assault the offender; even so, the thief continues to engage in his "trade."

## QUEEN

One of the most interesting roles is the queen. In this institution, as in adult prisons, queens are overt homosexuals. At the time of data collection, no queens were confined, although one youth was showing signs of adopting the appropriate behavior. Over the past four years six blacks and one white played this role, according to staff, imitating women in their gait, wearing fancy or colored (red) undershorts, and using lipstick and rouge when they could get them. A staff member noted that "they think they are girls." He claimed that these boys could be identified by the way they combed their hair, how they walked, and the "feminine" way in which they held their hands.

The most salient characteristics of these youths are their homosexual experiences in both the community and other institutions. That is, these boys arrive committed to homosexuality. Consequently, their relationship cannot be defined as exploitative because they select their own "lovers" from prospective partners. "Booty bandits," in particular, vie for their attention, and losers generate enormous animosity toward the recipient of the queen's attention. Writing notes to their sexual lovers, queens also play the games, "stay away closer" or "hard to get, but gettable" (Irwin, 1970). In fact, even aggressive youths get caught kissing the queens, and fall in love with this feminized male.[16]

Beginning their role performance early in their stay, queens tend to continue it throughout their institutionalization. In a setting in which the white is exploited both sexually and nonsexually, the black who flaunts his body in front of others confuses and upsets both inmates and staff. Staff are bewildered by his activities and try everything to discourage his flirtations and sexual activity. In spite of the harassment of staff and peers, the queen usually remains steadfast. He looks everyone in the eye and appears to be proud of his social role. In the end, staff give up, releasing the youth simply to get him out of the institution.

## SCAPEGOAT

The lowest-ranking social role is the scapegoat. Considered to have departed from the group's normative expectations, the scapegoat is isolated from the group. He typically has minor criminal offenses in his record, including limited involvement with drugs.

He normally is committed to the Ohio Youth Commission for incorrigibility and running away from other institutions (Bartollas et al., 1974a).

The process of becoming a scapegoat transpires over a period of time and consists of several stages. The first stage begins when the future scapegoat arrives at the institution much more fearful than the average inmate. In contrast to that of other boys, his anxiety does not subside, principally because he realizes that he is a "prime candidate" for extensive exploitation—being small, lower-middle-class, and white. The second stage involves the reactions of fellow inmates who are aware of his amenability to victimization and therefore harass him unmercifully.

If he cannot be sexually victimized in this second stage—which may last for a number of weeks—his peers will eventually let him alone. But if forced into oral sodomy, masturbation of others, or more than an isolated incident of anal intercourse, the publicity of this "dramatic event" becomes his "status degradation ceremony" and begins the third stage of his "moral career." In contrast to the gradual process of stereotyping deviant behavior in the community, this process of labelling is sudden, sometimes surprising, and always definitive. Following his "dramatic event," he is viewed as a social outcast, someone to be avoided. Peers proceed to make a "retrospective interpretation" of him in which their previous conceptions are reassessed "to fit" with his new status.

In the fourth stage of this identity-changing experience, the inmate—confronted by pressure from peers to conform to his new role—begins to accommodate himself to it. For him to create new "definitions of the situation" at this point would be next to impossible. Life in a total institution offers little room for "face-saving and moral-preserving detachment from imposed identities" (Lofland, 1969). "Role engulfment" takes place, in which the inmate shapes his new identity and learns to play a role which probably will be his career as long as he is confined. He is no longer seen apart from his role, for all his other identity is blended into it.

Scapegoats differ from cottage to cottage because boys and staff make their own distinctive input in shaping the scapegoat's role. In addition, some cottage staff are much more effective than others in restricting sexual exploitation. As already indicated, some cottages have more than one scapegoat, and some cottages have none. In recent years, more cottages have had one or more scapegoats.

How does the scapegoat feel about his new role? Whereas other inmates vent some of their anger about being exploited on less aggressive peers, the scapegoat generally displays little outward emotion. If pressured about his status when denial is impossible, the scapegoat usually acts resigned to his fate. Every indication still exists that deep down he feels guilt, shame, and indignation. Upon being labelled dirty by homosexuality, for instance, the scapegoat often begins to skip his daily shower, becoming physically dirty as well. Not infrequently, the scapegoat tries to hurt himself. Upon realizing that he had lost face with his peers, one went back to his room and set it on fire, nearly resulting in his own death and that of several others.

How does the scapegoat justify his sexual behavior to himself? This question is important because usually he has no deviant sexual history in the community and only brief sexual involvement (anal intercourse) in another institution. It is quite a switch to go from occasional anal intercourse to committing oral sodomy on several peers waiting in line. Scapegoats ordinarily neutralize their involvement by saying that they are either forced into homosexuality or that they now need homosexual relationships and cannot control themselves.

> If you're a punk and you've been a punk for a long time and you want to stop, it's very hard because you've got so many desires in you. If you enjoy what you was doing before and then after you do it, you get a guilty feeling—you don't know where to turn. Like you say, I want to stop and they you get to the point where it's just like you need a woman, you get horny or something like that. It gets to the point where you want to do it again, and you don't know what to do. You say you want to stop. But there's something in you that wants to keep going.

Preliminary findings indicate that scapegoats who do not escape from their roles (i.e., "get off the bottom,") during institutionalization remain social outcasts in the community. Since approximately one out of every three scapegoats who go through this "identity transformation" is able to fight his way "off the bottom" before release, this means that two out of every three remain on the bottom of their peer hierarchy as social outcasts in the community. Their reputation (label) apparently goes with them, and they continue to play this lowly role.

Further, few scapegoats complete their parole period successfully; as "loners," they quickly become involved in criminal pursuits. Serious property offenses such as armed robbery are frequent, and crimes of passion are occasional. This is quite surprising considering that minor offenses were committed to get incarcerated in the first place. If they are able to escape their status while in the institution, they seem to have about the same chance of community adjustment as do other released boys.[17]

Reaction from Peers and Staff

Once the scapegoat is successfully labelled, inmates "put him on a shelf" or isolate him. Feeling that he is now different because of the sexual activity, peers do not want anything more to do with him. He is not allowed to serve their food, smoke before or after them on the same cigarette, or even sit beside them. They usually act as if the scapegoat were not physically present in the room.

When a scapegoat is trying to escape his status, he is kept "on the bottom" by power games. Black exploiters want him there for future use; white peers not far from the bottom are aware that the scapegoat's rise may mean their descent. "Heavies" who desire to maintain equilibrium and order in the cottage are aware that the reshuffling of social positions upsets their ability to control. Thus, whenever something happens to get a boy "off the bottom," these boys react.

In recent institutional history, two scapegoats were helped by peers to escape their role engulfment. One peer was an extremely capable lower-class white (a "slick") who had a "don't give a damn" attitude and did not associate much with others in the cottage. He began to befriend the scapegoat, constantly telling him, "don't let them mess over you." The scapegoat eventually heeded his new friend's advice and stood up for himself. It took several fights and the support of his friend, but he was able to escape his lowly status. In another situation, a highly respected black student befriended a white scapegoat who was being harassed constantly. This black boy, who also was not dependent upon the peer social structure, was upset with the treatment of the scapegoat and began to stand up for him, resulting in the scapegoat's restoration to social respectability.

Youth leaders working directly with inmates initially respond with anger to a youth who lets others push him around. They warn him repeatedly that serious trouble will follow unless he defends himself. Youth leaders, aware of the dynamics of social processes, usually can foresee exploitation and are not surprised when a boy has been socially typed. But they feel, for the most part, that the scapegoat brings the trouble on himself: "If he wanted to 'get the kids off his back,' then he would 'kick a few asses.' " Hence, they tend to reject and ignore him like everybody else. They refuse to talk to him, do not choose him to do cottage assignments, fail to select him for dances, and overlook him when home visits are assigned.

Some youth leaders will eventually get to the point where they are "fed up" with what a scapegoat is doing to himself. Generally, these are the most treatment-oriented staff, and they offer the scapegoat help, encouraging him to stand up for himself. If they offer assistance and encouragement when the youth is ready to change, they can be quite helpful in dislodging him from his deviant role.

Surprisingly, social workers are, if anything, less responsive to scapegoats than are youth leaders. They usually are not close enough to the "interior" life in the cottage to be aware of its processes, and often become aware of the "dramatic event" only after the fact. Therefore, somewhat confused by the process of becoming deviant, they are influenced by other staff and inmates to ignore the scapegoat. Thus, boys who desperately need the intervention of social workers are deprived of this important resource.[18]

The scapegoat also appears to have problems establishing contact with other staff. This lack of interest is certainly not surprising considering the public knowledge of his sexual stigma. The chaplain, who frequently supports inmates ignored by everyone else, ordinarily has little contact with these victims. Part of the reason is related to the scapegoat's lack of religious response, but this, in turn, may be related to his feelings of worthlessness. Conversely, boys who escape this status seem to be more responsive to religious instruction. Two boys, in fact, recently had "conversion" experiences after ceasing to be engulfed in the scapegoat's role.

Although recreational staff are quite supportive of inmates, scapegoats receive no positive support from them because of their refusal to participate in either team or individual sports. They also fail to receive support from teachers and the principal of the high school, principally because of their poor performance and lack of interest. In spite of the length of their confinement, scapegoats generally collect few academic credits and little vocational training.

As a final note to this long chapter, inmates receive many labels, some of which reflect roles which boys come to occupy. Several of these roles, especially the "heavy" and the scapegoat, become a career during confinement. At least with the scapegoat, the negative stigma appears to affect his community adjustment and way of life. Therefore, while some roles and labels may only affect residents during institutionalization, others may stigmatize them throughout life.

## NOTES

1. Cooperative "heavies" are supposed to be "cool" and strong enough that they do not have to fight.

2. The interactions involved in leadership selection are part of the underlife of the cottages, making it difficult to be aware of the actual dynamics of what has transpired. This phenomenon clearly needs to be studied further.

3. Cooperative "heavies" outnumber aggressive "heavies" approximately three to one throughout the institution.

4. The "slick" will still continue to maintain social distance from peers.

5. The following incident relates behavior very unusual for a "slick." When certain staff had a youth report sexual victimization by other staff, a "slick" was called into the office. Asked whether these allegations were true, the youth replied that he did not know anything about it. Not being satisfied with his answer, the staff continued to press him. He became extremely nervous and asked for a cigarette. He was given a cigarette and, in a quivering voice, said that two staff members were sexually exploiting inmates.

He was obviously extremely uncomfortable, having abandoned his "playing it cool" self-management. Becoming more involved, this youth repeated "It just ain't right, it just ain't right," and then he went on to describe in considerable detail what was happening. The two staff members, in turn, brought the "slick" to the superintendent. As he repeated his version of staff sexual exploitation, the "slick's" voice began to break. Typical of most "slicks," this youth had never shown emotion before; but at one point, tears appeared in his eyes. He again repeated, "It just ain't right, it just ain't right." Somehow, this incident had become the motivating factor for him to deviate from his non-involvement.

This youth was then returned to his cottage, where he informed the other "slick" what had taken place, and something of the following conversation must have taken place: "Man, what are you sticking your neck out for those punks for? You are going to turn around and mess up your release." The superintendent and other staff meanwhile interviewed several youths who were named by the "slick" as being sexually exploited. When the superintendent requested a second talk with the "slick" who had informed, the cottage was called and staff were asked to bring the youth to the superintendent's office. Forty minutes later, the cottage was again called to ask why the youth leader and boy had not arrived. The youth leader showed up alone and said that the boy would not come. This youth, who had been perfectly compliant to every request of staff in recent months, would no longer cooperate. Indeed, he refused to talk about the matter ever again. He simply sat in a chair with his lower lip quivering, saying, "I don't know nothing about it." Having abandoned his social role for an hour or so, he obviously had vowed never to do so again.

6. Boys are given Jesness Personality Inventory at this and other Ohio Youth Commission facilities.

7. In his book, Irwin says that inmates in California prisons who are serious about changing are "gleaning."

8. Although the staff rated all twenty-five as sexual exploiters, evidence indicates that some may have engaged in sexual relations voluntarily. For example, two white scapegoats had sex with each other and six intraracially, passive youths "traded off." Early in their stay two black youths coerced whites into anal sodomy. The major point being made here is that no evidence exists that any of these ten residents were committed to sexual exploitation as a way of life while confined. For statistical purposes, all twenty-five youths were considered sexual exploiters, since it is doubtful they would have formed similar relationships if allowed to remain in the community. Clearly, just as was the case with "how to define a victim," further research must resolve who exactly is the exploiter. Here, as in other aspects of victimization, the subject's definition of the situation must also be explored.

9. The pressures put on blacks are subtle and do not involve the physical harassment they do with whites.

10. One staff member suggested that boys began peddling to keep their minds occupied.

11. Inmates are not permitted to carry money on their persons or to have money in their possession.

12. Usually, the peddler has to persuade his parents or siblings to bring narcotics into the institution. However, several staff have been accused of bringing narcotics into the institution for boys, and it is conceivable that a peddler was at the bottom of this.

13. Compared to adult prisons, the economic activity in this inmate society is much

less developed. Little "interest" is collected for lending, such as two or three cigarettes for one. Youths do not manufacture their own alcohol, nor is there very much gambling in this subculture. See Williams and Fish (1974) for an expansive treatment of the economic activity of the inmate society in adult prisons.

14. Unless, of course, the boys decided to "run game" on the staff member.

15. Both the "messup" and the thief experienced considerable rejection as children.

16. As noted in Chapter 6, these boys escape labelling because of their extreme aggressiveness and strength.

17. Three scapegoats who appear successful in their community adjustment to date have all left their communities. Two made a satisfactory adjustment to the armed services; the third moved to Florida and, at last report, was doing well.

18. Female social workers seem to be much less likely to ignore the scapegoat than male social workers.

# PART III

# OTHER EXPLOITATION DETERMINANTS
# AND ADAPTATIONS

CHAPTER 8


## THE EXPLOITATION TYPOLOGY


**The typology discussed** in the third chapter emerged after we requested staff to rate the exploitation potential of all in their cottages. We had assumed that the ratings would be fairly clear-cut, but it became quite clear that some modifications were needed in the typology. The findings suggested that exploitation was not an either/or phenomenon and that many boys exhibited varying degrees of being exploiters and exploited. Thus, we ended up with the fivefold typology.

But, given that the boys in the typological categories varied on the dimension of exploitation, did they differ on the other characteristics as well? Were there, in other words, certain variables which enabled the observer to predict which youths would exploit or be exploited? To determine whether specific characteristics might influence a boy's classification, chi-square and analysis of variance tests were run on their criminal history and physical characteristics. In addition, the Gough Adjective Checklist, the Jesness Personality Inventory, and the Machover Draw-a-Figure Test were all run against the typology. Inmates classified on each of the typological categories demonstrated certain distinct characteristics. Before we examine these characteristics, though, we will describe the typological categories.

Category 1:  Exploits Others and Is Not Exploited (Exploiters)

Generally made up of the heavies and their lieutenants, this group controls the cottages. Feared by residents because they have proven themselves in fights or psychological oneupmanship, they have risen to a position of leadership. Because they are "tough," they do not need to fear exploitation, and about the only time one of them receives less than he gives is when the lieutenant is requested to carry out the heavy's orders. As we suggested in Chapter 7, when an aggressive heavy controls the cottage, he and his lieutenants may be quite assertive and even brutal in exploiting other peers.

Category 2:  Exploits Others and Is Exploited (Give and Takes)

Although a few lieutenants are included in this category, the majority of these youths come from the middle levels of the exploitation matrix. Not strong enough to protect themselves completely, these boys are victimized on cigarettes, food, clothes, and occasional personal items. Even though they sometimes exploit others sexually, they are not victimized sexually. Interestingly enough, a few of these boys do choose to "trade off" sexually with peers. At the same time, they are able to take items from weaker youths further down the exploitation hierarchy.

Category 3:  Does Not Exploit Others and
Is Not Exploited (Independents)

As noted in Chapter 7, there are two basic types of independents. The first type, "boys who profit," is interesting because of its maturity and concern about self-improvement. Being somewhat older than their peers, these boys are able to take care of themselves and are not threatened by aggressive inmates. They are not interested in the exploitation hierarchy found in the cottage. The second type lacks any concern about improving themselves. Institution-wise, they know what is expected of them and merely "do time." Accepted both by staff and peers, they stay outside the exploitation matrix because participation in it can prolong their incarceration.

Category 4: Does Not Exploit Others but
Is Occasionally Exploited (Sometimes Boys)

These boys do not exploit others. The most likely reason for
this is that they are not strong enough to take things from others,
although they are capable of protecting themselves from being
seriously exploited. Their need for acceptance by peers apparently
compels them to remain in the exploitation matrix. Therefore,
they are able to rationalize giving cigarettes, clothing, food, and
other material goods away, but draw the line when it comes to
sexual exploitation. In fact, even though some of these youths
were exploited sexually once or twice early in their institutionalization, they now have become more resolute and are no longer
able to be victimized sexually.

Category 5: Very Definitely Exploited and Fairly Often (Victims)

There are two basic types of this final group. The first type,
extensively described in the previous chapter, is the cottage scapegoat. Five of the eight cottages, for instance, had scapegoats who
were labelled social outcasts and were isolated from others. Because their social role isolates them and gives them an unclean
status, they are no longer significantly exploited materially by
peers.

The second group receives extensive nonsexual exploitation.
Both close supervision of staff and their own resourcefulness
protects them from sexual exploitation. Nevertheless, as soon as
these boys receive any goods at all, such as food or cigarettes,
victimization begins. Boys are quickly relieved of their possessions.
Sometimes "beaten upon" by their peers, they seem to be in-
capable of protecting themselves.

## THE TYPOLOGY AND THE EXTENT OF EXPLOITATION

Initially, 159 names appeared on the roster of the institution.
By the time data collection began, the number of boys on whom
ratings could be obtained concerning their criminal history, demographic and physical characteristics had dropped to 150.[1] Table

8.1 indicates how these youths were divided up according to the typology. The largest group of boys, whom are called the "give and takes" for convenience, totalled about 34 percent of the entire population. They were followed in turn by the "sometimes boys" 21 percent, the "exploiters" 19 percent, the "victimized" 17 percent, and the "independents" 10 percent. Therefore, almost 90 percent of the youths were involved in either exploiting others, being exploited, or some combination of the two. Especially striking is the fact that over 70 percent of the boys were being exploited in some manner and that only 10 percent managed to escape involvement in the exploitation matrix.

In addition, sixteen of the twenty-five boys definitely exploited were regarded as chronic sexual victims who were considered to be cottage scapegoats. The remaining nine heavily victimized boys were probably also sexually victimized but were able to keep the fact of their exploitation secret.[2] Also, 91 (or 61 percent) were exploited on items such as food, clothes, and cigarettes, leaving only about 29 percent who were not intimidated or forced into a victim role at some time. The only boys escaping victimization were the exploiters and the independents.

Important is the reason why some of the inmates were made into victims and others escaped. Chapter 5 established that the number of previous commitments differentiated among boys who were leaned on sexually and those who had items exploited from

Table 8.1

DISTRIBUTION OF YOUTHS IN EACH
TYPOLOGICAL CATEGORY

| TYPOLOGY | CODE NAME | N | % |
|---|---|---|---|
| Exploits others but is not exploited | Exploiters | 29 | 18.8 |
| Exploits others but is exploited | Give and Takes | 50 | 33.6 |
| Does not exploit and is not exploited | Independents | 15 | 10.1 |
| Does not exploit, and is occasionally exploited | Sometimes Boys | 31 | 20.8 |
| Definitely exploited | Victims | 25 | 16.8 |

them. Age, weight, height, and number of previous offenses did not significantly differentiate among the categories. To determine whether the same variables discriminated among the typology's categories, an analysis of variance test was run, and the results are presented in Table 8.2.

The only variable which differentiated significantly among the five categories was the number of previous commitments. The exploiters were also taller than most of the boys, weighed more (with the exception of the victimized), had the greater number of previous commitments, and had fewer previous offenses than their peers.

Table 8.2

**EXPLOITATION TYPOLOGY BY DEMOGRAPHIC AND PHYSICAL CHARACTERISTICS, AND CRIMINAL HISTORY[a]**

| Typology | Age at Admission | Weight | Height | No. of Previous Commitments[b] | n | No. of Previous Offenses |
|---|---|---|---|---|---|---|
| Exploiters | 17.04 | 158.54 | 68.79 | 2.13 | 29 | 3.89 |
| Give and Takes | 16.72 | 146.88 | 67.76 | 1.04 | 50 | 4.56 |
| Independents | 17.07 | 153.60 | 67.80 | 1.47 | 15 | 4.80 |
| Sometimes Boys | 16.90 | 147.26 | 68.23 | 1.71 | 31 | 5.42 |
| Victims | 17.00 | 162.72 | 67.68 | 1.28 | 25 | 4.44 |
| Mean | 16.91 | 152.48 | 68.04 | 1.47 | 150 | 4.62 |
| F Test | 0.7960 | 1.4373 | 0.9547 | 3.7453 | | 1.0727 |

Between degrees of freedom    4
Within degrees of freedom    144

a. For other data related to the typological classification, see Appendix J.
b. Statistically significant at the .01 level.

## THE TYPOLOGY AND PSYCHOLOGICAL CHARACTERISTICS

Mendelsohn and von Hentig were two of the first researchers to point out that the psychological and social characteristics of the victim and the perpetrator contribute to victimization. Clearly, various psychological states should make a person more suscep-tible to being victimized or more likely to become an aggressor. The peculiarity of this institution, however, is that nearly all of its inhabitants have been aggressive in the community. Why, then, do some of these supposedly very tough boys end up being victimized?

The typology construction indicated that the different cate-gories of boys differed fairly substantially in their roles and position in the inmate hierarchy. These boys, therefore, should also vary in their psychological characteristics if a connection does exist between mental states and their classification. Since our hope was to discover certain personality traits related to boys who took advantage of peers and those who permitted themselves to be victimized, the boys were given three psychological tests.

The Gough-Heilbrun Adjective Checklist

The Gough Adjective Checklist (ACL) consists of 300 adjectives divided into 24 scales and indices. The adjectives were given to all boys who would take the test and a total of 135 boys responded. Of the ACL scales and indices, 21 were factor analyzed on the basis of how they differentiated among the exploitation cate-gories.[3] Analysis of variance showed that a total of 14 of 22 scales were statistically significant at the .05 level or better.[4] A definite patterning, then, emerged among the five categories of the typol-ogy. The 22 scale scores may be seen in Table 8.3 and their rank ordering may be seen in Table 8.4. Some of the scales did not differentiate among the categories at a statistically significant level. However, the rank ordering of a large number of the scales was identical.[5]

The number of adjectives checked was in the highest possible category for any population. According to Gough and Heilbrun (page 7 of the manual), checking a larger number of adjectives

seems to reflect surgency and drive, and a relative absence of repressive tendencies. Correlation with intelligence is slightly negative, so that the exuberance in behavior may possibly spring more from shallowness and inattention to ambiguities than from a deep level of involvement. The individual high on this variable tends to be described as emotional, adventurous, wholesome, conservative, enthusiastic, unintelligent,

## Table 8.3

### TYPOLOGY BY GOUGH ADJECTIVE CHECKLIST

| ADJECTIVE SCALE | POP. MEAN | EXPLOITERS | GIVE AND TAKES | INDEPENDENTS | SOMETIMES BOYS | VICTIMS | F | P |
|---|---|---|---|---|---|---|---|---|
| No. Adjectives Checked | 173.200 | 188.080 | 170.348 | 173.200 | 166.296 | 170.727 | 0.9556 | NS |
| Defensiveness | 23.919 | 24.640 | 22.870 | 20.800 | 20.222 | 31.955 | 3.4396 | .05 |
| Self-confidence | 36.593 | 36.440 | 36.043 | 34.467 | 35.444 | 40.773 | 1.5695 | NS |
| Self-control | 30.393 | 30.840 | 30.978 | 25.400 | 27.556 | 35.545 | 2.8372 | .05 |
| Lability | 38.378 | 42.480 | 37.870 | 35.733 | 35.667 | 39.909 | 1.6217 | NS |
| Personal Adjustment | 19.993 | 22.080 | 20.130 | 14.600 | 15.889 | 26.045 | 3.6981 | .01 |
| Achievement | 21.926 | 22.800 | 21.283 | 16.600 | 20.259 | 27.955 | 4.3023 | .01 |
| Dominance | 20.289 | 20.240 | 19.196 | 17.533 | 18.556 | 26.636 | 4.4229 | .01 |
| Endurance | 26.859 | 27.720 | 27.087 | 22.667 | 23.185 | 32.773 | 4.3822 | .01 |
| Order | 29.815 | 30.800 | 31.087 | 23.933 | 26.111 | 34.591 | 3.4576 | .05 |
| Intraception | 13.170 | 13.800 | 13.565 | 8.067 | 7.926 | 21.545 | 3.4108 | .05 |
| Nurturance | 11.481 | 13.040 | 11.109 | 6.600 | 6.074 | 20.455 | 4.5474 | .01 |
| Affiliation | 21.022 | 22.400 | 20.043 | 15.667 | 16.463 | 30.136 | 3.5314 | .01 |
| Heterosexuality | 23.252 | 25.800 | 20.870 | 22.467 | 21.296 | 28.273 | 2.2139 | NS |
| Exhibition | 50.585 | 50.080 | 49.391 | 52.867 | 50.778 | 51.864 | 0.9893 | NS |
| Autonomy | 59.207 | 59.760 | 56.957 | 64.333 | 61.444 | 57.045 | 2.2790 | NS |
| Aggression | 69.896 | 67.360 | 69.239 | 74.533 | 74.407 | 65.455 | 3.1214 | .05 |
| Change | 36.252 | 37.440 | 35.065 | 35.067 | 38.222 | 35.773 | 1.0346 | NS |
| Succorance | 71.059 | 72.760 | 70.696 | 71.200 | 73.556 | 66.727 | 3.4108 | .05 |
| Abasement | 60.200 | 62.640 | 61.261 | 57.133 | 60.074 | 57.455 | 2.9872 | .05 |
| Deference | 35.600 | 36.120 | 36.739 | 31.533 | 32.481 | 39.227 | 2.3847 | NS |
| Counseling Readiness | 70.689 | 72.400 | 71.326 | 71.067 | 71.407 | 66.273 | 2.8797 | .05 |

Between degrees of freedom   4

Within degrees of freedom   130

N = 135

frank, and helpful. He is active, apparently means well, but tends to blunder.

As Table 8.3 indicates, the mean number of adjectives checked was 173.2. The number checked ranged from 20 to 295, with a standard deviation of 43.75. In comparison with normal populations, then, these youths are in the upper limits of adjectives checked. Consequently, their description by Gough and Heilbrun would appear to be highly accurate with the possible exception of the "wholesome" and "helpful" labels. Any evaluation of these offenders must obviously take into consideration their institutional confinement: immersion in this milieu may help to explain why these boys answer so many adjectives compared to normal populations.[6] Further, on all but six scales, inmates' highest scores are lower than the median on the scale scores for a normal population. In other words, on these six scales, these incarcerated boys' most favorable responses fall in the low or unfavorable range which Gough and Heilbrun determined existed for a normal population.[7]

When the scale scores for the boys within each of the five typological categories were factor analyzed, a profile for each type began to emerge (see Table 8.4). The victims, for example, scored highest on thirteen of twenty-four scales.[8] On six of the scales, the victims scored highest, followed by the exploiters, give and takes, sometimes boys, and independents. The scales which demonstrated this pattern are as follows:

    Personal Adjustment      Endurance
    Achievement              Affiliation
    Dominance                Self-confidence
                             (not statistically significant)

The victims also scored highest on yet another seven scales, including self-control, order, nurturance, heterosexuality, deference, defensiveness and intraception.

The victim emerges, then, as a better-adjusted youth in the community. He has more self-control, better personal adjustment, higher need for achievement, more need to dominate, greater need for order, more endurance, higher intraception or desire to see

## Table 8.4

## RANK ORDERING OF TYPOLOGY BY GOUGH ADJECTIVE CHECKLIST

| Adjective Scale | Exploiters | Give and Takes | Independents | Sometimes Boys | Victims |
|---|---|---|---|---|---|
| No. Adjectives Checked | 1 | 4 | 2 | 5 | 3 |
| Defensiveness | 2 | 3 | 4 | 5 | 1 |
| Self-confidence | 2 | 3 | 5 | 4 | 1 |
| Self-control | 3 | 2 | 5 | 4 | 1 |
| Lability | 1 | 3 | 5 | 4 | 2 |
| Pers. Adjustment | 2 | 3 | 5 | 4 | 1 |
| Achievement | 2 | 3 | 5 | 4 | 1 |
| Dominance | 2 | 3 | 5 | 4 | 1 |
| Endurance | 2 | 3 | 5 | 4 | 1 |
| Order | 3 | 2 | 5 | 4 | 1 |
| Intraception | 2 | 3 | 4 | 5 | 1 |
| Nurturance | 2 | 3 | 4 | 5 | 1 |
| Affiliation | 2 | 3 | 5 | 4 | 1 |
| Heterosexuality | 2 | 5 | 3 | 4 | 1 |
| Exhibition | 4 | 5 | 1 | 3 | 2 |
| Autonomy | 3 | 5 | 1 | 2 | 4 |
| Aggression | 4 | 3 | 1 | 2 | 5 |
| Change | 2 | 5 | 4 | 1 | 3 |
| Succorance | 2 | 4 | 3 | 1 | 5 |
| Abasement | 1 | 2 | 5 | 3 | 4 |
| Deference | 3 | 2 | 5 | 4 | 1 |
| Couns. Readiness | 1 | 3 | 4 | 2 | 5 |

NOTE: Patterened scales are in boldface.

into the motives of others, higher nurturance or desire to engage in behavior helpful to others, and more self-confidence. Yet, in this particular context, these boys are the most poorly adjusted. In spite of the highest scores on heterosexuality, they often find themselves sexually victimized.[9] Although they are second on lability, or ego strength, the victims find themselves in an environment in which they are unable to handle more aggressive youths. It is important to note that they are lowest on aggression. Perhaps, because of their poor institutional adjustment, victims are lowest on deference—that is, their willingness to seek and sustain subordinate roles in relationship with others. They are also low on counseling readiness, which means that they are unwilling to seek or to profit from help.

In speculating why these seemingly better-adjusted boys find themselves victimized, several possibilities may be raised. First, their better adjustment may invite victimization from those more poorly adjusted. Feeling better about themselves and superior to those around them, these youths bring on exploitation simply because peers resent their air of superiority. Second, even though they are fourth in abasement or feelings of inferiority, some victims may emit cues for exploitation. These may arise from some need for punishment or merely from not knowing the rules or how to survive in this environment. Third, victims are primarily white and appear to lack the ability to organize themselves. Whites also tend to feel overwhelmed and receive little support from other whites in this facility. Experiencing a state of anomie, they may feel their best coping mechanism is to permit exploitation. Fourth, many of the white victims come from rural settings and are more prejudiced toward blacks than urban whites. This prejudice, in turn, creates animosity and causes retaliation from black inmates. Fifth, some of the victims' higher scores may reflect a need for self-control, dominance, and order in an environment in which they feel very much out of control. In other words, victims may be expressing the need to gain better control over their social world. Further, most of the victims are middle-class and find physically protecting themselves against aggressive ghetto youths who have much more experience in physical encounters very difficult.[10] Finally, many of the scales and the adjectives reflect a middle-class value orientation (Williams, 1970; Bronfenbrenner, 1958).[11]

The "give and takes," on the other hand, were intermediate on not only the eight scales mentioned above, but on four more. On the basis of the scale scores, the "give and takes" appear to be a mixture of middle- and lower-class boys. The scores may reflect partly the value orientation of the inmates. Taking several of these assumptions into consideration, the ACL scores are probably accurate in projecting a better-adjusted youth whose social background (more sheltered middle-class) and his present social setting (dominant black ghetto subculture) result in his becoming the most victimized youth. Psychologically more healthy in the community—although still below the normal population on scale scores—he is sociologically ill-equipped to deal with his present environment.

Significantly, exploiters have many personality characteristics in common with the victims. On defensiveness, self-confidence, personal adjustment, achievement, dominance, endurance, intraception, nurturance, affiliation, heterosexuality, change, and succorance, exploiters' scores were second following those of the victims. Of interest also is that aggressors ranked fourth on aggression, which certainly seems contradictory to their role in the exploitation matrix. On lability, however, which involves ego strength or tendency to push out, exploiters ranked first. The emerging picture is that exploiters and victims are relatively better adjusted when in the community. Lacking the material goods of the middle-class youth, they put pressure on peers to get what they want. The exploiters' feelings of abasement may also contribute to their exploiting others as they try to prove to themselves and others that they are not inferior or cowardly. Resenting the superior attitudes of the victims, and having some self-punishing needs, they apparently become involved in exploitative behavior knowing they will be punished.

Two additional statements need to be made about the exploiters. The first is that they score highest on counseling readiness, compared to the victims, who are fifth. Feeling inferior, they may want to reach out to staff, but, as adherents of the inmate code, are reluctant to relate to the "keepers." Second, the assumption about the victims' adherence to a middle-class orientation and value system does not hold true for the exploiters. These youths may want to achieve middle-class values as much as the victims even though they have not been exposed to those values to the same extent.

Much less can be said about the other three types. The give-and-take boys, for example, are intermediate on not only the eight scales mentioned above, but also on four more. In no case, do these youths rank highest on any of the scales. They are lowest on the heterosexuality, exhibition, autonomy and change scales, but not statistically significantly so. If the rank ordering of these boys is important, some clue is available to explain their position in the typology. The boys receive emotional satisfaction from interaction with peers; consequently, the participation of these youths in any type of exploitative relationship may provide satisfaction of basic needs. They appeared further to lack confidence in themselves (second in abasement) and, therefore, obtained satisfaction from conformity to others. Since exploitation is the norm for the institution, the assumption can be made that the boys feel status can be gained by doing as those around them do—i.e., exploit others—and at the same time, by permitting themselves to be exploited.

The "sometimes boys" are next to the lowest on the eight patterned scales, their scores indicating they are poorly adjusted youths. Although having similar difficulty dealing with the present environment, these inmates seemed to lack the community adjustment of the victims. Ranking first on both the change (which involves the need to seek novelty of experience) and succorance scales, these youths may permit themselves to become involved in the exploitation matrix out of some need for variety. But more likely is the fact that they gave up goods and occasionally sex to others because they felt they could gain emotional support from them. Certainly involved in their exploitation is some inability to withstand the aggressive overtures of peers. And perhaps also involved is some confusion on the part of these inmates who did not see any alternatives to victimization in this environment.

Finally, the independents are consistently the lowest scorers on ten scales. Yet, they are highest on exhibition, autonomy, and aggression. These traits may indicate why they did not need the attention of peers and had the ego strength to act independently of their fellow inmates. Nevertheless, the fact remains that on ten scales the independents received the lowest scores, suggesting that they are the most poorly adjusted youths in the community. Obviously, in view of their successful institutionalization, the lack of community personal adjustment fails to lessen their ability to perform well in this institutional context. Institution-wise from the past commitments, their present latent aggression apparently discourages overt aggressive overtures from others. As a result, they were able to "do time" and return to the community where the "slicks," particularly, will likely encounter problems because of their poor personal adjustment.

The Jesness Personality Inventory

As another check on the characteristics of those in different levels of the typology, the Jesness Personality Inventory was administered. Made up of 11 scales and consisting of 155 true-false items, the Jesness has been administered to numerous delinquent populations. Because this test was administered late in the data collection, and some residents had been released, only 75 percent of the 149 inmates were given this test.

Examinations of the results, nevertheless, showed no significant differences among the five typological categories. However, several of the scales did show some of the same type of patterning as the ACLs (see Table 8.5). Yet, there were some noteworthy variations with the ACL findings. For instance, on the Jesness social-maladjustment and the manifest aggression scales, the victims were highest; followed by the exploiters, give and takes, sometimes boys, and independents. A high score on the social maladjustment scale would appear to challenge the better adjustment of the victims as suggested by the adjective checklist. But the Jesness maladjustment scores may also reflect the inability of boys who hold this orientation to meet pressure from others in socially acceptable ways. Thus, although a boy may perceive his personal adjustment to be good, his social adjustment may be quite poor. The victims obviously are finding adjustment to their present

## Table 8.5

### TYPOLOGY BY JESNESS PERSONALITY INVENTORY

| JESNESS SCALE | POP. MEAN | EXPLOITERS | GIVE AND TAKES | INDEPENDENTS | SOMETIMES BOYS | VICTIMS | F | P |
|---|---|---|---|---|---|---|---|---|
| Social Maladjustment | 62.320 | 65.364 | 59.800 | 60.571 | 60.417 | 67.045 | 1.3271 | NS |
| Value Orientation | 56.090 | 58.455 | 53.175 | 54.357 | 56.500 | 59.682 | 1.7863 | NS |
| Immaturity | 54.066 | 54.955 | 53.600 | 52.643 | 52.792 | 56.318 | 0.3902 | NS |
| Autism | 59.270 | 58.545 | 57.800 | 54.857 | 59.750 | 64.955 | 2.0443 | NS |
| Alienation | 56.311 | 60.682 | 54.475 | 55.000 | 56.702 | 55.682 | 1.2838 | NS |
| Manifest Aggression | 53.123 | 54.409 | 52.700 | 50.143 | 49.667 | 58.273 | 1.9451 | NS |
| Withdrawal | 55.566 | 54.975 | 53.975 | 52.286 | 58.458 | 58.407 | 1.5853 | NS |
| Social Anxiety | 47.615 | 43.591 | 48.200 | 47.214 | 47.542 | 50.909 | 1.1449 | NS |
| Repression | 52.377 | 54.864 | 52.375 | 53.071 | 50.958 | 51.000 | 0.6385 | NS |
| Denial | 47.508 | 46.909 | 48.350 | 48.500 | 47.417 | 46.045 | 0.2119 | NS |
| Asocial Index | 64.574 | 68.818 | 62.725 | 66.286 | 61.208 | 66.273 | 1.1597 | NS |

Between degrees of freedom  4       N = 122
Within degrees of freedom   117

social environment quite difficult. On the manifest aggression scale, both victims and exploiters reflect this behavioral pattern, but in different ways. Manifest aggression means that youths have unpleasant feelings, especially anger and frustration, and experience discomfort as a result of those feelings. Not surprisingly, victims and aggressors express their reactions differently; victims are often depressed over their exploitation and speak out, while aggressors appear to express their anger and frustration through exploiting others.

It is of some interest that the victims were either the highest or lowest scorers on eight of the eleven scales (see Table 8.6). Most interesting is the fact that victims reflected an orientation to lower-class subcultural values, also contradictory to the ACL interpretation. The victims, according to the Jesness, were nonconforming, rule-violating, irresponsible, and alienated when relating to adults and peers. This, of course, may only be reflecting

Table 8.6

### RANK ORDERING OF TYPOLOGY
### BY JESNESS PERSONALITY INVENTORY

| Jesness Scale | Exploiters | Give and Takes | Independents | Sometimes Boys | Victims |
|---|---|---|---|---|---|
| Social Maladjustment | 2 | 3 | 4 | 5 | 1 |
| Value Orientation | 2 | 5 | 4 | 3 | 1 |
| Immaturity | 2 | 3 | 5 | 4 | 1 |
| Autism | 3 | 4 | 5 | 2 | 1 |
| Alienation | 1 | 5 | 4 | 2 | 3 |
| Manifest Aggression | 2 | 3 | 4 | 5 | 1 |
| Withdrawal | 3 | 4 | 5 | 1 | 2 |
| Social Anxiety | 5 | 2 | 4 | 3 | 1 |
| Repression | 1 | 3 | 2 | 4 | 5 |
| Denial | 4 | 2 | 1 | 3 | 5 |
| Asocial Index | 1 | 4 | 2 | 5 | 3 |

middle-class youths' rebellion against the organizational processing to which they were being subjected. In reaction to these rule-creators and enforcers, these youths constantly challenged and resisted their leadership. Since the families of victims have only recently become middle-class, many of their values could still be that of the lower class. Victims also ranked first in immaturity, autism, and social anxiety. Again, it would appear that this has more to do with their social adjustment than their personal adjustment. In this particular institutional context, victims are not equipped to deal with their daily social realities. As a result, they feel more anxious, immature, and want to set themselves apart from their peers.

Even though none of the Jesness findings are statistically significant, several tentative conclusions may be drawn. The Jesness may be helpful in understanding why victims—whose scores represented better social adjustment on the ACL—do so poorly in this training school. There are also some conflicts in what both of these instruments are trying to measure, raising questions about their validity. While apparently able to discriminate social characteristics, the Jesness may not be able to effectively discriminate personality characteristics. Obviously, much further testing and cross-validation of scales on this type of population is necessary before coming to any conclusions.

The Machover Draw-a-Figure Test

A third personality instrument utilized was the Machover Draw-a-Figure Test. This projective and clinical test was quantified into the categories of: sexual identification, aggression, and feelings of inferiority, maladjustment and anxiety.[12] In spite of the boys' reservations about taking this test, eighty-one percent agreed to draw the male and female figures.

Neither sexual identification nor any of the scales was statistically significant when run against the typology (see Appendix M). On their drawings, exploiters and victims were much lower on feelings of anxiety and inferiority than the other three groups (see Table 8.7). Of interest also is the fact that exploiters and give-and-

Table 8.7

MACHOVER SCALE SCORES BY TYPOLOGY

| Machover Rating | Tot. Pop. Mean | Exploiters | Give & Take | Independents | Sometimes Boys | Victims | F | P |
|---|---|---|---|---|---|---|---|---|
| Aggression | 3.160 | 3.000 | 3.222 | 3.071 | 3.160 | 3.273 | 0.3048 | NS |
| Inferiority | 3.191 | 3.160 | 3.422 | 2.786 | 3.320 | 2.864 | 2.1740 | NS |
| Maladjustment | 3.954 | 3.560 | 4.022 | 3.714 | 4.240 | 4.091 | 2.3544 | NS |
| Anxiety | 3.061 | 2.880 | 3.044 | 2.786 | 3.400 | 3.091 | 1.0135 | NS |

NOTE: For the rank ordering of the above scale, see Appendix M.

takes were very low on maladjustment, while the other three groups were extremely high. Unknown is whether the scale was measuring the social or the personal maladjustment of the victim. Consistent with their Jesness scores, victims scored high on aggression. But it is somewhat startling that the exploiters scored lowest on aggression, which is similar to their performance on the ACL. The three different scales either do not measure the same type of aggression or one or more of them lack validity. Considering the vast amount of psychological literature challenging the validity of the Machover, considerable reservation must be exercised before accepting any of its findings.[13]

This chapter has attempted to empirically analyze the exploitation typology and the factors which contribute to the typology's formation. Of the criminal history and physical data, only the number of previous offenses statistically differentiated significantly among the five categories. Three psychological tests possibly capable of identifying personality differences among the boys were also analyzed. To claim that personality traits related to exploitative behavior were discerned would be to transcend the data. One major problem is that personality characteristics are being related to behavioral dynamics. Another problem concerns the appropriateness of these three tests for this population. In spite of these reservations, the Adjective Checklist may be helpful in pointing out that the most victimized institutional boys are the healthiest psychologically. The Jesness Personality Inventory may document their inability to make an adequate social adjustment in this milieu. Future research is needed to document more clearly this relationship between personal and social characteristics in institutional adjustment. Prediction of who should be protected may eventually be possible.

## NOTES

1. After this initial rating of the boys, one more youth was lost for analysis, which reduced the number used in the study to 149.

2. Occasionally, boys are sexually victimized, but not often enough for peers to consider them scapegoats.

3. The scales not reported are "total number of adjectives checked," "number of favorable adjectives checked," and "number of unfavorable adjectives checked." However, the rest of the scale scores were computed taking the "total number of adjectives checked" into consideration. Unfortunately, the computer program used was not programmed to calculate the number of "favorable" and "unfavorable" adjectives checked. This information, no doubt, would be very interesting and useful if available.

4. Duncan's range test was also used to analyze these data. We are grateful for the assistance Dr. Alvin Smith of St. Andrew's College provided in that analysis. The results of that test are not reported here, but basically substantiate the findings of the analysis of variance tests.

5. Social class and number of previous commitments are two other important variables as indicated in the last section. Age, weight, and height were somewhat less important.

6. The boys have to develop their verbal abilities in order to survive.

7. This may suggest that institutional forces which are not found in society are working on these boys. Equally possible is that the inmate population is more poorly adjusted to start with than is a normal population found in the community. To empirically test which of these two explanations is accurate, the boys would have to be tested while still in the community and before getting into difficulty.

8. Not all thirteen scales differentiated significantly among the five typological categories.

9. The youths may react to their victimization by playing up their normal desires.

10. Previous analysis showed that the victims were overwhelmingly middle-class, whereas the exploiters, independents, and sometimes exploited boys were from the lower class. Further, this interpretation of the Adjective Checklist as measuring social class orientation is the authors', not Gough and Heilbrun's.

11. According to Robin Williams, major value orientations of the American society include some of the following: achievement and success, activity and work, material comfort, efficiency and practicality, progress, freedom, and external conformity. Bronfenbrenner cites studies demonstrating that the middle- and working-class parents have

different behavioral orientations toward their children. Some of the orientations (these orientations are not held in common) toward children include: the parents grant autonomy, are cooperative, equalitarian, democratic, punishment-oriented, share authority, are indulgent, and have excessive contact. The working class emphasizes the qualities of neatness, cleanliness, and order, whereas the middle class emphasizes happiness, consideration, curiosity, and self-control. The contention of the authors is that these major values and parental orientations are expressed differently in the middle and the lower classes. We believe that the Gough Adjective Checklist taps the differential responses of the various social classes to these values and orientations. This contention remains to be empirically demonstrated, however.

12. Professor Franco Feracuti quantified and analyzed the data on the Machovers.

13. For how the Machovers relate to the boys' demographic, physical and criminal history data, see Appendix M.

## CHAPTER 9

## SOCIAL CLASS, EMOTIONAL DISTURBANCE, AND VICTIMIZATION

A **dearth of appropriate** community facilities results in penal institutions being used to house the mentally disturbed.[1] Juvenile institutions in particular are housing increasing numbers of emotionally disturbed youths, who are housed with normal youths until their numbers warrant separate facilities. In this institution, the number of cottages reserved for the disturbed had increased from one to three during the past several years and created another dimension in the life of this training school.

Social and Psychological Characteristics of
Emotionally Disturbed Inmates

Until 1971, only a few emotionally disturbed lower-class boys were placed in this institution. Since then, an increasingly large number of disturbed boys have been transferred here. While more middle- than lower-class whites are currently being transferred to this facility, approximately one out of three of the recent arrivals are black.[2] Presently, four basic types of disturbed youths are being admitted: (1) the largest group is made up of middle-class whites;[3] (2) the smallest group is made up of middle-class blacks; (3) the second largest group is made up of lower-class whites and blacks; (4) the final group is made up of both whites and blacks whose behavior is considered bizarre.[4]

The disturbed usually come from broken families which are smaller than those of other inmates. Additionally, the disturbed almost always have experienced acute rejection in the home. Minor offenses such as incorrigibility dot their early court records, but more serious offenses, such as crimes against property prevail in their later criminal history. Loners in the commission of crimes, these youths are more prone to drug use than the average resident. Glue sniffing is especially popular. Once incarcerated, they often run away, and their present commitment frequently reflects the inability of other facilities to keep them secure.

The psychiatric history of the disturbed frequently includes time spent in a mental hospital, and they are often labelled "neurotic," "pre-psychotic," or "emotionally disturbed" by psychiatrists. They also very likely received tranquilizers at some time during their confinements. Descriptions in their case folders include: poor self-concept, neurotic guilt, anxiety symptoms, restricted ego capacities, little self-awareness, inability to control impulses, high degree of rejection, resistance to authority, a tendency to act out inadequacies, pathological relationships with family members, and a high degree of internal conflict.[5] These boys are usually assigned an "E" suffix by a psychiatrist because they are believed to exhibit sufficient emotional disturbance to interfere with their functioning in the community.[6] In addition, they are classified in the intake cottage either as an $I_4 NA$ or $I_4 NX$. (The $I_4 NA$ refers to a neurotic, "acting-out" youth, while $I_4 NX$ refers to a neurotic, anxious youth.) The "E" suffix and these I-level classifications are the primary ways that the disturbed may be identified, for often their actual behavior and characteristics are quite similar to those of their normal social peers.


## INSTITUTIONAL EXPLOITATION

Considerable emphasis is placed on rehabilitation in this custodial institution. Still, there are several reasons why the psychological states of the emotionally disturbed deteriorate even further as a result of institutionalization: (1) inability to deal with inflexible rules and procedures; (2) failure of staff to understand dependency needs; (3) inappropriate cottage assignments, and; (4) exposure to a value system much more anti-social than their own.

The institution's custodial goals stipulate that all residents are expected to follow institutional rules and procedures. Emotionally disturbed youths, however, find these rules particularly difficult to accept, apparently because of early problems in adjusting to "rule generators" and "rule enforcers." The emotional conflict and rejection experienced in previous environments are carried over into institutional life, giving them a world view not amenable to the demands of institutional living. This is clearly reflected in the fact that, until recently, disturbed boys were confined an average of a year longer than normals.[7]

In response to the interviewer's question, "What can be done to make this a better institution?" one emotionally disturbed boy responded:

> Have a little more freedom and slack up on some of the rules you got, even though it is a maximum security place. Still, I know kids ain't supposed to be in no place like Chillicothe and Mansfield [adult reformatories], but that's what it's like.

Another disturbed boy gave a similar response:

> Just a little thing sets you off inside and you don't care anymore. Why should you care when you got all this time in front of you and there ain't nothing happening? There isn't anything going for you. You are always pushed around like a baby. You are eighteen years old—seventeen or eighteen is the average in here—and you are almost grown up. The staff look at you and say, "Do this" and "Don't do that." You have to ask to use the restroom, when you can smoke. They got certain times now when you can smoke. All these things are childish.

> We look at ourselves and say that we are just as much as a man as the staff member is. If I was out on the street, I wouldn't be treated like this. It seems like they think that when we get locked up, all our privileges are taken away. We have no privileges whatsoever like a civilian would have. Like our mail is read. What is censorship of the mail? That's when you cut something out of the mail. . . . They tell us to open our eyes and see what privileges we have here and the good things of the institution. But that's not the way we think.

Even though staff fear organized resistance to their authority, only once in institutional history has a cottage protested as a unit. This took place when a cottage made up of emotionally disturbed boys decided to protest cottage rules. This mass protest began in a meeting called by youth leaders to resolve some cottage problems. Instead of resolving the conflict, the meeting motivated youths to bypass the cottage staff to implement change. The basic grievances involved the early bedtime, the limit on shower time, the inability to take a shower upon return from the athletic field, the inability to smoke when and where they wanted, the inability to go to the bathroom at night instead of using a "piss pan," and the lack of participation in decision-making.

After the cottage meeting, the most resentful boys got together and planned a mass protest directed at the superintendent. In lines of two the next morning, the boys started to school, but when they came to the corner leading to the school, all twenty-four turned right instead of left. In orderly fashion and followed by the two startled and speechless youth leaders, the twenty-four marched to the double doors, rang the buzzer, and marched through the then opened doors. Though faced with freedom straight ahead, the twenty-four turned right and marched to the superintendent's office. Since the superintendent was not present, they agreed to meet with the assistant director of guidance, who was in charge of custody. A lengthy, heated exchange followed, stormy since the director of guidance refused to budge on any of the boys' requests. The residents were finally told that they were not running the institution and they were returned to their cottage. Staff, in turn, were warned to keep residents under better control so that this type of incident would not recur in the future.

Exploitation by staff is one of the most surprising forms of institutional exploitation. Because of their high dependency needs, emotionally disturbed youths are an especially easy "mark" for staff interested in their pies, candy, cakes, and cigarettes. Boys often shine staff's shoes and boots or voluntarily give up their share of an especially good meal. Certainly, a most extreme form of exploitation is sexual, and every two or three years a staff member stands accused of sexually exploiting boys.[8]

Another form of staff victimization is the punishing of disturbed youths for "acting-out"—i.e., barricading themselves in rooms, urinating on the floor in their rooms at night, being defiant to staff, breaking and throwing cottage furniture, creating problems in school, drinking metal polish, and setting their rooms on fire—when all they are doing is trying to get attention. High dependency needs lead them to require warm, accepting, and meaningful relationships with concerned adults; yet, their "acting-out" results in severe negative sanctions which they interpret as a continuation of the rejection received throughout life (Konopka, 1962; Deutsch, 1950; Schulze, 1951). Feeling alienated from staff (whom they desperately need), disturbed boys then become more amenable to peer exploitation. Finally, hostile toward peers who are victimizing them and distrustful toward staff who are not fulfilling their needs, they feel very much alone. This condition of anomie may become unbearable if satisfactory relationships with either peers or staff are not forthcoming.

Disturbed boys are also exploited by the process of cottage assignment. From the founding of the facility until 1969, this form of exploitation was even more acute. The emotionally disturbed were placed frequently in cottages where protection from stronger peers was practically impossible. To attenuate their victimization, officials began, in the summer of 1969, to place the most seriously disturbed in one cottage with staff capable of dealing with their needs, a very successful maneuver.[9] Not only were two staff members in this cottage able to reach their boys psychologically, but they also were able to protect them from serious exploitation. In the winter of 1972, institutional officials decided to reserve three cottages for the disturbed, due to the larger numbers being admitted to the institution.

But, in spite of these efforts, cottage assignments continue to contribute to victimization. Indeed, normals remaining in cottages reserved for the disturbed have a "field day" with their more passive peers. Inmates are quite aware that the "sick" are placed in the three reserved cottages and single them out for attention. Too, disturbed youths regularly carry out the "self-fulfilling prophecy" which demands that "sick" boys play the "sick" role, and similar to exploitation matrices found in other cottages, the disturbed develop an inmate pecking order in which the aggressive exploit the passive.

Emotionally disturbed boys who are relatively protected in cottages still must go to school, play on athletic fields, take showers, and go to coeducational dances with nondisturbed inmates. To be expected, these contacts provide the more aggressive boys with an opportunity to exploit them. In terms of cottage placement, then, maximum exploitation occurs if these youths are assigned to cottages of normals. In a cottage with both disturbed *and* normals, a lesser amount of exploitation will take place; but the most favorable milieu is the cottage where only one type of boy resides.

Finally, the value system these boys are exposed to is much more antisocial than their own.[10] Until a boy's first confinement, extremely minor crimes are catalogued in his court record, but when a boy graduates from a juvenile institution, he usually shifts to more serious property crimes—e.g., auto theft. The boy is very quick to say that he knew little about crime before going to the institution; now, after being exposed to this setting, he feels ready for the "big time." Interactions with antisocial peers and hostility held toward the system for "messing over them" appear to be prime motivating factors for the participation in more serious crime.

## EXPLOITATION BY PEERS

Although all emotionally disturbed respond to the institution in basically the same way, wide differences exist as to how they are exploited. In fact, to understand the types and degree of peer exploitation, four different groups of emotionally disturbed must be identified.

The first and largest group is made up of white, middle-class boys. These boys have unique characteristics which contribute to their extensive exploitation. Of major importance is the fact that they are not "street-wise" and find standing up to physically aggressive lower-class youths very difficult. One experienced youth leader made this statement in describing them: "I don't remember any middle-class boy who was an exploiter of lower-class boys." Their attitude of superiority also galls peers and immediately leads them into conflict with the black-dominated, lower-class subculture. One middle-class white described his peers by saying, "They are all animals in here." He went on to say that he was indignant about being forced to live with ghetto youths. As previously mentioned, these middle-class whites receive far more material goods than do other inmates, including money for the canteen and packages of food from home, thereby creating jealousy. Since many of these youths have been sexual victims in other institutions, they are prime targets of "booty bandits." Tending to lack impressive criminal backgrounds, other peers do not feel that they belong here (i.e., "He is only here for chicken-shit."). Certainly significant, too, is the fact that their behavior and demeanor separate them from other, nondisturbed peers.

Specifically, they are the most withdrawn of all inmates. Attempting to "withdraw into the woodwork," they are always asking to go to their rooms. One leader noted, "They are there but not there." Their passive tendencies, in addition, result in their being very anxious. This apprehension can be perceived by the expression on their faces, their tone of voice, the look in their eyes, and the way they hold their hands.[11] As one experienced staff commented, "They look like they are burdened down with problems," and another added, "Many middle-class kids suffer nervous strain and lose weight." Further, these boys are simultaneously the most dependent on staff and yet are very resistant to authority. If they do not get their way, they often run around the cottage throwing and sometimes breaking furniture. If reprimanded by being taken back to their rooms, they may barricade themselves in the rooms and perhaps even set fire to them.[12]

These boys are also victimized by peers "beating on them"—i.e., using them as punching bags.[13] Of the eight inmates who are often "beat upon," almost all are white, middle-class, and emotionally disturbed. In an interview, one responded to the question, "How do they push you around?" by saying, "They hit on me. They call me names. I've been used to that. Things like punk, MF, SOB, and so on." When his peers were asked whether they beat on

him, they admitted that they did, and then, when asked why, they
said because "he bothered them." One boy said, "He simply gets
on my nerves."

Another emotionally disturbed boy described how it feels to be
in this situation:

> The guys pick on us. They take our stuff, push us around, call us
> names, embarrass us, talk to staff about us, and give everybody the
> wrong impression. We say to ourselves, now everybody got me laid out,
> they're wrong, but what chance do I have? They aren't going to listen
> to me; they think I'm a punk or something. And they approach us time
> after time for homosexuality.

Several other disturbed whites acknowledged being beat upon
by both disturbed and nondisturbed peers. Their situations were
similar to the one already noted, in that the abuse was not
committed for some ulterior purpose (i.e., to get food, cigarettes,
or sex), but as a means of externalizing aggression toward those
who could not defend themselves. Feeling "messed over" by the
institution and society, aggressors strike out at the weak.

Most importantly, the emotionally disturbed run a high risk of
being sexually exploited. Of the sixteen who were identified by
staff as chronic sexual victims, eight, or fifty percent, were disturbed; of the eight, five were white and middle-class. Further,
two or three times every year, a middle-class disturbed white will
be surrounded by a roomful of boys who wish to be masturbated
or have oral sodomy committed on them. If no staff member is
around to intervene, a gang rape may result.[14] Too, these youths
are much more likely to masturbate other peers and to commit
oral sodomy than nondisturbed or other disturbed peers.

A supervisor related how one of the middle-class white youths
was sexually assaulted while the group was taking showers. Instead
of supervising the boys, the youth leaders were elsewhere. Three
other inmates forced the boy into the corner of the shower,
rammed soap into him and then sexually abused him.

The second group is made up of disturbed middle-class blacks.
They have many characteristics in common with their white
counterparts but are pressured for little more than material goods.
Similar to whites, they are not good with their hands, but unlike

whites, will not permit anyone to run over them. A seasoned youth leader noted, "You back one of these youths up against a wall, and he will come out fighting." He went on to say that regardless of his background the black youth has something in him that makes him want to defend himself. Black middle-class youths likewise feel superior to other boys; in fact, their parents, who are upwardly mobile and recent middle-class arrivals, seem to implant very strong feelings of superiority in their sons. These feelings and the resulting behavior lead middle-class disturbed blacks into conflict with the dominant lower-class black subculture. Like their white counterparts, these youths receive extensive material goods from home, becoming a "have" in a world of "have-nots." Only a few have had homosexual experiences in other institutions, and they are more likely than other black youths to develop homosexuality as a style of life. As in the case of middle-class disturbed whites, minor crimes—such as incorrigibility and drug use—dot their early court records.

Although their behavior and demeanor separate them from nondisturbed peers, they are still closer to the normal or expected behavior than white middle-class disturbed boys, as they are not as withdrawn and anxious as middle-class whites. They do tend to be more anxious, more withdrawn, and moodier than normals, sometimes experiencing prolonged periods of depression. Family conflicts and problems particularly tend to result in this moodiness and depression. As a result, they frequently take tranquilizers and medication simply to maintain emotional equilibrium. Dependent on staff, these boys become "crybabies," as one staff member called them, for they are always running to staff saying, "Mr. _____ , somebody took my red badge," or "Somebody took my shoes." But, unlike whites, they do not tend to throw tantrums when they fail to get their way; pouting is more typical.

Consequently, having more in common with middle-class whites than either white or black lower-class disturbed youths, these boys feel alienated from their lower-class disturbed and nondisturbed "soul brothers." Because of this alienation, they begin to "buddy" with their white counterparts, and reap considerable verbal harassment from their black peers. Even though willing to give up some of their material abundance in order to win friendship, these boys resist more extreme exploitation. Of importance also are the admonitions of the black normative code against sexually exploiting blacks and the watchful staff, who usually protect these youths.

These boys generally are willing to give up their cigarettes and food received from home or purchased at the canteen, but they absolutely refuse to give away their AM-FM radios, rings, or watches. They, in addition, will not give another peer their clean institutional clothing. While they may lend a peer something to wear to a dance or a special function, they make certain that the item is returned.

In one way, simply lending items might not be considered exploitation because these boys have a choice of whether or not they grant the request. But, in a larger sense, they are in an environment where they feel friendship must be bought from other peers. Receiving more acceptance from whites, they tend to spend more time with them, thereby increasing their rejection by blacks. This, in turn, requires that the good will of black peers somehow be won back, which makes it very hard to turn away blacks who request something.

The lower-class black and white disturbed boys who make up the third group have few characteristics in common with their middle-class peers. Being street-wise and quite concerned about improving their position in the inmate pecking order, they are much more difficult to exploit. In fact, these youths tend to feel that they can "take anybody on." A youth leader paraphrased their attitude by noting that they say, "I can handle the other guy, if I am five feet and one hundred pounds and the other guy is six feet and two hundred pounds." Moreover, attempted exploitation of these youths is dangerous because the exploiter may end up getting hurt. A white lower-class boy expressed it this way:

> These blacks keep thinking they are big shits. I don't want to blow my cool. But if someone gets down wrong with me, I don't care who it is and I don't care how big they are. I'm going to fight them back. If they beat, don't turn on me. Cause I'm gonna get ya. Cause if you were on the outs and you hit me, you better look out, cause when you come out of the house, I'm gonna get you. I'm gonna blow you away.

Instead of feeling superior, these inmates want to be part of the dominant subculture. As a result, black inmates, especially, pick models of aggressive and popular boys to mimic. Some, for example, imitate the "institutional shuffle" or the "pimp walk." [15] Another behavior modeled after normals is sitting around the cottage slumped over in chairs. Very much involved in the politics of scarcity, these youths have few material goods. In fact, some of the lower-class whites resort to rolling their own cigarettes with "bug dust" (tobacco) furnished by the institution.[16] In contrast to the other two groups, it is difficult to distinguish the lower-class boys' behavior from that of normals because when they mimic others, they mask the emotionally disturbed symptoms. These boys are much more comfortable in the institution and depend on staff less than the other three types of emotionally disturbed. They have considerable rage toward staff but are usually able to control it. While few have had any homosexual experiences in other institutions, those who do usually have an extensive history of being sexually victimized. Also, they have more serious crimes in their background than middle-class disturbed youths, including crimes of passion. (For example, several of these boys in recent years had committed matricide.) Consequently, especially in cottages for the emotionally disturbed, these lower-class whites and blacks may become exploiters; nevertheless, even here, each youth is ranked in the pecking order and, unless very strong, is often exploited by those above him. Black lower-class emotionally disturbed emerged as the more aggressive youths in the cottage. Being labelled as "sick" apparently creates a type of "reaction formation"; hence, they try to prove their masculinity and pass for normal by exploiting others. In other words, the sick label is compensated for by increased aggression toward others (Cohen, 1955).

As previously suggested, these lower-class disturbed youths are reluctant to give up what they have and will fight to retain their possessions more than middle-class disturbed. But, in terms of sexual activity, these boys are the most interesting of all. In the first place, they appear to be the only group who willingly seek out sexual liaisons with each other. A lower-class white described the beginning of this "hands on" process in the following interview excerpt:

For instance, _____, he plays with me, feels my ass, and I keep telling him to knock it off because he's a little bit sick in a way. He plays a lot. He don't really know what's happening.

At this point, the interviewer raised the question: "Do you think he would like you to have oral sex with him?" The youth responded, "No, I don't think he would do that. He never, as far as I know, done that." The interviewer continued: "Has he asked you to screw him?" The boy's answer was:

Yes, playing around, but he wasn't serious. Sometimes, I'll be in a good mood, and I'll play with him like that. But I'll never touch him unless he touches me, and sometimes, it's with my fist—most of the time. I might be in a good mood and I'll say, "Hey, man, be cool," and I'll rub my hand against his leg, but I'll never—I don't think I would do it to him. I used to do that, but I don't like to because it's rotten. I don't like it.

This next step shows the steady progression toward the "trade off"—and demonstrates as well some of the ambivalence of the boys in deciding to go the final step. Also revealed is the attempt to "con" the researcher into believing that the youth is not interested in sex. The last step, of course, is the decision to "trade off." It would appear that six boys are involved on an intraracial basis in "trading off": "Today, it's my turn, but tomorrow it's yours." Although this comes closest to what is known as true homosexual behavior, most of the activity is undoubtedly a function of institutional living.

Of importance also is the affinity of lower-class whites to sell sexual favors for material goods. In the words of one inmate, "Hey, man, I'll turn you on for a couple of packs of cigarettes." Another youth informed on a lower-class disturbed white in his cottage: "Guys would come up and say, 'I'll give you some dope for some butt.' What they would do would be to give him some filed down aspirin, and he would swallow them whole, thinking he had a high. He never knew what was going on." A third inmate responded, "I was approached by _____ to buy some ass for two packs of ciggs.[17] So I gave him the two packs and punked _____ in the mop room at 8:45 in the morning." A fourth youth was overheard to say, "If you give me a pack of cigarettes, I'll masturbate you."

Finally, there are a few lower-class disturbed whites who are sexually "ripped off." In general, these boys are not as aggressive as the average lower-class youth. They are gang raped, or they are placed in a cottage of aggressive normals. However, these whites usually do not become scapegoats because they are able to terminate exploitation early in their stay.

The final group receives almost no exploitation and is composed of white and black disturbed youths who exhibit bizarre behavior. Profiles of these boys include the following characteristics. They usually are not "street-wise" and have little ability to defend themselves. Peers generally laugh at them, feeling that they are much different from everybody else. A boy mentioned that one of these bizarrely acting residents "gets all emotional. Everybody laughs at him."

These inmates also rarely have any material goods. Even if they come from a middle-class background, they no longer have contact with their parents; therefore, little can be exploited from them. Significantly, their behavior and demeanor sharply distinguish them from other disturbed peers. As one alert youth observed, "They seem to be living in another world." In a real sense, these youths frequently appear divorced from reality, and are often diagnosed as pre-schizophrenic. Highly anxious, they have nervous tics and exhibit "different" mannerisms. One youth leader claims that an astute observer can recognize these youths by the pain in their faces.

Usually dependent on staff, the disturbed still do not talk with staff very much because they feel uncomfortable around them. The total unpredictability of their behavior makes it difficult to know what to expect from them. These boys experience an inability to express themselves verbally, and their interpersonal relations with others are therefore greatly affected. Not surprisingly, many have been passive homosexual victims in other institutions. Although their criminal background usually involves minor offenses, their backgrounds seem to be more representative of the various types of criminal activity committed by the total inmate population than by the other three types of disturbed individuals. The gestalt of these characteristics presents an unpredictable, emotional, and maladaptive youth. Peers are afraid to push these boys, since they do not want to be responsible for driving them to suicide or some other irrational act. Staff, too, are very cautious about how other boys treat these inmates. As one said, "I don't want a suicide on my hands."

An example of the behavior of these boys is the youth who had been in the cottage for six or seven months and who suddenly acted as if it were his first day in the cottage. He forgot the names of all the staff, and was able to recall only a little of what had happened to him before. Then one evening, he suddenly proceeded to masturbate before all the inmates and staff. Another bizarre behavior is for a boy to begin screaming and to continue for some time. In the midst of his hysteria, he may run around the cottage, throw himself on the floor, and begin to foam at the mouth. Some place metal objects in their arms. In fact, every time one boy became upset he would fill his arms with various types of metal objects. Another continued to sniff glue, even after being warned that it was causing brain damage.

Boys who refuse to eat are also regarded as bizarre. (One boy refused to eat for more than two weeks.) Some suddenly refuse to bathe, consenting only when physically coerced by staff. In one case, a boy who was working in the kitchen at the diagnostic center grabbed a knife without provocation and proceeded to go looking for the deputy superintendent of the Ohio Youth Commission. Never having met this person, he greeted everyone by saying, "Are you _____ ?" and waving the knife in the person's face. A more typical behavior is to make inappropriate responses to interpersonal cues or to try to harm oneself.

## SELF-VICTIMIZATION

Emotionally disturbed youths, victimized by peers, staff, and organizational procedures and processes, are faced with difficult problems—the two most important being survival and release. The anger and frustration resulting from these problems is sometimes internalized, and the boys harm themselves physically. The most popular methods are to set one's room on fire, slash or cut one's wrist, hang oneself, or drink lye or metal polish. Those who harm themselves are divided into two groups—those with some ulterior purpose and those who harbor feelings of hopelessness. In general, lower-class whites make up the former group, while middle-class whites make up the latter.

In an interview, a white lower-class boy explained why he had drunk metal polish:

> The first day I got up in the cottage I got in a fight. I was pushed by homosexuality and I got in a fight. The "Man" blamed me for it, and made me do some work and all that. So as it went on, I was down in the school area, and I was approached about four or five times. I had to fight myself out of it. It really messed me up mentally, you know. I was really bothered by it. . . . So then they started bothering me more. And everything kept on building up, so I drank some metal polish. I thought that maybe if I drank some metal polish, they would take me to the hospital and I could run. Because this place was pretty well laid out; I couldn't run from it.

The metal polish was taken in order to gain admission to a hospital where escape would be fairly easy. Boys often set their rooms on fire, hoping either to escape in the commotion or to gain more attention from staff.

On the other hand, some hurt themselves because they have given up. There have been two suicides in the history of the institution. One of these was a despondent lower-class white youth who was returned to the institution after running away. He announced to everyone within earshot that he was going to kill himself. He indicated that he was "fed up" with the institution "messing over him." The next day he set his room on fire and subsequently died from the burns. The other suicide was likewise prefaced by threats, and then one day, staff found this youth hanging in his room.[18]   Several suicide attempts were thwarted only by the staff's quick reactions.

But much more frequent than suicide or attempted suicide is victimization which is brought on by interpersonal cues. As noted in the analysis of the exploitation typology in Chapter 8, there is evidence that some victims have an unconscious desire to be hurt and thereby produce the wrong cues—cues which, in fact, encourage their victimization. Apparently, these boys accept more harrassment and torment as a way of fulfilling certain of their needs.

These youths, too, seem to have special problems with masochistic behavior. They tend to see themselves as "losers," and positive reinforcement by staff generates considerable discomfort. The dissonance between the positive strokes and their own feelings of self-rejection leads them to act negatively. Two examples should clarify this self-defeating syndrome.

The first involved a youth who was informed that everyone was pleased with his progress. Furthermore, he was assured that a short stay was in order if his present behavior continued. Several days later he escaped from the academic area, and in the process, got a long gash on his face. Nevertheless, he made it to his home in one of the large urban areas of the state and remained there for two or three days before voluntarily returning. In talking with staff, he admitted that their positive feelings toward him made him very anxious, and he ran away to reduce the anxiety. Used to being a "loser," he apparently felt uncomfortable in another role.

A second youth, who had superior intelligence, had his release postponed time after time because he always got into trouble just before release. After being confined for nearly three years, he was finally ready to graduate in early June and be released after the graduation ceremony. In late May, he and his classmates took part in a car wash to raise money for the senior class to take an off-campus trip. At the car wash, he took lighters from several cars, knowing that they would be missed and that he would be "busted." When caught, he gave no explanation for his behavior.

These emotionally disturbed youths whose community offenses often are limited to incorrigibility clearly do not belong in a maximum security juvenile institution. Confronted by aggressive peers, intolerant staff, and the rigidity of organizational rules, they feel the time confined is a living hell. It is not surprising that many vent their anger toward society upon returning to the community.

## NOTES

1. We are grateful to Mr. James Roberts of the Ohio Youth Commission for his assistance on this phase of the study. Mr. Roberts is a co-author on a paper to be submitted for publication, which is based upon the contents of this chapter.

2. It is open to speculation why more emotionally disturbed blacks are coming into the OYC. While this may only reflect the labelling systems of this youth commission (I-level and "E" suffix), some important societal dynamics may be involved.

3. Most of the boys referred to as middle-class are actually lower-middle-class in origin. For ease in reporting, we are referring to them simply as middle-class.

4. Of the 149 inmates on whom data were collected, only 23 had an "E" suffix. When the $I_4$s were added to the "Es," 35 percent or 52 of the 149 were considered emotionally disturbed. Of these 52 inmates, 21 were white and middle-class; 19 were white and black lower-class; 6 were black and middle-class; and 6 were white and black residents notorious for their bizarre behavior. It should be noted that statistical analysis of the "Es" did not include boys classified as $I_4$s.

5. Nearly all of these youths have had at least one psychological workup and several psychiatric evaluations during their OYC institutionalization.

6. The diagnostic center has recently been phased out.

7. All boys, of course, find the rules difficult to accept, but the emotionally disturbed keep fighting the rules, whereas the normals adjust to them.

8. Staff exploitation of inmates is discussed in more detail in Chapter 12.

9. The institution has recently reversed this process and is placing disturbed youths in with others because of the stigma involved in being in a "labelled" cottage.

10. The disturbed appear to react more to the value system, have fewer extremely violent crimes in their record than middle-class normals, and use their institutional experiences as an "excuse" for going on in crime more than normals do. These observations, of course, need to be empirically validated.

11. Jim Roberts stated: "It is really hard to put in words how these middle-class whites act, but when you work with them a while, you can see consistencies in the looks on their faces, tones of their voices, looks in their eyes, and how they handle themselves (in interaction with others)."

12. This internal lack of control over impulses usually creates hostility and resentment among peers.

13. The boys may also be beat up by others who want to use them sexually. Use as a punching bag, however, appears unrelated to sexual exploiters.

14. If all youths who were occasionally sexually exploited could be identified, a number of staff feel that this correlation between emotional disturbance and sexual exploitation would be much higher.

15. This "institutional shuffle" or "pimp walk" is a swaying walk in which a boy has one hand swinging and the other in his pocket or both hands in the front of his pants. Youth leaders interpret arrogance in the demeanor and strut.

16. No blacks will use this institutional tobacco, and even heavy smokers who are out of cigarettes will do without before using "bug dust."

17. In this type of incident, the cottage's peddler makes arrangements for the "economic" part of the transaction.

18. This youth, too, was white.

*CHAPTER 10*

## MODES OF ADAPTATION

**Since Chapter 1,** where the observations of many of the nation's top experts on institutional life were discussed, this book has been devoted to describing and analyzing life in one juvenile training school. Primary emphasis has been on the process of inmate interaction, the exploitation matrix, the assignment of multiple labels, the adoption of social roles, and the adjustment difficulties of the emotionally disturbed. Even though most residents attempt to conceal their emotions, the quality of institutional life makes strong feelings surge toward the surface. These feelings can be grouped into the following clusters: righteous indignation; rage; fear and anxiety; shame and humiliation; and hopelessness and despair. Because some youths are not being exploited by peers and are progressing rapidly toward release, they can repress their feelings and avoid emotional reactions which may prolong incarceration; this reaction constitutes a sixth emotional response. This chapter considers these feelings, broader modes of adaptation, and runaways.

Every resident has a variety of emotions; nevertheless, one of the above clusters becomes characteristic of his institutional response. To illustrate, a boy may have feelings from several clusters, but the most predominant may be rage. The feelings, of course, range from very mild to very severe. Boys experiencing these feelings may differ considerably from their peers in the same category. In order to capture some of the depth of feelings experienced by these youths, mini-interviews have been constructed between an inmate and his social worker. In the sense that these statements are taken from interviews during the victimization study, autobiographical statements written by residents, and reaction of inmates during actual casework intervention, these are not actual exchanges between a youth and his social worker. Few boys choose to be this honest. These trenchant vignettes, then, are condensed from a much larger body of material.

### Righteous Indignation

*Social Worker:* Melvin, why are you so resistant to everything here?
*Inmate:* I've no reason to be here. I was set up by the cops.
*Social Worker:* O.K., maybe you did get a bad deal in the community, but why don't you try to make the best of your time here? Otherwise, it's just wasted time.
*Inmate:* 'Cause I don't like being confined. I don't like the environment I'm in here. I'm not saying I'm hard, but some of there guys in here are weak. The guys in here are far below my level.
*Social Worker:* I think there are some things you can work on here. Take, for instance, your—
*Inmate* (interrupts): Man, I've been messed over ever since I came here. Staff expect more from us than they can do themselves. They promise me this and promise me that. Staff are just "Uncle Toms," all they care about is "whitey."
*Social Worker:* If you program, you can get out in five or six months. Why don't you take a course in welding?
*Inmate:* I just want to be out. I don't want to wait another five or six months. I don't feel this institution is doing anything for me. They are just keeping me here for really nothing. They're trying to ruin my life. [voice becoming louder]
*Social Worker:* You're getting upset again.
*Inmate:* Damn right, I'm upset. I just want to get out of this place.

This youth has few problems with peers, but clearly feels exploited. In fact, he is likely to be an exploiter. His umbrage arises from society robbing him of his freedom, placing him in a setting in which he has difficulty attaining release, and making him comply with institutional requirements. One way he can handle this indignation is to externalize aggression toward peers.

### Rage

*Social Worker:* If you continue to act out here, you're going to get sent to Mansfield.

*Inmate:* Send me there. I don't care. You fuckers have messed over me long enough.

*Social Worker:* Fred, why are you having so many problems here?

*Inmate:* 'Cause when you go to bed at night, all you can see is those green walls and those bars. And then you get a visit, your mother, and man, you just want out of here. You feel you would rather be dead than to stay here the rest of your life. I know what it's like out there because I haven't been locked up all my life.

*Social Worker:* But why did you attack Mr. Jenkins? That wasn't very smart.

*Inmate:* Ever since I came here, that bastard has been on my back. He thinks he's tough shit. These youth leaders come off the streets with hard feelings and take it out on us. Jenkins is always getting on my case, and I ain't going to take it anymore. I'd like to meet him on the streets.

*Social Worker:* What about your constant fights?

*Inmate:* Some of these dudes keep getting in my face. Some of these fuckers are all the time playing hard.

*Social Worker:* It seems to me like you're pushing your peers around. You're the one who plays hard.

*Inmate:* Are we finished now?

*Social Worker:* Fred, why are you so angry?

*Inmate:* I become angry when things don't go my way. I become angry when people mess over me. I become so angry at times that I would like to kill somebody. Sometimes, I can't control myself.

This composite portrays one of the more aggressive inmates. He challenges new or weak youth leaders, as well as peers who resist his dominance. Feeling strongly that he does not belong here, he can quickly and unpredictably become violent toward those who attempt to impose power or control over him. Little irritations can create an enormous reaction from him. He is an extremely frustrated youth who is full of pent-up anger. After a physical confrontation with a youth leader, staff members often seek to have him transferred to an adult facility.

## Fear and Anxiety

*Social Worker:* Don, you wanted to talk with me.

*Inmate:* Yeah, this place is a real jungle. I don't think I can make it here. I'm terrified all the time. Everybody gets pushed around, jumped on all the time. I'm scared of everything.

*Social Worker:* You've got to stand up for yourself. If you don't, you'll be in real trouble.

*Inmate:* Man, I can't stand up to these dudes. They're animals. You can't trust anyone in here. They're all animals.

*Social Worker:* Have you asked staff for their help?

*Inmate:* This is just a jail. You know, nobody cares about you here, they just lock you up for time. Everybody here is just getting a paycheck.

*Social Worker:* How do you plan to handle your anxiety?

*Inmate:* I don't know. I hope that I get released soon.

Deeply fearful, this boy does not know what to do. He is hopeful that the social worker, youth leader, or someone else will rescue him from the overwhelming atmosphere. If the pressure continues, he is likely to begin emitting nonverbal indicators of his anxiety, such as a nervous tic, stuttering, poor appetite, or inappropriate impression management.

## Shame and Humiliation

*Social Worker:* Why did you let Terry beat on you all night?

*Inmate:* Man, it wasn't like that.

*Social Worker:* Are you telling me that he didn't work you over all night? My God, look at your eye.

*Inmate:* I couldn't help it. I couldn't stand up to him. He kept beating on me. There wasn't anything I could do.

*Social Worker:* I also know that Tim has been sexually exploiting you.

*Inmate:* That is a bunch of horse shit.

*Social Worker:* Tim told me.

*Inmate* (after long silence): You think I like that? You think I like getting beat on all night? You think I like getting fucked in the ass? It's not funny. I never did those things when I was on the outs.

*Social Worker:* If it bothers you so much, why don't you stop it?

*Inmate:* Damn right, it bothers me, but those black dudes keep pushing me around. I just can't stand up to them. They think they're one bad MF. They think they can kick the whole world's ass. When I think about what I've done here, it brings back some bad thoughts.

> But they won't let me quit. I'm not proud of myself, but they won't let me quit.

This youth, like other residents, has become involved in behavior which is quite atypical for him. He might have been a lady's man "on the outs," but in this setting, he is exploited by stronger boys. Shame and humiliation overwhelm him.

### Despair and Hopelessness

*Social Worker:* When we pulled you out of your room last night, I thought you were a goner.

*Inmate:* I don't care. I wish I would have died.

*Social Worker:* You've a lot to live for. You have your whole life in front of you.

*Inmate:* I just can't make it in here anymore. I just can't make it. Life is no good. I'm miserable. I would like to be nothing.

*Social Worker:* Don't you have people who care for you? How about your aunt? She's always writing. How about Pam [girlfriend]?

*Inmate:* I'm weak. I'm kind-hearted. Take, for instance, my cigarettes. People keep coming up and asking for one and I would say, "Yeah, take one." But they would take the whole pack. And then I began to give up sex. I'm always tense and anxious. I've always been degraded. I would rather be dead than continue to suffer in this hellhole.

Faced with unmanageable problems, this resident tried to take his own life. Unless staff transfer him to another facility, he probably will again try to destroy himself. Staff know this and quickly attempt to get rid of him. The trauma of this milieu has been so great for this youth that he sees no point in going on.

## BROADER ADAPTATIONS

Other adaptations boys make are the roles they play. Whether the emotional states result *in* or result *from* a boy's taking over a particular role is not known. Nevertheless, boys who play these roles generally are adapting to institutional living in one of several fairly typical ways.

Residents vary according to the degree to which they give the appearance of inculcating staff values (Goffman, 1961). The "inmate who profits" is the most receptive to staff's values, while the "ass kisser" feigns receptivity simply to expedite his release. Because of the inmate code, staff exploitation and indifference, and the fact that many of these boys arrive from large institutions in which personal contact with staff was very unlikely, these youths simply are not prone to accepting staff norms.

A larger group of boys make the most of institutional life (Goffman, 1961). This is without question the most popular mode of adjustment. These boys are very sensitive to their creature comforts. They quickly discover ways to get more food, to get out of doing unpleasant tasks, and to be given more institutional privileges than deserved. Although few would choose life in the institution over life in the community, many are able to survive quite well in this milieu. Residents from poor backgrounds seem to be more prone to utilize this adaptation. They are used to deprivation and have learned how to make the best of it. As one staff member said, "This is the first time many of these kids have had three square meals a day." "Heavies" and those labelled "manipulators" by staff are the most effective in getting their needs met.

A third possible mode of adjustment is "playing it cool" (Goffman, 1961). In this adaptation, the inmate gives allegiance to neither staff nor fellow inmates. "Playing it cool" allows minimal commitment to both worlds, permitting its perpetrator to "do his time" without paying homage to either. In pursuing this mode, the resident keeps his emotions under control and "bends with the wind." Learning little from either world, this youth passes from the institution only embittered. The "slick" is the best example of the boy who "plays it cool."

Another form of adaptation is rebellion, which consists of inmates confronting the institution and staff at every possible turn (Goffman, 1961). Very much filled with rage, one youth said, "It was a matter of me against the institution, and I just tried to whip the institution." Boys often attempt to demonstrate to peers and staff that they are so strong that neither institution nor peers can achieve anything resembling victory over them. They therefore refuse to go along with the rules, obeying orders with obvious contempt and taking every opportunity to demonstrate their strengths to peers. It is significant that more residents do not pursue this mode.[1] The reason appears to be related to the degree of anger necessary before a juvenile will take on the system. Most boys realize that rebellion will only prolong their institutionalization.

Inmates could certainly riot, set fire to the institution, and take staff as hostages. Even though this institution has never been close to a massive uprising, three or four boys on several occasions did gang up on staff members. This activity still does not come close to the massive, large-scale riots in adult facilities.[2] Three types of youths do utilize this mode of adjustment. They are the aggressive "heavies," his lieutenants, and some emotionally disturbed residents. The aggressive "heavy" and his lieutenants are concerned about mitigating the power of staff. The incorrigible or disturbed youth is more concerned about authority figures "bossing him around."

The final type of adaptation is withdrawal. The anxiety, humiliation, and hopelessness of scapegoats, "sickies," and others further down the status hierarchy can drive them to this type of adjustment. This obviously is inadequate coping, and can be placed under the rubric of inmates' responding to unmanageable problems (Bartollas, 1975c). A wide variety of techniques are utilized, ranging from isolation from others to withdrawal through drugs, mental breakdown, runaway behavior, and suicide.

The mildest form of withdrawal is choosing not to associate with other peers. Placed in this restricted context of residential living, privacy is difficult to attain, unless a youth such as a scapegoat is regarded as an outcast and ignored accordingly. Representing a greater degree of withdrawal is the youth who constantly gets high on glue, paint thinner, or any other available substitute. He considers his environment so unpleasant and unmanageable that he escapes with drugs. One youth sniffed so much glue that he suffered brain damage and, shortly after his transfer to another facility, died. Even greater is the withdrawal of those who experience mental breakdowns. Several boys, in fact, incurred so much psychological damage that they had to be heavily medicated, placed in strait jackets, and transferred to psychiatric facilities. The most extreme form of withdrawal, of course, is suicide. As described in Chapter 9, there have been two suicides in the history of this institution. The rapid intervention of staff prevented many other inmates from destroying themselves.

But residents can choose another mode of withdrawal. They can escape. In a real sense, there is defiance or rebellion in this behavior, which requires considerable ingenuity, endurance, and desire. Since so many choose to run, the remainder of this chapter will be devoted to this form of adaptation.

From July 1, 1970, through July 31, 1972, 125 boys escaped and 39 attempted to escape. Eleven variables statistically differentiated runaways from a control group of non-runaways.[3] Runaways were two-thirds white, tended to have drug and alcohol abuse on their records, had a runaway pattern in other institutions, had fewer "R" and "E" suffixes than non-runaways, had more disciplinary meetings held against them, became involved in homosexually more often, had been confined longer, had fewer home visits, graduated from high school less often, had poorer grades in school, and less frequently received "satisfactory" releases from aftercare.

Besides these salient characteristics, runaways were motivated to escape when they encountered an unmanageable problem which was unshareable (Bartollas, 1973, 1975b, 1975c).[4] A number of problems weighed heavily on these absconders and became very difficult for them to manage. When they concluded that these problems were unshareable with staff, pressure rapidly built up inside them, and it was not long before they chose escape as an alternative. Once this happened, they seemed to be emotionally compelled to flee. It would appear that this process explains the sense of desperation found in boys on the run, boys who are emotionally charged to the point that they are able to scale almost any wall or traverse any field in their escape attempt.

An upset youngster discussed in an interview an unmanageable problem which led to his running away:

> Then after two and a half or three months of having my pre-release, I went before the psychiatrist to get my "E" cleared. The psychiatrist . . . felt that I should not have my "E" cleared, that I would not be able to

make it on the streets, that my ideals were too much involved with fantasy, and that I would be more or less a potential drug user if I ever got back on the streets, so, she did not clear it.

He paused a few moments, took a deep drag on his cigarette, and then continued:

People on the outs and my parents were all dependent on me to be out by Christmas, and this seemed to fall through now that I could not get my "E" cleared. So when all this confusion hit me the only thing I could see myself clear to do was to run and that's what I did.

Distrustful of staff and distant from the boys, this youth ran a few days after the psychiatrist refused to clear his "E" suffix or give him any clue as to when the "E" would be cleared.

Another boy developed an unmanageable problem when he lost his pre-release badge and was informed by staff that he would have to start all over again. He had been in the institution sixteen months when he became involved in a serious incident which set him back:

After I lost my badge—you know I had lost it a month ago—I was supposed to go to the other staff and see how they felt about my receiving it back. So I went to one staff, and he told me that I had to start all over again. So, I got to thinking, and you know if I had to start all over again, I'll probably be better off trying to split. I might make it, that is, when I really started thinking about having to start all over again. So, then I just decided one day that I got to leave here. I got to make it, and I did not care how I went. Either it was breaking out of here, or going the right way, and I was turning 18 on Friday. So, I decided that I had been locked up two birthdays, I got to make it, and I just decided to leave.

Because, you know like I say, losing my badge and the fact that I had to start all over again seemed so terrifying that there was nothing else to do. There was a conglomeration of things building up inside. I just could not go out any other way. All I could see was just my freedom and I had to get it.

A third boy, subpoenaed to be interrogated for a crime which he and others were accused of committing, also felt unbearable pressure. In spite of the fact that his friends had agreed to "plea bargain" for a lesser crime, this youth refused to "cop" his plea.

He was then assured that he would be brought before the Grand Jury in a few months, be tried as an adult, and spend the rest of his life in jail. Here are his experiences:

> Well, I went back to Calvin County Jail in Cleveland in January, and while I was there, I was told I would be sent to Mansfield for first degree murder. I did not cop out, and the other young man copped out and he got one to twenty.... If I would have went on and fought the case, I would have got twenty to life. So right then I started thinking about AWOL. Maybe, if I would tell my P.O., just to send me back to the present institution because Grand Jury is six months' away, maybe I could scout up.

Following his return to the training school, he continued to think about his date with the Grand Jury. He was afraid, however, of sharing his feelings with either staff or peers because staff might employ more stringent security measures against him. When he heard that he would be returned to Cleveland the next day for his scheduled Grand Jury appearance, he quickly made his decision—"I made up my mind that I would leave before the day was over"—and he ran that night.

Generally, then, serious and significant problems were perceived by boys as ones which needed to be reconciled; otherwise, they felt unbearable pressure.[5] Analysis of interviews indicated that sharing problems with staff deterred boys from running, but that, for a number of reasons, boys believed staff to be unapproachable. They believed that sharing problems with staff would not help; the inmate code cautioned them against sharing deep feelings with the "turn-key"; staff would not understand their problems; and the boys did not know the staff well enough.


## CONCLUSION

Inmates have strong feelings about life in this institution. Righteous indignation, rage, fear and anxiety, shame and humiliation, and hopelessness and despair are the strongest. Because of the intensity of their feelings some boys rebel and others withdraw from institutional life. It is significant that so many feel compelled to cope in ways which are self-destructive. Unmanageable problems, in particular, put pressure on residents to withdraw in maladaptive ways.

## NOTES

1. It is germane to mention here that the entire institutional population is taken out on the recreation field during nice weather. It would be a simple matter for the inmates to begin racing off in all directions toward the fence a hundred yards off. Lacking firearms, the few staff members would only be able to capture a few of the absconding inmates. But this has not happened.

2. In one instance, a staff member was stabbed several times and nearly lost his life.

3. See Appendix G for the degree of significance of each of these variables. For the runaway study, a roster of runaways and attempted runaways was compiled as one cohort. The youths admitted to the institution immediately following each run and attempted run constituted a control cohort. Analysis indicated that both the runaways and the controls were representative of the population at large.

4. Other popular explanations of runaway behavior include the following: Focusing upon personality characteristics as the basis for differentiating those who escape from those who decide to stay; inmates who are disappointed with either the institution or their progress toward release run in order to assuage their disappointment; escapees have a tendency to learn escape behavior as an acceptable or feasible response in other settings, and once having run in order to reduce the stress of a setting, adopt flight as a means of escape whenever faced with problems; escapes may not be understood without considering the structural features of the institutions involved; finally, escape is looked upon as simply a normal response to an abnormal situation.

5. In reply to questions as to why they had chosen not to escape, most of the controls admitted fantasizing about absconding. But these youths gave three basic reasons why they did not run. Some claimed that there was no reason to because they had had no serious problems during incarceration. Others felt that they were able to handle serious problems by discussing them with a staff member. They suggested that this process of externalizing the problem helped bring relief. Some controls contended that their problem was unshareable with staff, but they were able to find a "just cause" providing them with a rationale to avoid running. The most popular "cause" was the nearness of release. To handle the pressures of their problems, they often either withdrew into themselves or became aggressive toward peers.

# PART IV

## STAFF AND INSTITUTION VERSUS THE INMATES

## CHAPTER 11

**INMATE GAMES: THE STAFF AS TARGET**

**Our purpose in this** and the following chapter is to examine how boys exploit staff and how staff exploit residents. As the next chapter demonstrates, the self-serving needs of some staff members lead boys to regard them as "the enemy." The control which the staff exercise is resented, and boys do whatever they can to wrestle away this control.[1] Inmates know, additionally, that by exploiting staff they can gain the approbation and respect of peers.

But only the most aggressive can overtly exploit staff. The remainder engage in a more subtle type of guerilla warfare which demeans and debases the opponent. One way of defining these overt and covert interactions is to look upon them as game-playing behavior. Transactional analysis has made us aware in recent years of these games. Eric Berne interprets these games as "ongoing series of complementary ulterior transactions progressing to a well-defined, predictable outcome" (1964: 48). He goes on to say that every game is intrinsically dishonest and is adopted to escape boredom and to keep individuals from becoming close emotionally with others. These boys play games, in addition, to gain an advantage. In this institution, ulterior transactions are performed to manipulate staff as well as other inmates. These boys, therefore, play physical, psychological, therapeutic, theological, educational, and materialistic games. Since some significant differences are found between the psychological games of TA and the games played by inmates, only part of the TA formula for games is utilized (Berne, 1964). Specifically, the con (inmate) hooks the mark (staff) into the game and then moves to the payoff for the boy. The "switch," the "crossup," and the staff's "payoff" are not considered in this analysis (Berne, 1972: 23).[2]

## The Staff Victim

Veteran youth leaders feel that all staff are victimized at some time in their career, whether they know it or not. One staff member observed:

> They tell us here, "I used you man, ah, man, I used you. You ain't nothing but a chump—you're a pushover." They'll set up a little game with you, or play little games among themselves, at staff's expense. And, of course, it's up to you if you want to be involved or not. In a lot of cases, it doesn't really matter if you're involved or not. You don't even have to know you're being a part of the game. You may be completely unaware of this. . . . I'm certain that I was subjected to this kind of psychological hanky-panky. Many times in the beginning, as a beginning youth leader, before I began to understand what actually was happening, what actually was taking place, I watched a student talk one of the staff members into bringing him three cartons of cigarettes within a week's time. It's not against the rules, bringing cigarettes to the kids, but this one particular kid had something going. He had gained some kind of favor with the staff to be able to make that kind of demand and have it complied with.

Their early weeks on the job are an especially vulnerable time for staff, and many are overtly victimized. Contraband (money, food, clothing, and radios) may be stolen from them; they may be physically pushed around by aggressive boys, or perhaps even violently assaulted. But, much more frequently, the types of games are such that staff are not aware of being victimized.

For someone to recognize that he is the victim of a game is a delicate art. The background of lower-class black staff members, especially, appears to sensitize them to the dynamics of exploitative games. Ghetto living, along with working in an institution for several years, makes them more aware of when someone is coming on straight or conning them. Therefore, they are able to challenge boys on their games. On the other hand, middle-class black or white staff are much less sensitive to boys' "putting them on." The staff have not had the experience of struggling for survival on the streets. Not exposed to the everyday transactions of ghetto living, they tend to shun violence and see no reason to worry about losing items "not worth fighting over." Subsequently, exploitation may either not be recognized or its importance may be ignored. Paradoxically, while these middle-class staff may be more likely to leave the boys alone, they are also more likely to be confronted both mentally and physically.

## THESAURUS OF GAMES

Physical Games

Since out-and-out physical attacks on staff are generally doomed to failure, boys normally must invent other means of maneuvering into a dominant position.[3] These games are used to put pressure on leaders to attentuate their control over inmates.

### "You Ain't Shit"

*Con:* An aggressive youth approaches a new youth leader and acts very friendly toward him. This youth frequently talks with the leader and expresses how pleased he is that the leader is working in this cottage. The boy's aim is eventually to intimidate the leader physically so that the youths can control him.

*Hook or gimmick:* Desiring the boys' approval, the youth leader takes this opportunity to win the boys' acceptance.

*Processing of game:* Suddenly and seemingly irrationally, the youth picks a quarrel and dares the youth leader to battle it out in the toilet area. He taunts the youth leader by saying: "You ain't shit."

*Payoff:* If the staff member accepts the challenge, the youth accompanies him to the toilet area. However, the youth quickly backs off after several swings and before they are injured. No payoff accrues in this instance, and the game is over. Should the staff member refuse to fight, the game has been won by the inmate and the staff member loses his reputation. In extreme instances, the entire cottage population may be able to intimidate a staff member who is afraid to fight.

### "Excuse Me. You're in My Way."

*Con:* The extremely aggressive youth can intimidate staff by acting very negatively and sullenly. A physical confrontation actually does not have to be employed. One technique is to graze past a staff member, bumping, but never acknowledging the act nor expressing regret. The game's purpose is to enable the boy to achieve dominance. By combining an appropriate "presentation of self" with backhanded acts of confrontation, the game can be won.

*Hook or gimmick:* Some inmates are eighteen or nineteen years old, over six feet in height, and very strong. Observing the demeanor and activities of an aggressive youth, some staff get the idea that they cannot handle him. Staff then choose to ignore his bumping into them or other acts of defiance.

*Processing of game:* The aggressive boy then increases his belligerence. In one instance, a staff member was closing the door of a boy's room when the combative youth forced his way through the door. With complete disdain for the staff, the youth initiated a search for "squares" he concluded were stolen. This youth had been permitted to get away with small infractions by the staff member in the past, but this act of defiance was completely unexpected.[4]

*Payoff:* An unpunished infraction such as this usually indicates that staff are losing their control over the boy. If questioned, two possibilities are open to the inmate: He may rationalize the act away by pretending to be so furious with a peer that he lost all control, or the inmate can try to push the confrontation further by challenging the staff member to a fight. Regardless of the inmate's decision, the fact that the staff member is willing to fight thwarts the inmate's efforts to achieve the desired dominance.

### "What's Wrong with a Little Horseplay?"

*Con:* A more advisable and safer way for boys to challenge staff is by talking or maneuvering them into "horseplay." The object is to test the youth leader's strength to find out how strong he is physically.

*Hook or gimmick:* Feeling that he should not back down from a challenge, the youth leader usually will consent to arm or leg wrestling.

*Processing of game:* If the staff member is defeated, boys begin to play up the defeat, much to the chagrin of the youth leader.

*Payoff:* Once boys realize that a youth leader is weak, they begin to harass him even more. Around him, boys act more insubordinate, recalcitrant, argumentative, refuse his requests more often, and threaten him with the use of force.

### "I Will Get You"

*Con:* The large amount of say that social workers have over the length of an inmate's stay is well recognized by the boys. Ways of physically intimidating the social workers are explored, as are other types of threats.
*Hook or gimmick:* Social workers usually fear the physical strength of these boys. One of the most effective ways the youths have of generating anxiety is to threaten the social workers' lives.
*Processing the game:* Telling the social worker that he will "get his" after the boy is released or escapes, the youth then cultivates the social worker's friendship. In light of the youth's threats, this act of friendship confuses the social worker.
*Payoff:* Social workers often jump at this chance to get on the boy's good side. Youths receive privileges and occasionally have their release speeded up as a result.

The outcome of these physical games is that inmates are occasionally able to usurp staff control. Indeed, in extreme cases, weak staff actually may be controlled by practically all of the inmates in a cottage, resulting in the boys giving the orders. One controlled staff member came upon a group of boys having sex with a peer and was told to leave the room. Another youth leader was dragged by his heels around the cottage. Other intimidated staff were locked in rooms during escapes. Yet another staff member was detained by three boys while they took the food cart into a back corridor, rammed it into an exit door until the door broke, and then escaped. Weak staff, in fact, often have boys sneer at them and tell them to "go to hell." Physically intimidated weak staff have also brought cartons of cigarettes to aggressive inmates, and some evidence exists that staff have smuggled in drugs. Finally, boys sometimes prevail upon weak staff to hide them in their homes following an escape.

### Psychological Games

Psychological games entail fewer risks and rewards than do physical games. The purpose of the psychological games is more to upset youth and social leaders than to control them. Control is a secondary gain, but the youth's primary aim is to get the staff to overreact to problems, forget to do their jobs, and, perhaps, resign.

### "You're Not Quite Yourself Today"

*Con:* The boys study the emotional status of the staff until the staff's frame of mind can be recognized simply by looking at them. A youth leader or social worker who is under the weather from illness or a hangover is a prime-target. Boys quickly take advantage of this opening.

*Hook or gimmick:* Staff find frustration more difficult to deal with when they are ill or depressed.

*Processing of game:* Inmates make it a point to approach the ailing staff member with some request. A discussion with the staff member, for example, will be demanded by practically every boy in the cottage. Problems thought resolved are again brought to the attention of the youth leader or social worker. For example, an inmate who long ago agreed that a group home placement would be acceptable says that he now does.not want the placement—after the staff member had spent weeks arranging the details. Or a youth who is well liked and accepted by the youth leader begins to "act-out." Overwhelmed, the youth leader or social worker finds his or her day going from bad to worse.

*Payoff:* If the youths succeed in disappointing or discouraging the staff member, the game is successful, especially if the staff member shows his feelings for several days.

### "He's Stupid! How Did He Ever Get To Be a Youth Leader Here?"

*Con:* Cottage leaders are extremely sensitive about their intelligence. Boys recognize this and use the knowledge to "get to" staff. A particular leader will be singled out for attention and boys will say, "He's stupid! He's dumber than anybody in the cottage." The label is deliberately passed on to the target, just in case he did not hear the original comment.

*Hook and gimmick:* Mental acumen is a very touchy area to many staff since some did not finish school, get high grades, or go to college. Many, in fact, have developed feelings of inferiority about their educational background.

*Processing of games:* Youths make sure the youth leader knows they think he is "stupid." The leader is then called "stupid" or "dumb" in a cottage meeting where everyone is present. The boys will laugh, as do the other youth leaders if they feel the label is correct.

*Payoff:* The youth leader, of course, becomes very upset and the game is considered successful. In one case, the labelling played an important part in a staff member's resignation.

### "I've a 'Wooden Leg': Don't Expect Too Much from Me"

*Con:* Labels assigned by staff and institution are recognized as being very useful by the youths. If labelled physically or emotionally ill, boys recognize that staff are reluctant to push them too hard to perform various institutional tasks.[5]

*Hook or gimmick:* The suicide risk, for example, will say, "Hey man, I'm a psycho. You can't make me do that." Not wanting to drive the youth to suicide, staff are afraid to force them to do things they don't want to do.[6]

*Processing of game:* The youth cuts his arm slightly, faking an attempted suicide. Fearing he might succeed and disturbed that they might be blamed, leaders react, "Let's get him the hell out of the cottage."

*Payoff:* Receiving privileges and preferred treatment from social workers and youth leaders is the boy's goal. The staff do have to be convinced that the boys have a "wooden leg," though, and boys therefore must put on a convincing performance.

### "I Don't Belong Here. This Place Is a Jungle."

*Con:* Victimized whites try to make new white social workers feel sorry for them. They hope to convince the social worker that they are different from their peers and that their pro-social orientation makes survival with all these "psychopaths" impossible.

*Hook or gimmick:* After being victimized by one or more aggressive peers, they report what happened to the social worker, vividly embellishing and falsifying the account. The social worker, especially if the aggressors are black, may feel indignant about this victimization.

*Processing of game:* Once the youth has captured the social worker's attention and pity, he then begins to spend as much time as possible with the social worker. He talks about all the "pro-social dreams" which he hopes to attain upon release. He communicates to the social worker how much he has helped him.

*Payoff:* White youths are playing for "big stakes," for they hope to gain release. If the game has been played well, chances are good that the social worker will do everything possible to get the boys released—even if it means ignoring the advice of other staff or boys who come to the social worker and say, "You think you know so and so, but you don't know the first thing about him."

## Therapeutic Games

Therapeutic games are employed for the amusement of the boys. They are also played to convince staff that the boys are being genuinely helped by the treatment program.

## "You've Really Helped Me"

*Con:* A staff member is told how much help he and the institution have been to the boy. Often relating information about themselves learned in other institutions, boys attribute the "insight" to the efforts of the staff member. The goal of this effort to impress and compliment the staff member is to receive a good report at the next review.

*Hook or gimmick:* New staff members, particularly, have their egos inflated by the youth's comments.

*Processing of game:* At the next review, the boy develops the game a step further by telling all present how much help this youth leader or social worker has been. The complimented staff member is so flattered that he defends the youth from all negative comments, even those from other staff. Occasionally, when a youth has been turned down for a higher status or release, the supportive staff member has stalked out of the review meeting.

*Payoff:* If other staff are convinced as to the boy's improvement, the youth has won the game.

## "Look How I'm Fouling Up"

*Con:* This game is played by the boy who does everything wrong. He is involved in fights with inmates and perhaps even an altercation with staff. He tries to escape once or twice and receives an additional eighteen months of dead time—time which he must serve—before he can receive pre-release and work toward release. Running around the cottage screaming hysterically or even trying to injure himself is relatively common behavior for this kind of youth.

*Hook or gimmick:* Cottage staff are quite concerned about the boy's welfare, while at the same time afraid that his destructive behavior may make them look bad.

*Processing of game:* Often, this only becomes a game when the boy realizes how much staff want him to do better. Hence, he begins to spend considerable time talking with staff, assuring them that he needs their help. He also verbalizes the conflict he has between positive and destructive behavior. "No matter how hard I try," he says to his cottage leaders, "I seem to end up failing." In response, staff are anxious to reinforce any positive acts. Suddenly, the "messup" becomes an ideal inmate; this confused, rebellious, and disturbed boy develops surprising control.

*Payoff:* Giving themselves credit for the "hopeless inmate's" improvement, staff decide to give him an early release—in spite of his "dead time" and initial negative behavior—and the game is successful. These boys sometimes have the shortest stay of any in the cottage as staff often circumvent the regular institutional processes in their cases.

### "Give Me a Chance To Prove that I'll Come Back"

*Con:* Some boys decide to develop a positive program so that they will be given pre-release and become eligible for home visits. These boys have decided that escape from within the institution is impossible, but if they can get home for a visit, that is a different story.

*Hook or gimmick:* Upon being denied a home visit, these youths "cop their plea": "Give me a chance to prove that I'll come back." "Trust me."

*Processing of game:* Since cottages no longer are given mass punishment when an inmate fails to return, these boys have a much greater chance of getting a home visit than formerly. Their strategy is quite simple—continue to badger staff until they give in to get them "off their backs." Additionally, when a questionable youth returns, boys are quick to say, "See, he came back. I'll come back, too."

*Payoff:* The game is successful when the boy walks out of the institution with a bus ticket in his hand and a smile on his face.

### "What Did You Think of the Group Meeting?"

*Con:* Audio-visual tapes are used as one means of evaluating leaders who conduct group meetings. Inmates realize that if they help the group leader look good in the taped sessions, he will probably help them get privileges and an early release. Once the boys know what the group leader wants, they perform the way he wants them to when being taped.

*Hook or gimmick:* Delighted with his boys, the group leader is even more delighted by the compliments he receives from his superiors.

*Processing of game:* On a sub rosa level, the boys let the group leader know how dependent he is upon them for those good tapes. They further suggest what he must do if he wants to continue having good tapes.

*Payoff:* The group leader takes the hint and backs up his boys when they come up for review, are involved in disciplinary hearings, or are being discussed by other staff.

## Theological Game

Deep religious experiences are occasionally undergone by youths during their incarceration. For the most part, however, boys fake religious experiences or conversions to convince the chaplain and other treatment staff they have reformed.

### "Are You Saved?"

*Con:* Staff look quite favorably upon boys who become interested in religion. The chaplain has sufficient power to help boys he feels are religiously oriented. The youths know they can count on him to support them if they show the appropriate motivation and interests.

*Hook or gimmick:* The boys, therefore, attempt to convince the chaplain that he has been an important factor in their spiritual development.

*Processing of game:* Going to the chaplain's office often, the boy describes how others are taking advantage of him. Accusing staff and peers of exploitation, he engages the chaplain's sympathy. Once the chaplain begins to listen and give him help, the boy requests him to intercede in his behalf.

*Payoff:* The chaplain is convinced of the boy's sincerity and need and helps expedite his release.

## Educational Games

Boys go to school from 8:30 a.m. to 3:45 p.m., five days a week throughout the school year, surrounded by male and female teachers. Several factors influence the games boys play in the school area: the principal or vice principal are part of the decision-making team which ultimately decides whether the boy will be released from the institution; two teachers from the academic area are assigned to each cottage team and have votes in the review process; some of the female and male teachers are afraid of these inmates; and boys have considerable resentment about being forced to go to school.

### "Teach Me To Read"

*Con:* Boys discover who the two teachers on their cottage team are. They want these teachers to become involved and interested in them, so that they will say good things about them at their reviews.

*Hook or gimmick:* A youth will approach one of these teachers, a female, saying that he is aware he must learn more than he knows in order to make it in life. Looking directly in the eyes of the teacher, he says, "Teach me to read."

*Processing of game:* After convincing the teacher that he wants to learn, the youth begins to confide in her. Slowly becoming involved in his problems, she becomes more and more concerned about his welfare.

*Payoff:* The inmate hopes that she will go out of her way to speak up for him at his reviews.

### "What Are My Eyes Saying?"

*Con:* Some black inmates have considerable resentment toward certain white teachers. One way to express this resentment is to stare at the teachers and make them feel uncomfortable.

*Hook or gimmick:* The white teachers may feel that these black inmates desire them sexually.

*Processing of game:* Once a boy discovers that he is making a teacher uncomfortable, he focuses his attention even more on her breasts, hips, and legs. He is trying to make the teacher feel that all his waking moments are spent in the fantasy of sexually conquering her. If she becomes so uncomfortable that she speaks to him about staring at her, then the inmate feels that the teacher is in a more vulnerable position.

*Payoff:* The payoff is how uncomfortable the boy can make the teacher. Some teachers become so intimidated that the quality of their teaching is affected.

### "I Want To Stay and Graduate"

*Con:* In reflecting upon how much longer he has before release, the inmate realizes that he will probably be confined another ten or twelve months. When he discovers that he can graduate in seven or eight months, he therefore approaches staff and informs them that he wants to stay and graduate from high school.

*Hook or gimmick:* Inmates hope that staff will be impressed by their maturity and will be certain to release them on graduation day, a customary procedure for many youths.

*Processing of game:* As soon as he informs staff of his decision, the boy suddenly becomes much more interested in school and seems to acquire more pro-social values. Over the months, he spends more and more of his time talking with staff about his new values.

*Payoff:* If the game is successful, several months of time are gained, because staff will see to it that he is released upon graduation.

## Material Games

These games are employed to better the boys' lives and to help them realize a more pleasant stay in the institution. Most items the boys desire are in short supply, and little freedom is possible. Manipulating staff is one of the ways freedom and scarce items are achieved.

### "If Not that One, How About this One?"

*Con:* Youths realize that staff can be manipulated. If the game is played well, staff can be convinced to compromise and allow the boys to do things not normally permitted.

*Hook or gimmick:* Especially threatening to staff are violent emotional outbursts by strong and influential inmates.

*Processing of game:* A staff member is approached by a boy who has a request. The boy realizes that his request is extreme and will not be granted. Once the request is refused, the boy then asks staff for a second favor which is more acceptable. Staff usually jump at granting this second request because they are afraid that a refusal will trigger a violent temper and acting out behavior.

*Payoff:* The game is fruitful if the youth is able to enhance his standard of living and enjoy life a little bit more.

### "Hey, I Know Something"

*Con:* Staff are always trying to discover what is taking place "backstage." The only real way they have of discovering what is happening in the interior life of the institution is when boys tell them.

*Hook or gimmick:* Thus, a boy will come and inform staff that something is taking place. Staff know that the social control of the cottage demands they be kept informed.

*Processing of game:* Playing the role of the informer, a resident goes to staff and gives them a little information. For instance, he tells them that he thinks someone is going to escape, that a boy was sexually victimized, or that a fight took place in the school area. From time to time, he feeds them a little information.

*Payoff:* The payoff is to get cigarettes, institutional privileges, and food from staff members who want to sustain this source of information.

### "Excuse Me. I Have a Problem."

*Con:* Boys who want to enhance their own or others' well-being sometimes encourage staff to talk with them. If staff are busy, other peers are freed to do whatever they want.[7]

*Hook or gimmick:* A youth approaches a youth leader to talk about a problem such as school, his girlfriend, goals in life, or family. The youth leader agrees to talk, flattered because the youth has selected him, but then forgets about his supervisory duties.

*Processing of game:* With the youth leader engaged, sexual exploitation, an escape, or an assault may be initiated in the shower area, dormitory, or private room.

*Payoff:* Youths are able to exploit peers or participate in prohibited activities without fear of detection.


## CONCLUSION

Staff are in control of this institution. Boys employ every trick possible to reduce that staff control. One administrator suggested that fifty percent of the waking time of boys was spent in trying to manipulate others. Physical games are employed to engage the attention of staff and to achieve more freedom. Psychological games enable the boys to safely direct their belligerance toward staff. Therapeutic, educational, and theological games are used to convince staff to release them. Finally, material games allow the boys to survive at as high a level of material living as is possible in this setting.

## NOTES

1. Of special assistance on this chapter were Mr. Donald Jenifer and Ed Redd of the Ohio Youth Commission. Discussions with these men laid the groundwork for the games discussed in this chapter.

2. "C + G means that the con hooks into a gimmick, so that the respondent responds (R). The player then pulls the switch (S), and that is followed by a moment of confusion or cross-up (X), after which both players collect their payoffs (P)" (Berne, 1972: 23). This chapter does not utilize the concept of the "switch," "crossup," or "payoff" fully. (For an attempt to analyze these two facets of games in this setting, see Miller et al., 1975.)

3. Inmates are also reluctant to attack a staff member because this act can result in a transfer to the adult reformatory.

4. Because residents are not permitted to go into the room of another peer, this is considered an act of defiance.

5. This game is similar to "wooden leg" found in Berne (1964: 159-163).

6. The memory of the two suicides described previously is still fresh in the minds of those in the institution.

7. Since there are two staff members now working on each shift in the cottage, it is more difficult to play this game.

## CHAPTER 12

## THE STAFF CODE AND INMATE VICTIMIZATION

**In earlier chapters**, the nature of the relationships found among
inmates was described. The previous chapter described how inmates exploited staff; this chapter deals with staff exploitation of
inmates.

Working in a "punishment-centered bureaucracy" induces staff
to take advantage of the system whenever possible. Staff power
over inmates is the greatest in the institution, and they frequently
use it to their own advantage. Indeed, even management techniques which seem beneficial are sometimes harmful to boys.

Staff treatment of the boys depends, in part, upon the nature of
the staff's previous employment and the length of time worked in
similar facilities. They go through a series of stages or "plateaus"
during their careers. Perhaps predictably, their relations with students vary with the plateaus reached and the promotions received.
Of equal importance is the staff code which provides the guidelines for acceptable and unacceptable behavior. This code is
divided into two sections, one of which is concerned with staff
orientation to other staff, who will "make it" in the institution,
what kinds of behavior to accept from others while on the job,
and the acceptable attitudes toward various components of their
work. The second part of the code concerns the staff's approach
to the youths, and consists of a series of tenets which are ranked

from acceptable to unacceptable from the viewpoint of the staff.[1] As will be seen, little in either part of the code actually works to the betterment of the boys, even though new staff are quite excited and optimistic when they start work.

*The orientation:* The first days on the job are bewildering. Job orientation sessions alert the new staff member to the danger of working with these youths, but when he walks into the cottage, he finds his fellow youth leaders relaxed and the boys friendly. This unexpectedly relaxed atmosphere encourages him to get involved with inmates to give them the "wisdom" of his experiences. Enthusiastically "rapping" with the boys to help them straighten out their lives, he communicates involvement and concern. He brings food from home and buys hamburgers for all. His favorite boys are treated from the canteen, and much time is spent playing pool, cards, and ping pong with residents.

Pleased with his effectiveness, he is unaware that the boys are "setting him up" and that he will soon be faced with protecting himself in a physical confrontation. When it comes, it comes as a complete surprise and he usually overreacts, shocked because he believed that his popularity was too great for such an attack to occur. Afterward, he withdraws from intense relationships with the boys and becomes more receptive to the counsel of the experienced youth leaders. Becoming very sensitive to infringements upon his authority, he tends to overreact to the slightest threats, and quite stormy relationships with inmates result. During his initiation to institutional life, he views his job as quite enjoyable, although he is jolted into a more realistic perspective by his confrontation.

*First Plateau:* Generally, in three or four months, a plateau is reached where the enthusiastic initial involvement wanes. The job is looked upon as work and not very interesting work at that. Relationships established with the other Youth Leader IVs, such as drinking after work, reinforce job indifference. Joining the union, too, tends to further heighten job dissatisfaction.[2]

Growing more and more indifferent, the average new youth leader becomes amenable in toto to the youth leader code. This code, which is maintained and sanctioned by older, experienced youth leaders, provides him with a more comfortable existence.

He also at this time begins to aggravate institutional officials by chronic tardiness and absenteeism.

With the exception of a few Youth Leader IVs who manage to maintain a healthy involvement in their job, the majority react to the negativism of this first plateau and resign within three years. Youth Leader IVs who remain usually are older, have more job experience, and are more stable in their family lives. Some are retired and have had successful careers in the armed forces; others work a day shift at a nearby factory before coming to work.[3]

*Second Plateau:* Those who maintain involvement in their jobs are rewarded by promotion to Youth Leader Vs. The involvement and enthusiasm held in their early months returns following promotion. Instead of seeing themselves as therapeutic agents, however, they become enthusiastic about running a "tight ship" and try to tighten security to control "acting-out" behavior. As well as maintaining an incident-free cottage, they prod boys to keep neat rooms.

Taking the supervision of their subordinates seriously, these new Youth Leader Vs soon become involved in the socialization of new Youth Leader IVs. Like other Vs before them, they instruct new leaders about the code and impose negative sanctions for violations. If a new informal rule or reinterpretation of an old rule is needed, Youth Leader Vs get together informally to decide upon the innovation or change. This action by the leaders keeps the code's qualities dynamic.

*Third Plateau:* Youth Leader Vs promoted to Youth Leader VIs become wing supervisors. Once promoted, they adhere more firmly than ever to certain parts of the code, especially those having to do with security and control.[4] Representing the administration, they no longer hold to such tenets of the code as "Don't do more than you get paid for," "Take advantage of the system," and "The administration will screw you."

At the same time, Vs who are not promoted begin to challenge the code's custody and control tenets because of increased interest in treatment. They sometimes become effective and even remarkable treatment agents. Contrary to their advice to youth leaders under their tutelage, these Vs now become considerate of student needs and spend a considerable amount of time discussing problems with them. Their new involvement breaks down the inmate-staff conflict, results in their becoming effective role models, and leads them to help boys plan for the future. Treatment success on this third plateau is indicated by the number of boys who see them as "significant others," and who write and visit them following release.

The loyalty these leaders generate is pointed up by the following example: One of the boys most hostile to the institution answered the question, "Do you like Mr. _____ ?" by responding, "I'll tell you the truth, I love him. He's just like a father to me. He'd do anything for me, in reason." What was so surprising about this response is that this boy had just finished berating nearly every youth leader in the cottage. In this particular cottage, significantly enough, many boys call this youth leader "father." Boys receive great warmth and acceptance from him, and many look upon him as the closest thing to a father figure they have ever had.

### The Code and the Institution

As staff progress through orientation into the various stages of their careers, the staff code guides most of their activities. The norms are part of the oral tradition of the institution and provide staff with guidelines on how to approach their fellow workers, their jobs and institutional requirements. Violation of the code's maxims brings punishment from code enforcers found in the ranks of the older youth leaders. The newcomer who insists upon going his own way finds his stay made quite uncomfortable as a result of the admonitions and punishments of these veterans. In fact, prestige of youth leaders depends upon their allegiance to the code.

## THE CODE

### Only Blacks "Make it" Here

Reference group norms strongly affirm that the white youth leader "will not make it." A former Youth Leader IV and volunteer coordinator reported it this way:

They [the boys] will accept the dictates of black authorities in situations like this more readily than they will the white leader. First of all, it has been my experience with white youth leaders that . . . they're so damn uncertain of themselves. They just don't handle the psychological stresses that are put on them when working in one of the cottages with 24 kids staring them down. That's a very difficult thing to get used to.

This youth leader explained why he felt white leaders met with more resistance than blacks. First, black inmates resent white youth leaders more because they believe that whites should have more important jobs. Dealing personally with the dirty work of the cottages is a form of status degradation of whites. Again,

I think it's a kind of programmed thing—the mechanism of the mind that whites most of the inmates' lives have always held the upper hand in any business and any area that he would go into [sic]. He is used to seeing white people well-dressed, the white banker, the white judge, and the white cop, so that to see him working here as a youth leader is beneath the pedestal in his mind that he has placed him on. And so he resents him here.

In addition, since white youths are dominated by a black subculture in this institution, impotent white youth leaders are resented because their weaknesses are attributed to white youths also. Thus, the code reinforces white leaders' inadequacies in the eyes of the students and hastens those leaders' exits from the facility.

Unless You Have Been There, You Don't Know What it's Like

Similarly, the code claims that a youth leader must come from the same social background as the boys. Although more and more middle-class inmates are being processed through this training school, the majority are lower-class ghetto youths who have struggled for survival all their lives. These youths know what it is like to go to bed hungry, to lack warm clothing, to be part of a subculture of violence, and to be kept under the watchful surveillance of the police. To work effectively with this type of boy, a youth leader is thought to need experience with a similar background, struggling against the same demonic forces of the ghetto. As one youth leader remarked,

I think the quality of the youth leader depends upon what he has been subjected to himself. This comes into play here quite a bit. I have to use the term deprivation. There aren't many black people working here that haven't suffered some form of deprivation. I can remember when I walked around the streets of Baltimore with a piece of cardboard on the sole of my shoe, a pair of my sister's underwear on because I had none of my own, one pair of decent pants to wear to school. I have been exposed to a lot of nonsense that a lot of these kids have—maybe even more, and there are many, many black youth leaders here who have experienced the same thing. They understand what it is.

Implicit in this criticism of the white youth leader is the feeling that middle-class youth leaders are reluctant to use the physical force necessary to work with aggressive delinquents. Too, the lower-class youth leader can tell the inmates what a "bad dude" he was, describing in scintillating detail his antisocial escapades, his narrow scrapes with the law, his prowess with women, and how good he was in cutting people if they "messed" with him. But now he drives the car he wants, lives where he wants, and buys what he wants. Indeed, he is a sermon in action both that crime does not pay and that rising above the jungle-like ghetto is possible.[5]

## Be Secure

The staff code is also clear about the importance of youth leaders maintaining good security practices. Since this institution is primarily custodially oriented, a high priority is placed upon being eternally vigilant about escapes. Therefore, leaders need to be always checking doors and counting boys to make certain that none have escaped. The wise youth leader also constantly analyses his own behavior patterns, because inmates use knowledge of these patterns to plan escapes. He is instructed to be sensitive to what is taking place in the cottage, and to develop inmate contacts who can provide needed information.

## There Is a Certain Way To Inform on Staff

Sanctions for security violation are among the most severe of all, since violation of these practices damages the cottage's reputation. A violation of security, for example, will result in the Youth Leader V criticizing the violator to his face. If the violation continues, the second step is to go to the wing supervisor. The third step is to place the violation on the leader's evaluation form, and the final step is to go to the superintendent and say, "You've got to get this guy the hell out of here before we lose the entire cottage."

## Don't Take No Shit

Inmates quickly test a new youth leader to discover how capable he is physically. They begin by setting him up for a confrontation and may continue the harassment until he resigns his job—especially if he is weak. In this power struggle, the youth leader must always try to achieve the upper hand. If, therefore, any youths "show their ass," the code advises the staff to assume immediate leadership, for once weakness is shown, loss of control may follow. Thus, "instant therapy" or a little "ass-kicking" are recommended prescriptions for the aggressive inmate. Staff are warned that hesitation in asserting their power will result in serious problems.

## Be Suspicious

The code warns that the wise youth leader should always be suspicious because inmates will manipulate him at every opportunity. In view of this counsel, staff tend to look upon all inmate activities with mistrust. Moreover, the code argues that inmates are dangerous and that becoming comfortable and forgetting the extent of their dangerousness can be quite costly. Youth leaders are, therefore, advised to be alert for any "furtive movements" or deviation from normal, since sexual exploitation, escape, or a fight may be taking place in the back halls. The seriousness of such student behavior usually results in severe sanctions against any staff negligent enough to permit them.

## Be Loyal to the Team

Loyalty to the team is also important. If inmates become aware of or are able to create conflict on a cottage's team, this conflict may be used to attenuate staff control. Loyalty to the team results, too, in a genuine reluctance to "rat" on other staff. Only such behavior as sexually exploiting inmates or aiding and abetting an escape will alienate "loyal" team members. Ordinarily, the goal of keeping all problems within the cottage to negate outside criticism is attainable. Staff members, in addition, try to help each other do their jobs, especially if someone is "under the weather." Violators of these team norms are avoided and otherwise rejected until they fall into line.

Take Care of Yourself

According to the informal code, taking care of one's own affairs on the job is acceptable. Youth leaders, for instance, spend considerable time on the telephone with personal calls, and bring portable television sets to the office to watch ball games. Occasionally some leaders keep students in their dormitories on weekend mornings, or even lock them up in order to catch some sleep. Leaders have also been known to "bum" food which inmates receive from home (e.g., cakes and pies), and nearly all will take off "sick time" to do their thing in the community.[6] If a leader takes care of himself too well, though, the Youth Leader V will complain to his supervisor.

Stay Cool, Man

Seriously injuring a youth is a severe violation of the code. In one case when a staff member split a boy's head open with a cue stick, fellow youth leaders made no attempt to protect him from official sanctioning because, in their opinion, he had overreacted and probably lacked the control necessary to work with delinquents. Other forms of unacceptable behavior involve coming to work inebriated, mistreating inmates, and taking personal problems out on charges. The importance of these violations is indicated by the emphasis during orientation on not "losing one's cool" or overreacting to an emotional situation.

The Administration Will Screw You

The conduct norms warn that the administration "down front" will exploit the youth leader in every possible way. These "anti-administration" norms were generated early in the institution's history when administrators were white, had professional degrees in social work, and were considered *outsiders* brought in to run a "tight ship." Even now, in spite of the fact that there is a black, college-educated superintendent who has held various jobs in the facility over the past ten years and that other important administrators are black, this suspicion remains. Youth leaders still remind one another that "they" are up to something "down front." In fact, this lack of trust at times approaches paranoic proportions, and new youth leaders are advised: "Do not make yourself vulnerable to those down front, because if you do, you will pay for it."

The failure to believe that "the administration will screw you" is seen as a serious violation of the code. Cottage staff are extremely fearful of the people "down front," and Youth Leader Vs become quite anxious about anyone who appears co-opted by these institutional elite. Further, if a particular Youth Leader V is unable to convince the Youth Leader IV of the danger of his relationships with administrators, the V will often begin to spread stories about the youth leader's shortcomings, and the new man's position in the institution may be seriously threatened.

Don't Listen to Social Workers

The contribution which social workers make to the cottage is both underplayed, and at times, ridiculed. Youth leaders believe that social workers, who are usually white and middle-class, do not know what it is like to be a delinquent on the streets—especially a black delinquent from the ghetto. In addition, they believe that someone with a social worker's background is easily manipulated because he or she depends on book knowledge and will make poor decisions about inmates. Since social workers tend to see this job only as a stepping-stone to a better job, the acceptable strategy is to put so much pressure on them that they are co-opted to staff values and do not interfere with the cottage's functioning.

Don't Do More than You Get Paid for

The informal code reminds new youth leaders that they should not do more than that for which they get paid. According to the union, which is an excellent vehicle for transmitting the code, this means doing work not stated in the job description. New youth leaders, for instance, spend much of their time talking with inmates. Code enforcers, nevertheless, remind new staff that therapists get paid $25.00 an hour to do the talking. Until recently, when they were given a promotion for becoming group leaders, Youth Leader IVs likewise felt that leading groups was beyond the call of duty. Similarly, when social workers ask youth leaders to help with inmate progress reports, these staff often refuse because they do not consider this to be part of their jobs. Obviously, the refusal to share their extensive knowledge with social workers militates against institutional effectiveness.

## THE CODE AND THE BOYS

The second part of the code is concerned more specifically with how the staff orient their behavior toward the boys. Examination of this part of the code yields three basic behavioral orientations. Practically every tenet of the code in some way works to the disadvantage of the youths. These tenets still appear on the surface to be quite normal and natural ways of working with youths. Specifically, these staff orientations involve negligence, exchange, and out-and-out exploitation.

Negligence is for the most part the result of staff unhappiness with their jobs and leads them to bypass regular duties to make their jobs easier. Very much related to "taking care of yourself," this differs only in that agreed-upon regulations are not enforced. The result of staff not doing their jobs is that inmates are sometimes exposed to victimization by peers. If negligence leads to an inmate being seriously injured, then staff members are seriously punished. Most of the actions constituting negligence do not result in injury or blatant victimization of boys; and staff receive little "flack" from their supervisors. The boys are unquestionably the losers when everything is considered.

Exchange is another type of staff-inmate relationship which enables staff to maintain control. Often developing over a long period of time, the actual nature of the exchange is not recognized by new staff, and even veteran youth leaders are often totally naïve as to its implications. Typical of most exchange relationships, both staff and some inmates gain from what the other has to offer. That is to say, the benefits are reciprocal for those involved. But as Chapter 7 suggested, an imbalance always exists in the exchange because staff are able to summon whatever amount of power is needed to control inmates. The fact that staff maintain a clear edge leaves the boys resenting and opposing staff programs.[7]

The opposition to the staff which was depicted in earlier chapters is a classic example of the split generated between staff and inmates by this imbalance of power.

Finally, and of no small importance in cottage living, is the fact that staff power is sometimes so great that no semblance of exchange is present, and out-and-out exploitation is possible. Differing from negligence and exchange, this victimization seems to stem from a desire to better their own life as well as occasionally to satisfy vindictive aggressiveness against those whom they dislike. The staff code defines this type of exploitation as the most deviant, and efforts are made to impose negative sanctions against violators.


## NEGLIGENCE

### Staff Not Making Regular Checks

The major type of negligence involves the failure of staff to make their regular thirty-minute check of youths on maximum restriction, their failure to police the shower area, and their failure to supervise boys who go back to the sleeping or toilet area during the day. Ever since a suicide and the setting of several fires by boys on maximum restriction, failure to check rooms has been looked on with a great deal of intolerance. A fire receives publicity throughout the institution and the community, and irresponsible youth leaders who do not make regular checks receive considerable pressure from all. Code enforcers, therefore, let institutional administrators impose negative sanctions. When no serious incident takes place and the infraction goes unnoticed, experienced youth leaders begin to tease the guilty. The point is generally well taken, and the once negligent leader begins to regularly check boys on maximum restriction. Code enforcers, too, are sensitive to youth leaders who do not police the shower area. "Everyone knows" that showers offer the greatest opportunity for sexual exploitation. Experienced youth leaders, in fact, can cite cases of mass sexual victimization. Unless staff watch boys carefully, a sexual exploiter will persuade a sexually victimized youth to go back to the toilet and the exploiter will follow in a few minutes. After Youth Leader Vs remind these youth leaders of past happenings, Youth Leader IVs usually become more aware and responsible in their duties.

Observing the staff neglect their duties obviously does not make boys appreciate their own situation. In particular, those who are exploited as a result of staff negligence interpret this behavior as indifference to their plight. It certainly is a contributing factor to despair, hopelessness, and impotence.

## EXCHANGE

### Exchange Transactions with Boys

The everyday operation of running the cottages requires that boys help with scrubbing and waxing floors, cleaning walls, washing windows, setting up tables, cleaning toilets and showers, serving food, and keeping their rooms clean. Presumably, staff should choose the boys to do these and other tasks without prejudice, assigning each a fair share of desirable and undesirable tasks. But, as it turns out, staff clearly have their favorites and permit boys to do tasks depending, for the most part, upon the value of youths to the staff members. Thus, even though many of the tasks are routine, the exchange nature of the staff-inmate relationship dictates who performs them.

"Heavies," for the most part, escape the routine tasks and end up giving orders to the other boys. The "heavies" are also the recipients of many special privileges denied to the rest of the youths, as discussed in Chapter 7. The lieutenants are only too happy to volunteer to do favors, run errands, mop floors, and do other cleaning to convince staff of their worth. If they are able to convince staff of their intrinsic worth to cottage life, lieutenants know that they may be allowed to become "heavies" upon the release of the old "heavy." The "slicks," on the other hand, do not permit themselves to be used to any real extent until near the time of their release. In fact, neither they nor the staff press one another on important issues. Slicks, then, attempt to convince staff of their readiness for release and begin to volunteer to do the high-status jobs ordinarily reserved for the staff's favorite boys. The "boys who profit," too, have an exchange relationship with staff, but in a manner different from any discussed so far. Few in numbers, these youths are the only ones who staff feel are growing and are seriously contemplating their futures. Although staff act as sounding boards for these boys, the boys give staff members some of the few moments of satisfaction in their institutional careers.

Needless to say, the "mess-up," the peddler, the thief, the "queen," and the scapegoat find their relationships with staff unsatisfactory. Staff assign them low status and undesirable jobs, very much ignoring their needs. Although there is some payoff for these boys because staff expect less from them, the value of this payoff is questionable since the boys receive less attention, less reinforcement, and fewer institutional privileges than their peers.

## Unsanctioned Privileges

One of the clearest forms of exchange is the unsanctioned privileges granted for good behavior. Institutional rules and structure imply that the food served is to be eaten, that refrigerators are for institutional use, and that a schedule is to be followed in all phases of institutional life. Yet, if inmates do not care for certain food, cereal and milk may be substituted if the staff approve. Boys are permitted to keep soft drinks in the refrigerator, and some favored students are even permitted to cook food on a hot plate in the kitchen.[8] Other unsanctioned privileges include staying up later than usual, going back to their rooms for a nap when school is not in session, and staying out of school when upset. In addition, boys on maximum restriction may spend more time outside their rooms and have more smoke breaks than are usually allowed.

These privileges become normative very quickly, and boys soon find it difficult to conceive of existence without them. The politics of scarcity govern relations between the staff and boys and the fear of loss of privileges operates as a strong lever in keeping the boys in line. Staff explicitly say, "Don't give me any trouble and I'll give you more than you're supposed to have." Inmates are thereby taught that the violation of rules and beating the system are possible. Certainly questionable as a rehabilitative technique, it is nevertheless an effective means of social control. Since staff reputations depend on keeping control over their charges, the blatant manipulation of institutional benefits makes that control possible. For their part, boys are willing to do staff's bidding in order to receive the benefits.

## Use of Reviews

Before pre-release status may be received, boys must remain in the institution for five months. They must then stay out of trouble for another three months before staff can recommend them for release.[9] The power of staff is especially apparent here. A critical review will add three months to the boy's stay.[10] Staff may also decide not to send the boys to the psychiatrist to have their "R" (aggressive) and "E" (emotionally disturbed) labels removed, and may decide against allowing the boys a home visit.[11]

Highly conscious of their power, staff continually remind boys to behave or they will cause the boys difficulties. One youth said, "You have to 'kiss ass' to get anything around here." Comments such as this reflect how offended youths are about the review process being used to degrade them. That statement also reflects the exchange nature of the staff-inmate relationship. In this instance, boys must not only keep a "quiet" institution, but must show subservience to staff before being granted their "rights." Additionally, further conflict is engendered in residents since peer approval depends upon their rejection of staff contact and values; yet this rejection of staff prolongs their stay.

To evaluate boys according to whether they are compliant and subservient circumvents the institution's treatment philosophy. Staff sanctions are sometimes based upon personal grievances against particular boys, so youths must be very careful lest their comments be interpreted as personal attacks. Thus, although the boys' comments may be a result of personal growth, the portent of a negative review keeps them from expressing their ideas.

## EXPLOITATION

Deception of inmates, encouraging inmate victimization, physical brutality, aiding escapes, and sexual exploitation of boys are ways by which staff exploit inmates. While deception is still considered normative and acceptable, the others are considered deviant and subject to negative sanctions from experienced youth leaders. Unlike most of the behavior discussed above, when the last four situations take place, experienced youth leaders get together and decide what action is needed.

### Deception

Deception of inmates is exploitation because of the one-sidedness of this staff-inmate interaction. Lying to inmates may bring about calm and order, but the inmates have no recourse for grievances. This deception is practiced to a great extent at special meetings called to handle cottage or institutional matters upsetting the boys. Frequently, the youths present a list of changes and demand their introduction into the cottage milieu. Staff, rather than seriously considering the demands, simply encourage the students to externalize their frustrations, and promise, in turn, to rectify some of the grievances. But as soon as everything cools down, staff go back to their old ways and no changes are made. In talking about these meetings, one staff member said, "It does them good to blow off every now and then."

Deception becomes less acceptable when staff make promises

they have no intention of keeping. Such promises are often made in exchange for information. For example, staff promise not to chastise a boy (a cheap form of bargaining) for informing on his collaborators in some activity. After he tells, the boy is punished just like everyone else.

Although deception demonstrates staff power and facilitates inmate control, the possibility of establishing positive relationships is severely damaged. Boys tend to respond affirmatively to those whom they feel they can trust; that is, if a genuine personal exchange is possible, boys will participate in a give-and-take fashion.

### Physical Brutality

Staff agree that the amount of physical brutality has been decreasing over the years. Those who became involved in frequent physical confrontation with inmates were punished, and nearly all left the institution. Yet physical force is still occasionally used. If employed because of drunkenness, or as a reaction to a personal problem, or if a leader is unable to restrain himself and attempts to seriously injure a boy or uses a weapon on a youth, the aggression is considered unacceptable.[12]

Following such an attack, an investigation is usually conducted by the administration. [13] This is considered outside interference by cottage staff, however, and they refuse to help in the investigation. But they do have their own way of punishing brutal leaders. One of the more effective is to complain to their supervisors about how these violent leaders are afraid of the boys or overreact. The supervisor then generally counsels and harasses the accused leader.

### Encouraging Inmate Victimization

Staff occasionally will encourage a mass assault on an unliked boy by intentionally leaving a door open. Some have even given the key to a room to inmates so they can "work over" the room's resident. When this happens, code enforcers usually meet with other enforcers to decide how to handle the situation. They are often so antagonized that they request the superintendent to take whatever action he can.

## Aiding Escapes

Helping runaways is both normatively unacceptable and against the law, but still it happens every year or so. Why staff become involved in this activity is not known, but it is undoubtedly related to physical intimidation on the part of the inmate, altruistic feelings of staff, the outcome of an exchange relation between staff and the escapee, or general camaraderie between the staff and inmate.

Helping a runaway takes place in one of two ways: (1) The staff member can leave a door unlocked, or (2) he can keep an escapee at his home, providing food, money, and a place to sleep. It would appear that the more frequent occurrence is for an escapee to come to a staff member's home for temporary assistance and shelter. In all probability, the shelter is arranged prior to the youth's escape.

If a youth leader is rumored to have helped an escapee, code enforcers do everything possible to expose and punish him. Some have even engaged in their own investigation to determine the truth of the rumor. Youth leaders know that aiding escapees not only jeopardizes their role as custodial agents, but that the boys are victimized because the returned runaway will have to spend seven to ten months of additional time in the institution.

## Sexual Exploitation of Inmates

Every few years, a staff member becomes sexually involved with inmates. One incident took place seven years ago and one took place three or four years ago. In a most recent series of incidents, youths accused several leaders of forcing them to participate in homosexual relations. The purely exploitative aspects of these incidents are difficult to verify, for after they make accusations about being forced into performing these acts, boys often end up admitting they were somewhat willing partners. These youths are divided into two groups: those who are weak and coerced into behavior they consider undesirable, and those who feel they may be able to bargain for some favor by engaging in sexual relations with staff. Enticed into the relationship by the promise of some valued commodity such as cigarettes, protection from other peers, or a promise of an early release, the boys may agree to participate. If the boys' accounts are to be accepted, the following is probably typical of the dynamics involved. One of the boys talking about his relations with a youth leader said:

> He had some intercourse with me about every two weeks. I did not want to do it, but he talked about getting me out of [here] faster and I wanted to get out because I have been here a long time. I think the reason I did it was I just came back from AWOL, and I thought I had a long time to go so I thought I would get out of here.

Another boy related:

> Mr. _____ called me into his office approximately two weeks after I arrived in _____ Cottage. We talked about people we knew in common. He began to talk to me about my homosexuality. I interpreted it that he was trying to help me. Then he began talking about sexual acts that he enjoyed. He asked me whether I enjoyed fellatio and anal intercourse. I felt that he was trying to persuade me that we should indulge. He also implicated several other students about being gay. He said that he had known several staff that "messed around" and if I got tied up with one of them I might get out faster.

When word spreads that certain staff are sexually involved with boys, other youth leaders quickly try to determine the truth of the rumor. If the rumor is deemed factual, all of the youth leaders who support the code socially reject the accused. The accused also often loses labor union support because the "code enforcers" control the union. Abandoned by his peers, the accused usually either resigns his position or is fired.

In summary, the informal code discourages youth leaders' involvement in treatment and other legitimate institutional affairs. While some of these leaders may later violate the tenets of their own norms, the code in the meantime has had its effects. Of interest also is the fact that informal codes either support or detract from explicit organizational goals. Certainly, to the extent that staff ignore, mistreat, or exploit inmates, their morale is lowered, and the impact of their stay becomes more negative.

## NOTES

1. The actual ranking of the code's tenets by all staff remains to be empirically demonstrated; the ranking here is based upon participant observation for over four years.

2. Probably the main tenet of those in the union is: "Don't do more than you're paid for." Union officials are suspicious of institutional officials and thwart many legitimate attempts to provide a better atmosphere for the boys.

3. An Air Force base is in the city where this institution is located, and the training school actively recruits men who are in the process of retiring from their military careers.

4. On each shift, one Youth Leader VI supervises all the youth leaders on his wing of the institution. Thus, there are a total of six Youth Leaders VIs employed. Because this leader has risen through the ranks, he has considerable power in the institution.

5. One reason for this "affluence" is that nearly all of these youth leaders have two full-time jobs.

6. Institutional staff are given 9.2 hours of sick time every four weeks. Many staff have minus sick leave, which means that they have taken more sick time off than they have earned. In fact, except for supervisors, it is unusual for youth leaders to have accumulated more than a few hours of sick leave.

7. Blau states, "Opposition to power arises when those subject to it experience shared feelings of exploitation and oppression," and goes on to say, "Whenever it [power] rests on coercive force or on the supply of benefits that meet essential needs and cannot be obtained elsewhere, power can be used to exploit others by forcing them to work in behalf of one's interests" (Blau, 1967: 228). Both of these statements apply to the staff-inmate relations described here.

8. The food is prepared at another location, and cottages are not supposed to allow boys to cook their own food.

9. Cottage staff must recommend both pre-release and release status for the boys. Then the status must be approved by an administrative review.

10. It is possible to give a boy a special review in less than three months.

11. Social workers used to make the decision as to when to send a youth to the psychiatrist for the clearance of his suffix, but this is now being done by the cottage staff at reviews.

12. Any advantage, of course, accrues only to the leader, as he is able to take his own aggression and frustrations out on the boys.

13. Institutional administrators conduct an investigation on every major physical force incident, which is defined as one in which a youth requires medical attention. Nevertheless, youth leaders are generally adamant about refusing to cooperate in these investigations, even when they have strong negative feelings about the incidents.

## CHAPTER 13

## ORGANIZATIONAL PROCESSING

**In addition to the informal** staff norms discussed in the last chapter, inmate victimization also results from the formal rules and processes utilized by institutional administrators. Administrators assume that close adherence to formal rules will result in a well-run, quiet institution. Therefore, they spell out staff and inmate duties and behavior in detail. The rules are so important to officials, in fact, that they place them in a "big black book." New staff are directed to spend much of their first several days on the job reading this book.

These all-encompassing directives severely limit individual freedom and choice. The atmosphere becomes repressive and punishment-centered. Not surprisingly, then, both staff and inmates attempt to achieve freedom from these rules. Most staff talk about leaving as soon as a good job becomes available elsewhere, and inmates tend to regard the institution as a prison. The purpose of this chapter is to examine some of these features of the organization's structure and the implications that structure has for its participants. Organizational goals, structural characteristics, staff processing of inmates, and cottage assignment are all discussed in the pages that follow.

## ORGANIZATIONAL GOALS AND INMATE EXPLOITATION

According to Etzioni, "An organizational goal is a desired state of affairs which the organization attempts to realize" (1964: 6). Correctional institutions, like mental hospitals, churches, and universities, are organizations with multiple goals. Characterized in terms of the importance they place on custodial or treatment goals, some are almost purely custodial, some have mixed goals, and others have almost purely treatment goals (Zald, 1962b: 335):

> Custodial goals are operative when an organization devotes a large part of its energies and resources to the control and containment of inmates; treatment goals are operative when a large part of organizational re- sources and energies are devoted to the rehabilitative and positive social change of inmates.

This institution's administrators have received a clear mandate from the Ohio Youth Commission, the state government, and from the community at large. Not only must they attempt to rehabilitate residents, but these hard-core delinquents must be controlled and kept in custody. To enforce this latter mandate, administrators are forced to set up a social structure which dis- courages violence, escapes, and riots. Staff are reminded that they must do everything possible to control these aggressive youths, even if treatment must be neglected.[1]

Evidence of this custodial emphasis is that superintendents are evaluated by the annual number of runaways. A certain "kiss of death" for a superintendent is when the runaways of any year equal the runaways of the last year of the former superintendent (Bartollas, 1973). Superintendents learn very quickly that treat- ment programs create custodial problems. Helping a person grow, for example, requires that the helper exercise responsibility for his own behavior. This necessitates placing him in more and more positions of trust. But if a youth is permitted to leave the institu- tion without staff escort, the staff are gambling that the boy will return. Predictably, staff members are sometimes wrong, and the superintendent must report another runaway to the Ohio Youth Commission. When the runaway count starts to climb for the year, superintendents begin to rescind off-grounds visits and to drasti- cally decrease home visits and off-campus jobs. In their desperation for a more secure institution, some superintendents become oblivious to staff's methods of maintaining institutional security.

## Centralization, Formalization, Stratification, and Job Satisfaction

As a highly centralized formal organization, this facility places the responsibility for decision-making in the hands of a few top administrators (Hage and Aiken, 1970: 19). The decision makers, who include the supervisors of the line staff, appear to feel that youth leaders and social workers are not capable of important decision-making. The top elite, in addition, are constantly concerned that youth leaders and social workers—both of whom work directly with inmates—are deliberately failing to perform their responsibilities. Thus, top administrators create a "punishment-centered bureaucracy" to ensure the maintenance of control. In the process, they lose the allegiance and diminish the morale of staff (Gouldner, 1954: 207-214).

Formalization, too, is related to intraorganizational conflict and refers to the number and organization of rules and how strictly they are enforced. The rules are characterized by a high degree of formalization; officials frequently remind workers that regulations must be followed. The big black book contains between two and three hundred pages, and top administrators are quite insistent that its directives be enforced. In this regard, Rushing (1966) points out that formal rules are used more often when organizational parts fail to attain minimum performance.[2]

Youth leaders bitterly resent this lack of trust in their judgment and the amount of control over their behavior. As a result, they create a "reactive subsystem," which regards the administration as an enemy (Young, 1970: 297). In the past, the administration and youth leaders were mutually dependent on each other. Youth leaders were primarily lower-class blacks who lived hand to mouth on a near poverty level and who needed their jobs desperately. The administration, in turn, depended upon these staff members to control these aggressive and "acting-out" delinquents. This dependency on each other led the two groups to cooperate and provide each other with assistance when needed. Now, however, youth leaders receive a more adequate income as a result of improved salaries and "moonlighting" on other jobs. They have their union and, ultimately, the review board, if the administration pushes them too much.[3] OYC officials fear confronting this newly organized AFL union, primarily because officials have lost almost all their cases to the review board regarding employees' dismissals. Hence, youth leaders have far greater power than ever before in the thirteen-year history of this training school.[4]

Another important area of conflict is precipitated by the institution's stratification system. Staff are rewarded with varying amounts of prestige and money. Education is used as the standard for evaluating job classifications, and social workers, social work supervisors, teachers and their supervisors, all of whom have college degrees, are given much greater prestige, higher salaries, and better hours than custodial staff. Social workers in addition, are free to arrange their own schedules as long as their supervisors approve. They may leave the institution at lunchtime, and some go to graduate school during the day. Youth leaders, meanwhile, work a set shift, cannot leave the institution, and are jealous of the higher salaries, prestige, and privileges of treatment staff.[5]

In spite of their greater rewards, treatment staff are far from satisfied with their jobs. Until May of 1970, social workers were cottage directors and supervisors of the youth leaders in the cottages. The institution's organization was then changed, which resulted in social workers losing their supervisory capacity. They, in effect, were taken out of the line of authority, and have no more say than youth leaders on cottage matters. Custodial staff, as a consequence, make decisions on treatment matters such as home visits, off-campus jobs, and restrictions of students. Treatment staff deeply resent this infringement on their decision-making.

Academic and vocational teachers feel very much alienated from other staff members.[6] The principal of the high school has formal authority but teachers lack both formal and informal authority. Teachers are aware that social workers unite with youth leaders to challenge their treatment efficacy and that little support will come from anyone if they become involved in conflict with residents. Therefore, teachers, like youth leaders and social workers, have problems with morale and job satisfaction.

Job satisfaction is attenuated among all staff by lack of demonstrated appreciation by supervisors, the anger and resistance of residents, the lack of a feeling of achievement because inmates fail so often upon return to the community, and the absence of feedback to staff concerning the progress of released boys. Certainly not to be ignored in the lack of job satisfaction are the long, drab hallways, constant complaining by fellow employees about jobs, poor salaries compared to other state employees, and working in a building that is cold in winter and hot in summer.

The result is withdrawal from job involvement. This, in turn, increases tardiness, and absenteeism. Since the work habits of many staff are unpredictable, boys find the forming of "significant other" relationships difficult. Of even greater effect on inmates are indifferent and careless staff who refuse to help residents who are struggling and reaching out for help.

Staff Processing of Inmates

To comply with the institution's custodial goals, youth leaders sometimes resort to techniques which are physically and psychologically harmful to residents. Some of the techniques were abandoned well before this study began, but some are still used.

*Physical Brutality:* One brutal technique no longer used involved four or five youth leaders who, as a group, pursued runaway boys. Called the "goon squad," these men were not only very adroit in catching a runaway, but in convincing him that he should never attempt to escape again. Many youths were severely "worked over" by the "goon squad." Another former approach used to discourage runaways from a home visit group sadism. The returnee was simply placed in the midst of his peers for a few minutes while the staff turned their backs.[7] Since all in the cottage were punished when someone failed to return from a home visit, peers greeted escapees with the observation, "If it weren't for you, MF, I would have gone home for Christmas."

Inactive since 1969, the mop squad was also impressive. Troublesome boys were given a very short mop, and for the next six or seven hours they moved that short mop as fast as possible up and down the hallways. Weary with aching muscles and soaked with sweat by the time the day was over, even the most recalcitrant would be soon pleading to return to his regular school program. With tears running down his cheeks, he would promise not to cause any more problems.

An approach which is still used by some youth leaders is to take the returnee back to his room and beat the hell out of him.[8] And, as suggested in Chapter 12, some leaders still overreact to problems, beating youths with pool sticks, flashlights, and clubs.[9]

Physical discomfort is indeed involved when boys are locked in their rooms at night. Even if they need to go to the toilet or become ill, no relief is normally available until 7 a.m. the next morning. In one incident, a boy complained about a stomachache to the Youth Leader III on duty. Since he was known as a "crybaby," this youth's complaints were ignored by the youth leader. When the youth leader finally called his supervisor, who was the only one permitted to allow the youth to leave his room, the Youth Leader VI decided that the youth was only pretending. He felt that the inmate wanted to be sent to the hospital from which he could escape. By the time the boy was seen by the nurse the next morning, his appendix had burst and he nearly died before emergency surgery could be performed.

*Psychic Humiliation:* The institution has various ways to assault the self-respect of inmates. Some are quite typical of "total institutions." For example, hair is cut one way—short—and beautifully groomed Afros or wavy hair cultured for years is quickly shorn. Already mentioned is the restriction against going to the toilet at night. The boys are also run through the shower like cattle and given a limited time to dry. If contraband is stolen or the rumor spreads that someone has contraband, all residents must stand in line while a search is conducted. This involves stripping the boys to their shorts and socks. Even the usually pleasant emotional experience of eating is reduced to a dull, commonplace ordeal. The cold, bland, and distasteful foods are a constant dehumanizing experience. Finally, to be greeted by a hard slap in the ribs each time he returns to the institution—which is supposedly necessary for search purposes—infuriates even the mildest mannered youth. As one said, "The MF doesn't have to slap us that hard."

The boys also feel the staff are indifferent to their plight and do not really care what happens to them. Even some of the hardest-core delinquents are bothered by the staff's attitude. This indifference was grossly expressed by one official who, coming upon the scene of a suicide, first said, "Are we alright?" He meant, have we freed ourselves from all blame in this matter? Will we be safe when the newspapers write up their reports?

More unusual is the "reformatory express."[10] The superintendent or the assistant director of guidance (who is in charge of custody) usually instigates this ruse to hoodwink boys into revealing information or "ratting" on a fellow peer. Feeling that someone knows where a missing key, a hacksaw blade, or some dope is, staff put the "squeeze" on him. If physical force or verbal threats are not effective, tight-lipped boys have been loaded into a car and taken toward the adult reformatory sixty miles away. Continuing to "work on" the boy, the driver reminds him what a bad place this adult facility is and what a rotten shame it is that he has to go there. The "reformatory express" reportedly went so close to the reformatory once that the buildings were in full view.[11]

In contrast to the infrequently run "express," which is basically apocryphal, maximum restriction is experienced by nearly every boy at one time or another. Normally preceded by a disciplinary meeting, maximum restriction consists of isolating the "troublemaker" in his room for a specific number of days. Other than a mattress on the floor and perhaps a writing pad and pen, the room is bare. Meals are served in the room. The room is left only for three occasions—a daily shower, several trips to the toilet, and one or two smoke breaks. In general, a fight receives seven days "on the floor"; sex play, ten to fourteen days; and assault of a staff member or return from running away, twenty-one days. Isolation is very difficult on some inmates, for sobbing, shouting, and becoming hysterical before their time is up are not uncommon.[12]

*Violation of Privacy:* The need for control also generates invasions of privacy. Although personal mail was read less at the completion than it was at the beginning of the study, some was still being read. Much more disturbing to residents are room searches by staff. When boys are in school, rooms are sometimes searched for contraband. Personal belongings are often scattered around the room, letters thrown on the floor, and personal photographs of family or girlfriends ripped up. Some staff even sneak around listening to boys' conversations while they are in their rooms.

*Chronic Exposure to Meaningless Programming and Programless Boredom:* Finally, organizational processing results in youths sitting around much of the time without anything to do. Tensions build up, tempers flair, and conflicts explode. Weekends are especially boring unless families are visiting; an unlikely event since all but one of the major urban areas of the state are a considerable distance away. On the weekend, most of the time is spent sitting around—watching television, sleeping, playing cards, or doing nothing. Broken only by a movie or a trip to the gym, this boredom is faced from Friday afternoon until Monday morning. School, of course, breaks the monotony during the week, but non-academically oriented students find educational programs only one more part of their stultifying experience.

## COTTAGE ASSIGNMENT

This phase of the study is somewhat speculative, as the institution was in a state of transition during the year of data collection. Since wing directors assigned inmates to cottages on the basis of the youth's characteristics, each cottage had developed a distinctive "character" over the years. But, during this year, an intake cottage was started and the I-level classification system was initiated. Because boys already assigned remained where they were, some cottages received boys radically different from its previous residents. Our impressions are that "mixed" cottages generate more victimization than "unmixed." Another reason for the speculative aspect of this phase is that no in-depth study of the way staff ran each cottage was made except for the understanding that emerges from working in the institution for four years. A third difficulty in exploring the victimization of cottage placement is the lack of empirical data relating I-level (world view) to exploitative behavior. An additional concern is that the process of classifying boys was done by staff who were quickly trained. Staff

experienced with this classification system may well have perceived many of these youths differently.[13]

To attempt to come to some understanding of the importance
of cottage placement in inmate victimization, the decision was
made to construct a profile of each cottage based on the exploitation typology. Using the number of youths in each of these
categories as the starting point, an analysis was attempted of each
cottage in order to determine how the interplay of all the known
factors affected the amount of exploitation.[14]

## Pine Cottage

A special feature in understanding the dynamics of this cottage
is that it contains the most seriously emotionally disturbed ($I_4$)
boys. Its leaders, fortunately, are particularly effective in working
with this type of youth. One, for instance, is a "father figure" and
the other is an excellent male role model. Boys receive affection
from one leader and a strong masculine pro-social role model from
the other. Since this cottage is at the end of the one hallway—a

Table 13.1

**TYPOLOGY BREAKDOWN BY COTTAGE**

| Cottage | Exploiters | Give and Takes | Indepen- dents | Sometimes Boys | Victims | N | % |
|---|---|---|---|---|---|---|---|
| Pine | 1 | 13 | 0 | 3 | 4 | 21 | 14.1 |
| Elm | 3 | 1 | 5 | 3 | 4 | 16 | 10.7 |
| Maple | 0 | 3 | 1 | 5 | 5 | 14 | 9.4 |
| Scioto | 1 | 4 | 4 | 8 | 0 | 17 | 11.4 |
| Forrest | 7 | 4 | 2 | 3 | 4 | 20 | 13.4 |
| Adams | 4 | 8 | 1 | 0 | 4 | 17 | 11.4 |
| Regal | 7 | 11 | 1 | 4 | 1 | 24 | 16.1 |
| Washington | 5 | 6 | 1 | 5 | 3 | 20 | 13.4 |
| Totals | 28 | 50 | 15 | 31 | 25 | 149 | 100.0 |

quarter of a mile from the front offices—it also receives less supervision than the other cottages on the same wing. The result is that this cottage's staff have more administrative freedom than leaders in cottages closer to the front offices. Of special importance is the skill of these leaders in ferreting out sexual exploitation. The $I_4$s are especially vulnerable to exploitation from stronger peers since they seem interested in winning approval in any way possible, even to the extent of giving up their possessions and manhood. Youth leaders, as a result, consciously try to protect potential sexual victims.[15]

The typological breakdown indicates only one exploiter, probably due to the tight supervision of youth leaders. It may also be that seriously disturbed $I_4$s find the sustaining of the exploiter role difficult. Another thirteen boys are "give and takes," perhaps related to their attempts to prove their normality and masculinity and to confusion resulting from their disturbed state. Three inmates are "sometimes exploited" and four inmates are "often exploited." Again, this is quite logical when the victimization of these youths by boys from other cottages and their psychological amenability to exploitation are considered.

## Elm Cottage

This living unit became an intake cottage in January of 1972—only six months before these data were collected. With the attainment of this new status, remarkable rapport and cohesiveness developed among staff members. As with the senior youth leader in Pine Cottage, the senior youth leader in this cottage has considerable experience and is called "father" by many boys. One early decision of the intake staff was to develop a core group of favored boys who were near release. These boys remained in the cottage to help new peers adjust to incarceration. The rapid turnover, however, made it difficult for this core group to work effectively with new residents.

Because new inmates are especially vulnerable to victimization, stronger residents who seek to gain power and prestige begin to exploit them soon after their arrival. It is not surprising, then, that three boys fell into the sometimes victimized group and that four others could be classified purely as victims. But only one "give and take" youth was found in this cottage. This latter category apparently takes some time to develop, which leads to the contention that cottages start out dichotomized between exploiters and exploited and only later do "give and takes" emerge. Elm Cottage also has a large number—five—in the independent category. Staff ranked five of the six core group members in the independent category, feeling that these youths were exemplary and were not involved in the exploitation matrix.

## Maple Cottage

Maple Cottage only a few months before the data were collected became a cottage for $I_4$s. Some of this cottage's salient characteristics were as follows: The population was contaminated heavily by the former population—inmates who were typically $I_3$s and $I_2$s; a new social worker had some difficulty working effectively with the dependent, emotionally disturbed youths; one staff member was often accused of physical brutality by residents; whites believed that two of the morning shift youth leaders racially discriminated against them; and no leader was considered a father figure who could lend emotional stability to the cottage. In addition, one "booty bandit" was released and another escaped shortly before data were collected.

The absence of these two "booty bandits" and the strictness of supervision appear to explain why there were no exploiters. That this cottage was in transition also appears to explain the existence of only three "give and takes." As with the intake cottage, the exploitation cycle was still in its either-or position. With the cottage made up of two different types of boys, it is to be expected that five inmates were classified as "sometimes" and five as "often" exploited. Adding to the exploited ranks, of course, was the fact that many of these anxious youths were victimized in other parts of the institution.

## Scioto Cottage

Scioto Cottage, until the recent change in the classification system, was assigned boys who had committed serious personal crimes in the community. Institutional administrators saw this cottage as appropriate for sociopathic personalities, principally because staff were tightly knit and maintained firm social control. But shortly before the l-level classification system was initiated, this cottage lost several of its strongest staff members. Remaining staff members subsequently began to have more difficulty controlling the population. Still, the decision was made at the intake cottage to send older and more aggressive $I_3$ MPs to this cottage; officials felt that this staff remained able to control aggressive inmates. Nevertheless, the intake staff sometimes refused to send weak $I_3$ MPs to Scioto Cottage because they questioned these boys' abilities to survive.

The skill of this debilitated staff in controlling inmates is clearly reflected in the fact that only one exploiter was found in this cottage. This, of course, is remarkable considering the aggressive nature of the cottage's population. Since severe exploitation obviously is sanctioned strongly, the only victimization left is to take the possessions of peers. As material exploitation is often overlooked by staff, it is not surprising that eight were "sometimes victimized."

Four "give and take" inmates tend to be a fairly large number considering that these youths are so aggressive; what apparently is taking place is that both the stronger and the weaker youths find themselves unable to dominate others of equal strength or weakness. It is more difficult to explain why four residents would be independent of the exploitation matrix. Perhaps more "slicks" are found in the ranks of older youths.

Forrest Cottage

Throughout the institution's twelve-year history, this cottage maintained a good reputation for working effectively with inmates, chiefly because staff members exercised tight control over their charges. Some of the institution's finest custodial staff, in fact, received their training in this cottage. Several key resignations adversely affected the quality of leadership the preceding several years. In addition, one of the most therapeutically oriented leaders in the institution, who is both respected and trusted by inmates, went through a period of job indifference. He lost some of his contact and involvement with boys. To bolster this ailing staff, a very strong youth leader was brought from another cottage to become the senior youth leader, but his conflict with the social worker largely negated his positive impact. The breakdown of strong supervision, then, permitted exploiters more freedom than formerly had been possible. Over the past three years, mildly disturbed boys were sent to this cottage by the wing director who was guided by a principle—if an inmate is severely disturbed, send him to Elm Cottage, but if he is only mildly disturbed, then send him to Forrest Cottage. After the introduction of I-level, this cottage continued to receive emotionally disturbed $I_4$ s.

Some disturbed boys exploit peers to prove their normality, which probably explains why this cottage ends up with considerable numbers of boys heavily involved in exploitation. Indeed, this cottage is tied with Regal Cottage for the highest number of exploiters in the institution—seven. Part of the reason appears to be attributed to more aggressive black $I_4$ s in this cottage than in either Elm or Maple Cottage. Only four "give and takes" are found, demonstrating further that this cottage is basically divided into the exploiters and the exploited. Three boys are "sometimes" and four are "often" exploited. Unless there is strict staff supervision, it would seem that cottages in which boys stay for only a short period of time, along with cottages in which there are large numbers of emotionally disturbed, may end up with this peculiar pattern of exploitation.

## Adams Cottage

Adams Cottage, similar to Forrest, maintained until recently the reputation of being a well-supervised cottage with few problems, even though it housed large, aggressive inmates. As was typical of other cottages, the resignation of key youth leaders resulted in a decline in the quality of staff leadership. A large number of immature and passive boys were further assigned to Adams Cottage over the preceding two years. When the I-level system was initiated as a means of classifying boys, $I_3$ Cfcs were assigned to this setting. These youths are immature and cultural conformists, tending to be easily influenced by their environments.

Eight boys, for example, are sexually exploited. Although four of these eight are often victimized sexually, the sexual victimization of the other four is not well enough known for them to be labelled scapegoats by their peers. Knowledge of the internal dynamics of this cottage suggests that some of the boys are "trading off" with each other. This partly explains the eight boys placed in the "give and take" category, the four who are sexual partners but not labelled, and the fact that only four exploiters are found. Boys' immaturity and dependency needs seem to contribute to this type of arrangement where they are constantly giving to some and getting from others.

Regal Cottage

In the past, this cottage seldom experienced problems; it had, for example, very few runaways. As in other cottages, rapid changeovers depleted experienced staff over the last two or three years and resulted in a marked decrease in the remaining staff's effectiveness. Regal Cottage has been a type of "catch all" cottage, accepting youths who do not seem to belong elsewhere. Since I-level was initiated, Regal Cottage has received $I_3$s but, even here, manipulators are sometimes mixed with immature and neurotic boys. The mixture of these different types of youths results in problems with exploitation, which is substantiated by the typological breakdown.

This cottage has seven exploiters. The different types of boys apparently result in a wider spread on the exploiter-victim continuum. Eleven inmates are "give and takes," reflecting the nature of interaction taking place within this contaminated population. Containing only one "independent," this cottage has four "sometimes" and one "often" exploited. Although accounting for seven exploiters and only one "often exploited" in this cottage is difficult, this exploitation may only be nonsexual. The two highest "give and take" cottages house, respectively, the most seriously emotionally disturbed in one case and the most heterogeneous population in the other. Anxiety is the one characteristic the boys in these two cottages seem to have. Different types of boys living together may generate considerable anxiety and conflict and "giving and taking" may be attempted to reduce the felt anxiety.

## Washington Cottage

Washington Cottage, like Pine Cottage, is a quarter of a mile away from the front offices. Unlike Pine, this cottage is not isolated from the rest of the institution, principally because of the nature of the cottage's population and its past history. Tradition relates, for instance, that Washington Cottage has always been a jungle and that the weak do not have a chance.

This cottage consistently receives the physically largest boys in the institution. White youths find survival difficult, since the black subculture is extremely strong. Interestingly enough, the number of runaways—a typical reaction of whites to exploitation—have always been very high from this cottage. So many youths escape that special screens were installed. Superintendents, too, anticipate their most serious institutional problems will come from this cottage. As is typical of many cottages, part of the reason for Washington Cottage's problems stems from the lack of staff leadership. Good staff simply do not want to become involved in this very tough milieu. One very fine youth leader on the other wing threatened to resign, for example, when requested to transfer to Washington Cottage. Of interest also is the fact that this cottage changed little in population type after the introduction of I-level, since the $I_3$s and $I_2$s sent to this cottage blended in well with the cottage's residents.

The cottage contained five exploiters, five "sometimes" and three "often" exploited. $I_3$ MPs and $I_2$s are youths whose exploitation of others exceeds any other I-level type; $I_2$s especially, are exploitative, although the few received in this institution only make up a small part of this cottage's population. "Black Nationalism" and other black militant groups have always received stronger support in Washington Cottage than in any other cottage; thus, blacks tend to be highly intolerant of whites. Constantly in a state of turmoil as they try to improve their status in the cottage hierarchy, those less capable of taking care of themselves end up giving and taking a lot. This may explain why there are six "give and takes."


# CONCLUSIONS

This institution is merely carrying out society's expectations—it controls hard-core delinquents. To accomplish this end, administrators feel it is necessary to create a formal organization. Being "punishment-centered," the repressive atmosphere of the institution affects both the morale of inmates and their keepers. Relationships among staff members are characterized by high intraorganization conflict. Organizational processing of boys, in addition, creates an environment which is antitherapeutic at best and only a step from the chain gang at worst. Even using the I-level for cottage assignments does not prevent the stronger from victimizing the weak.


## NOTES

1. Since the completion of the data in May 1973, the Ohio Youth Commission has opened up another youth facility for these older and more aggressive delinquents. This new facility is scheduled to become the end-of-the-line institution, while the present one will work with more disturbed youths.

2. The authors did not empirically test how well organizational parts were functioning; nor did they empirically compare this institution with other, similar institutions.

3. Buttressed by the union, line staff are relatively free to develop their own culture, which they do through staff's informal "code."

4. The union was at this point more interested in consolidating gains and experimenting with power than with the welfare of the boys.

5. Race has been a major source of division between professional and nonprofessional staff because, until recently, professional or treatment staff have been white and custodial staff black. Now, although custodial staff are still predominantly black, more and more treatment staff likewise are black.

6. Vocational and educational staff are considered part of the treatment staff.

7. When a youth failed to return from a home visit, the whole cottage was held responsible, and no other home visits were permitted for ninety days. This was changed in 1971; mass punishment is no longer utilized.

8. Similar to other institutions, runaways are required to serve at least seven months of additional time.

9. In all fairness, a concerted effort has been made to remove adults who frequently physically maltreat inmates.

10. "Reformatory express" is a name used by the researchers, not those in the institution.

11. This is only a rumor, and may or may not be true.

12. In winter, a heating problem has sometimes resulted in inmates on maximum restriction being bitterly cold.

13. See Chapter 2 for the characteristics of $I_2$s, $I_3$s, and $I_4$s.

14. The actual cottage names are not being used in this study.

15. They are, of course, unable to control the exploitation when their boys are in other areas of the institution.

## CHAPTER 14

## INDEFENSIBLE SPACE

**The ecological design** of this institution also contributes to victimization.[1] The setting and its meaning, the construction of the hallways, the layout of the cottages, the location and atmosphere surrounding the educational and recreational areas, all influence the interaction among inmates. From the viewpoint of the boys, practically all areas of the institution hold some risk, but some are clearly safer than others.

In Oscar Newman's book, *Defensible Space* (1972), the effects of physical design on preventing victimization in urban dwelling units are traced.[2] According to Newman, the elements of defensible space combine to produce "an environment in which latent territoriality and sense of community in the inhabitants can be translated into responsibility for ensuring a safe, productive, and well-maintained living space" (Newman, 1972:3).[3] The development of a secure environment requires the utilization of four elements (Newman, 1972:9):

The territorial definition of space in developments reflecting the areas of influence of the inhabitants. This works by subdividing the residential environment into zones toward which adjacent residents easily adopt proprietary attitudes.

The positioning of apartment windows to allow residents to naturally survey the exterior and interior public areas of their living environment.

The adoption of building forms and idioms which avoid the stigma of peculiarity that allows others to perceive the vulnerability and isolation of the inhabitants.

The enhancement of safety by locating residential developments in functionally sympathetic urban areas immediately adjacent to activities that do not provide continued threats.

In applying these principles to correctional institutions, several problems arise.[4] Prevailing correctional philosophy denies Newman's premise that individuals must have private settings. Few recognize that extensions from these settings must exist, in which individuals may conduct their own affairs (Newman, 1972: 2). Also denied is the statement that "for one group to be able to set the norms of behavior and the nature of activity possible within a particular place, it is necessary that it have clear, unquestionable control over what can occur there" (Newman, 1972: 2). Correctional officials, of course, abhor any suggestion that prison residents be given control over the prison. They claim, quite accurately, that many prisons are already under the control of inmates, and with far less than satisfactory results.[5] Prisons, too, are unwilling to set up facilities which "make it possible for both inhabitant and stranger to perceive that an area is under the undisputed influence of a particular group, that they dictate the activity taking place within it, and who its users are to be" (Newman, 1972: 2-3). Present prison philosophy simply does not allow prisoners to have the freedom of action to set up a viable, comfortable, and safe prison community.

Because of the massive size and density of institutions, inmates arrive as strangers, develop a pathological community, and leave embittered, depressed, and no closer as human beings. Indeed, considering the conditions found in most, if not all, U.S. prisons, the development of co-operative communities is extremely unlikely, if not impossible.[6] Nearly every facet of institutional life precludes such a development, and no guarantee exists that simply changing the structure would improve the situation.

## INDEFENSIBLE SPACE AND THE PRESENT SETTING

The facility's design is attractive and built in the best tradition of ranch-style living. The building is located on twenty-one acres of land and is surrounded by green grass and overgrown wooded areas—not at all an unattractive setting (see Figure 14.2). Too, a cottage approach was utilized, moving the design far from that utilized in many detention homes, jails and other penal facilities. The facility is neither multistoried, excessively large, nor open to outside influence. Although its location is symbolic of traditional thinking, the primary concern with the building is its inside construction.

Even though located within the limits of a large city, the plot of land the institution occupies gives the impression of isolation. Much of the surrounding city is not in view because of woods and undeveloped park areas. Some open grass areas separate the facility from the wooded sections, and the visitor feels as though he is a considerable distance from civilization. This feeling is enhanced by the fact that the road to the facility goes through the grounds of one of the state's largest asylums for the mentally ill. The foreboding character of this asylum lends an ominous air to the trip as the visitor realizes that he is passing from the territory of one group of society's deviants to another.

Thus, one of the most serious drawbacks of the facility is the overwhelming aura of stigma associated with its construction. The setting and the institution's security features drive home the point that the residents are different and not to be trusted. With the surrounding fences, locked doors, and barred windows setting off the buildings and residents from those on the outside, the "differentness" of the boys is brutally emphasized. The point is made even more salient when viewing the outside from within. To view the out-of-doors through bars or screens, to have to pass through locked doors whenever going from the individual rooms into the cottages and other sections of the institution, and to have to conduct all sports activities within the boundaries of a high fence and under the watchful eyes of a large number of youth leaders, emphasizes further that the institution is for the criminal.

The isolation of the boys takes on yet another, more extreme form. They are separated not only from any community which will give them support in protecting themselves from aggressors, but from the institutions which give them support as well. The church is only minimally present, in the form of a chaplain who is looked upon as one to be manipulated; the family is absent and unable in most cases to give support even when its members do care; political and economic institutions are segments of a different world and have relevance only in providing the values which motivate youths to acquire all they can when the opportunity arises; the educational institution is present, but constitutes only another boring obstacle for many to tolerate. The only roots the boys have is in the peer hierarchy—no other form of social organization is present to give them the security and protection they so desperately need.

## INDEFENSIBLE AREAS

### Lobby and Hallways

The institution's lobby is the focal point of all who enter or leave, (see Figure 14.1). First off the lobby are administrative offices, a conference room, and rooms in which records are kept. The location of the lobby and administrative offices is excellent from the point of view of keeping the institution secure. Since the youths must pass through the lobby and past the administrative offices to enter or leave, the lobby and front offices act as both a real and a symbolic barrier between the boys and freedom.

Straight ahead from the lobby's entrance is a narrow passage which separates this section of the institution from the residential area. As the youths go through the passage to their living, recreational and educational areas, they must pass through two heavy glass doors electronically operated by a switchboard operator sitting in the lobby reception area. Anyone desiring passage to or from the residential area must ring a buzzer. The switchboard operator then opens the doors.

After going through this passage, the visitor must pass through a

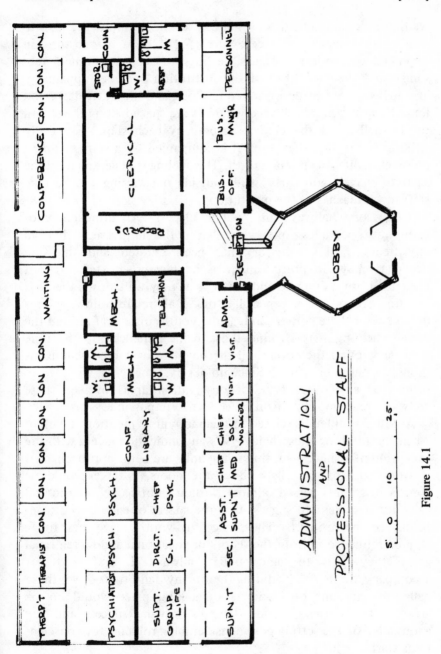

Figure 14.1

waiting area and into a long hallway leading toward the institution's main intersection, (see Figure 14.2).[7] Here, as one turns in
order to get to the cottages, feelings of security immediately
vanish and the "totality" of the institution becomes apparent.[8]
The hallways are made of concrete block and are bare, drab, and
long. Long and narrow barred windows are spaced along the length
of the halls, and the echoes accompany each step.[9] Especially
striking is the fact that, even if accompanied by a staff member,
one feels as if lost in a labyrinth. This feeling is heightened by the
sight of electric golf carts sitting outside the waiting area to take
staff to far reaches of the institution.

These long hallways are "public places." An atmosphere of
anonymity pervades, one which gives the impression that an
unprotected public territory has been entered and that the
occupant may do pretty much as he pleases. If staff are not
present or are trailing behind the boys as they walk down the halls
or turn corners, this is especially true. Staff relate following boys
up to one of these corners and, as the youths disappear around the
corner, hearing fists striking those being harassed. By the time
staff get around the corner, all the boys are in line or walking as
though nothing happened. Since no observation desks, windows in
offices or any other type of observation areas oversee these
hallways, reducing victimization is next to impossible.

Another problem is related to the anonymity mentioned earlier.
At no point along these hallways is any indication given, with the
exception of a single sign, that living units are being approached. If
it were not for the signs above the doors, cottages could be
approached and passed almost without notice. No structural
evidence is present to suggest that the spaces outside the cottages
belong to the residents. Thus, once the youths leave their living
area or return to it from the school or vocational and recreational
areas, they pass through public hallways. If staff did not
accompany these youths during their many daily treks down these
halls, the amount of victimization taking place would be far
greater. The corners, bends, lack of viewing spaces, and the
anonymity of the setting pose considerable problems for conscien-
tious staff.

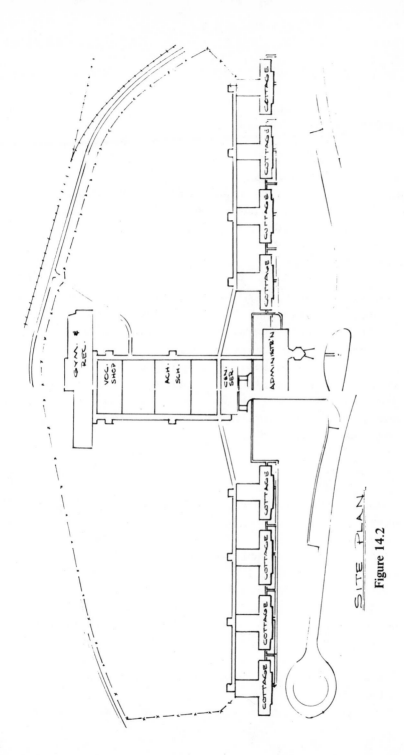

SITE PLAN.

**Figure 14.2**

The Vocational Shop

In this area, equipment, corners, and doorways do not permit surveillance of hidden spaces (see Figure 14.3). Many of these rooms are large and filled with equipment which blocks the view of staff. Smaller rooms adjoining main equipment rooms are difficult to survey visually, and devious activities taking place in them are easily concealed. Although shop officials keep a tight rein on the boys, and few youths are in the shops at one time, passive inmates are sometimes pushed around physically.

The Academic Area

Of major concern here is the lobby between the two corridors passing through the academic area (see Figure 14.4) Examination of this area shows that, with the exception of the doors with windows in them in the classrooms, no supervision of the lobby and the connecting corridors is possible. When the academic personnel's lack of sensitivity to victimization is considered, the extreme dangerousness of the section becomes apparent. Many boys are, indeed, victimized here, as well as in the toilet just off the lobby.

The Recreational Area

The recreational area has two major structural problems, the shower area and the large size of the gym (see Figure 14.5). The shower area reflects a prime example of poor construction, as it contains at least four separate sections. A staff member must be constantly on the move if he is to keep all the boys in sight. The numerous corners make constant supervision impossible and even elimination of the place for baskets has only minimally reduced the problem. The walls surrounding the basket area still remain standing and prevent easy viewing into the shower and boys' restroom. This area is so difficult to keep safe that staff have ceased using it and have the boys take their showers in the cottages.

The gym, on the other hand, is extremely large. Unless the gym

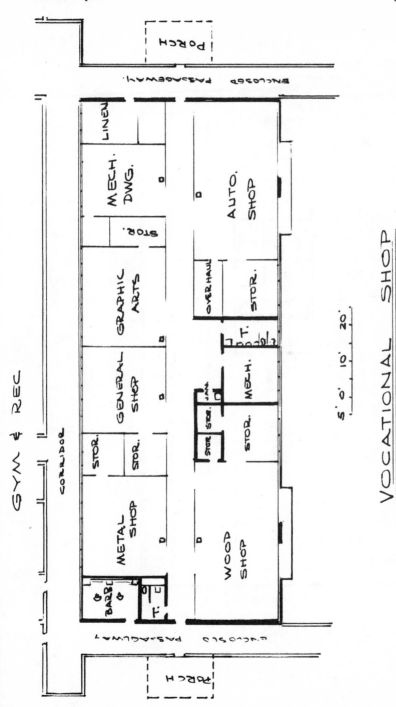

VOCATIONAL SHOP

Figure 14.3

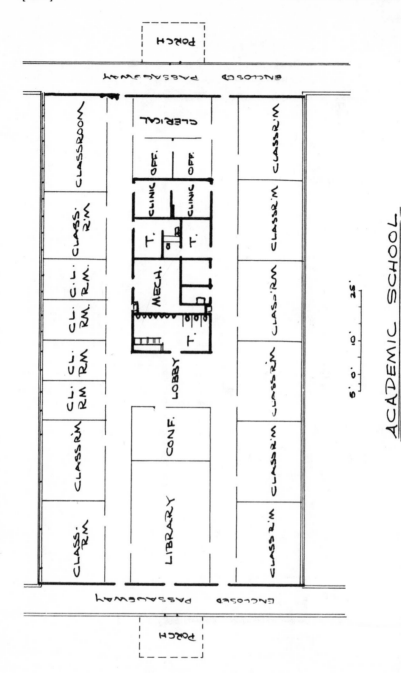

ACADEMIC SCHOOL

Figure 14.4

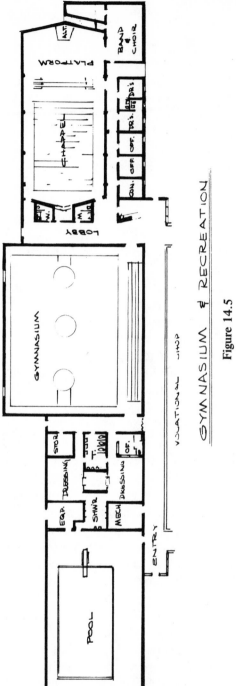

GYMNASIUM & RECREATION

**Figure 14.5**

instructor is exceptionally vigilant, boys on the opposite side of the gym from him are able to get into considerable mischief. A weak gym instructor is practically helpless if a large number of youths are using the facility at one time. While he is at one end of the floor, youths can be taking advantage of a passive peer on the bleachers at the other end.[10]  Or a stronger inmate interested in sexual exploitation can force a passive youth into the hallway leading to the shower area and do what he wants to the weaker youth.

The Chapel Area

One of Newman's points about the willingness of residents and others to take care of hallways defined as an extension of their living areas is dramatically illustrated by the chapel setting. Figure 14.5 also shows the layout of the chapel, which is at the end of the long hallway extending from the passage leading from the main entrance. The folding gate found in Figure 14.5 is usually left open, giving anyone who desires ample opportunity to drop out of view. One small corridor goes off to the right immediately as one passes through the folding gate. It is necessary only to take two steps to the right of the gate opening to disappear from the view of staff in the main hallways or gym.

Newman points out that such concealed halls and indefensible areas quickly become the territory of anyone who enters. The condition of this particular area suggests that few want to spend much time there. On one visit, the floors were dusty and large pieces of plasterboard type of material were scattered along the hall, indicating that staff do not define the section as either desirable or important and, therefore, do not have the youths clean these halls as much as the other floors. The drawbacks of this particular hallway become more apparent as one passes down its length toward the band and choir room. Yet another turn is approached which leads to a door to the outside grounds. This small hallway, too, is dirty and shows little upkeep. In addition, youths apparently discovered this secluded spot long ago. The door to the outside shows signs of tampering, and someone has attempted to force a large cold air screen from one of the walls.

Proceeding straight ahead from the folding gate to the end wall is yet another short hallway leading into the chapel. Thus, another corner is provided which can conceal deviant activity. Another surprise is that the men's and women's restroom doors are occasionally left unlocked. Since no observation or checkpoints exist for staff to control these halls, and since no rooms with observation windows are in these areas, the potential for victimization of the weak or carrying out escape plans is great.

## The Cottages

The long distances from the cottages to the school and other sections of the institution lends to the impersonality of the setting. The cottages are identical in design, emphasizing the routine of the facility, and the fact that all of the boys are considered alike (see Figure 14.6).[11] With all the cottages built the same way, a sameness pervades the units and infuses the feeling that one really has nothing to defend as one's own.

The program (recreation, dining, and living) area is easily supervised by youth leaders and the social worker watching through large picture windows enclosing their offices. Still, this room has structural problems, the first being the kitchen. The kitchen is simply a cement block room with only a door and a serving window through which observation might be impossible. The door, moreover, is on the wrong side of the room for surveillance from the staff offices, and the serving window is usually closed. Even if open, these do not permit easy viewing because of the angles, size and elevation involved. Subsequently, youths working in the kitchen can easily take advantage of others. A second problem is the corner of the youth leader's office nearest the dining area. This corner is made of concrete blocks and is approximately two and one-half by three feet on two sides. A desk placed anywhere in the office loses visibility of certain parts of the program area. The boys recognize this fact, and many, in fact, use this corner as a shield from observation. They stand on the side opposite from the staff, leaning against the corner.

The corridor leading to the single rooms and four-bed dormitories shares many of the features of the major enclosed

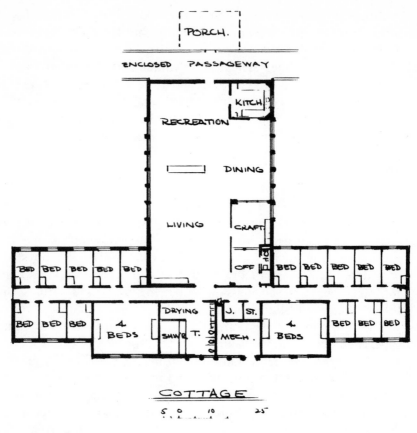

**Figure 14.6**

passageways.[12] In spite of the fact that the offices are enclosed with glass, surveillance down the corridor is impossible for more than a few feet. Staff can see just slightly past the door to the nearest four-bed dormitory door—if they get as close to the corner of the office as possible. The view in the other direction toward the toilet and shower area is also limited.

Examination of the single and four-bed dormitories shows them to contain other elements of indefensibility. The windows in the doors of these rooms, for instance, are only about four by six inches, simply not large enough to allow staff full view of the room. In some cases, the glass has been broken out, and weak staff must be careful that they are not grabbed or punched through the broken window. The small size of the window prevents examination of the room's corners and the defensibility of the four-bed dormitories is especially open to question. The single rooms are so small that a boy who wants to harm himself or barricade himself in his room finds the task rather easy. All he has to do is place his bed, chair, or other cottage materials in front of the door, effectively blocking the entrance.

It is not difficult, finally, to understand why the toilet and shower area are the most difficult areas to police. Boys can hide around the corner of the door in the toilet area and right up next to the last washbasin. Staff coming down the hall are unable to see a youth standing there unless they actually look around the door frame. In addition, even though the door to the drying room is kept locked, staff must be particularly vigilant once the youths are allowed in the showers. A staff member standing at the door to the toilet could easily miss exploitation taking place around the double set of corners. Even though a viewing window is placed around the double set of corners. Even though a viewing window is placed in the wall between the drying area and the shower, exploitation is possible if someone is not standing right in the window observing the boys.

The single rooms in which the boys sleep are places where youths are put on maximum restriction as well—not necessarily places where the boys may retreat to gain security and privacy. The windows in the boys' rooms do not allow much outdoor viewing, nor does the window in the door contribute to the feeling that the hallways are an extension of the territory represented by the rooms.[13] All windows are barred. For all practical purposes, nothing gives the boys a feeling of homeliness or security.

Finally, with none of the boys' living spaces defined as their own, with no extension of their rooms emphasizing that they have a right to privacy and safety, and with what space they do have being a battleground on which others attempt to take their goods, no area in the cottages or institution exudes the feeling that it may be approached with safety. Neither their rooms nor the cottage program area, the hallways beyond the cottages, the school or vocational areas, nor the front offices housing institutional officials offer the youths the hope of achieving either security or safety. Even if aware of its possibility and the ways to implement it, the very important goal of "self-help" is impossible for the boys to achieve. They have been forced to surrender all shared social responsibilities to parents, police, judges, youth leaders and their stronger peers for so long that the conceptualization of any other style of life no longer seems plausible (Newman, 1972: 11-12).

## SEXUAL EXPLOITATION

Somewhat predictably, the nature of victimization varies according to the section of the institution. The lack of surveillance and the hidden nature of the spaces described in the last section affect whether boys are forced into sexual activities. In order of decreasing frequency, the following are the areas where sexual exploitation takes place: single rooms and shower area of the cottages; the recreational and educational areas; last, the vocational area.

### Single Room and Shower

Surprisingly, little sexual exploitation takes place within the four-bed dormitories. Staff are quite aware of the possibility of sexual activity taking place here, and they keep a close watch on the dorms' inhabitants. Weak youths, in addition, are put into single rooms at the earliest opportunity as a protective measure— the staff then assume they are safe. Unfortunately, this assumption is not always correct, as weaker boys are occasionally accosted in their own or someone else's room. Aware of this possibility, experienced staff make every effort to prevent boys from going to their rooms alone. Inexperienced or busy staff, nevertheless, often forget to keep a close watch, and attacks do take place.

The shower area, because the boys are undressed, is an especially high-risk area. Sexual activity takes only a very short time, particularly under these circumstances. Again, experienced staff are well aware of the potential danger to weak youths and, therefore, stand at the shower door, allowing only one or two youths to enter at a time.

The toilet too is a high-risk location. Boys on the program area take advantage of the fact that staff often forget that another youth was just granted permission to go to the bathroom and request to go themselves. Or, even if staff do remember that another youth was granted permission to leave the program area, it is easier to forget to check on what is happening.

Recreational Area

Once outside the cottages, the recreational area is the most likely place for sexual exploitation to transpire. Supervision is not as tight, and boys are exploited particularly often in the shower area. As noted, staff now have the boys take showers back in their cottages. In this section of the facility, then, ample opportunity exists for assaulting peers verbally and physically. During warm-ups and moments between play, for example, inmates from all over the institution come together for recreation. Being together, combined with the relative lack of supervision, means that peers who are safe in cottages may now be exploited, and their aggressors can very likely escape punishment.

Educational Area

The amount of exploitation taking place in the educational section is very close to and may equal that taking place in the recreational area. Supervision, again, is the basic reason. Staff in the school are not as experienced as are those in the cottages and are not as sensitized to the dynamics of exploitation. Since the image of the educational area does not include exploitation, staff further are not on guard and leave youths by themselves. Many teachers in this area—men as well as women—are afraid of the boys, and in fact, are unable to control them physically.

Of major importance in the school area is harassment by "booty bandits," who call peers names or grab them in an effort to set them up for sexual exploitation. Even though the grabbed youth may not know who did it in the crowded hallway or lobby, it is still part of the exploitation process. In this area, too, mass sexual attacks occasionally take place.

One youth, for instance, was ordered by several others to masturbate them while the teacher was still present in the room. Unable to do anything about it, the teacher stood by, permitting the group masturbation. In another situation, the teacher was ordered to leave the room while one youth was compelled to commit oral sodomy for other boys. In still another incident, a college female was visiting a class, and when she went outside the classroom for a cigarette, she was attacked by several inmates. It took a valiant effort by school personnel to avert a rape.

## NONSEXUAL EXPLOITATION

Nonsexual as well as sexual exploitation takes place in all areas of the institution, and in the following order of decreasing frequency: cottages, and educational, vocational and recreational areas.

### Cottages

Most nonsexual exploitation transpires in the cottages where the boys keep their material goods. Cigarettes, food, and clothes are the major items taken, while other possessions (such as radios, shaving lotion, and facial soap) are occasionally "borrowed." Because most material exploitation is considered minor by staff, staff show little concern when boys lose their possessions.

### Educational Area

The major form of nonsexual exploitation in the educational areas concerns cigarettes. The weakness of teachers results in the taking of cigarettes with impunity in the classrooms and halls. Verbal and physical attacks are commonplace; more fights, in fact, take place in the school area than in all others combined.

Vocational Area

Even though some taking of personal possessions such as cigarettes transpires here, the most serious nonsexual exploitation involves stronger inmates forcing weaker ones into taking contraband out of the shop, usually for the purpose of escaping. Hacksaw blades, screwdrivers, and saws are all smuggled out of the shops by intimidated boys. In a recent incident, a weak inmate smuggled a screwdriver out of the woodshop to aid a potential escapee. He was told that if he did not, he would be beaten.

Recreational Area

Other than sexual victimization in the shower, the most that usually happens on the recreational program is the "beating on" and verbal abuse of the weaker boys to set them up for further exploitation. In addition to this verbal and physical harassment, many fights take place here. Youths are constantly trying to improve their "reps" by fighting. Some fights are between equals, jockeying for top positions in the cottage. Other fights are between those unequal in size and represent the strong exploiting the weak.

## CONCLUSIONS

It is obvious in this institution that the residents are not able to "perceive and control all activity taking place within it" (Newman, 1972: 4). These boys clearly do not have to worry about outsiders taking advantage of them, but the major concern is with those within the institution. Much of the victimization that does transpire takes place in public areas that are hidden from view. Values of the present milieu keep residents from helping newcomers, keep inmates from questioning illegal activities, and also keep them from coming to the assistance of those in need. The boys quickly learn to be detached from practically all that is happening unless it pertains either to themselves or to a close friend.

Admittedly, a basic change in the construction of this institution would entail certain risks, and a number of dilemmas would remain even if the physical plant was modified. The greatest risk is that changes in physical structure would be made without careful attention to the attitudes, values, traditions, and social structures of the inmate and staff world.[14] The way the inmate world is presently structured, to decrease staff surveillance would be to expose the weak to every whim of the strong.

## NOTES

1. In the following discussion on indefensible spaces, the authors generally are referring to structural and ecological problems which diminish the boys' abilities to defend themselves from their peers. A number of structural elements, however, also keep the staff from effectively protecting the boys. Both of these features are discussed in this chapter.

2. Newman's book focuses on the rather typical high-rise apartments found in our cities, but many of his principles may be applied with equal facility to correctional settings.

3. A number of parallels may be found between a city and this facility. First, many disadvantaged youths live next to those who have all they need. Second, all inhabitants are in milieus in which third parties are in positions of formal authority. With only two youth leaders watching these boys at a time, the boys are granted considerable anonymity in their behaviors. Also, officials are able to keep only small segments of behavior under surveillance. Third, hidden places allow criminal or forbidden behavior to transpire unobserved. Fourth, as boys and staff do not trust each other, they withdraw further and further from mutual interaction. Fifth, informal codes do not reinforce the idea that boys should go out of their way to stop undesirable activities. Sixth, all but the most flagrant violation of the law or rules are ignored.

4. Although some jails, detention homes, and prisons are multistoried and, therefore, approximate the conditions found in certain housing projects, few, if any, come close to six stories in height, a point at which Newman feels the character of the units changes so as to make the buildings even more indefensible. Height, however, is not the only determining factor.

5. To simply allow prisoners to assume control would constitute a disaster. Values, traditions, and philosophies would have to be developed and ongoing in a prison before Newman's ideas would have a chance of succeeding. Under the present system, this will probably never occur.

6. Many prisons, detention homes, and other juvenile facilities continue to be built with the idea of further segregating the inmates and placing them in cells, along impersonal hallways, and in large rooms devised for the handling of masses of anonymous humanity. No serious attempt is made to develop a genuinely livable and healthy environment.

7. Often, some type of activity is taking place in the waiting area. A secretary may be behind the desk, or youth leaders may be talking and bantering good naturedly. Boys

sometimes are being prepared for or returning from home visits in this area. However, with the exception of certain times of the day when there is no activity, the visitor feels secure. The presence of staff officers and the fact that the visitor is usually easily visible to any staff who are in the halls is quite comforting. Unfortunately, staff offices on either side of the waiting area have large picture windows only on the side facing the small hallways, and not on the side facing the waiting area. Were windows present which allowed staff full view of this entrance area, the feeling of security would be enhanced. If no staff are to be found in the small hallways to the left and right of the waiting area, the visitor feels very alone indeed.

8. The barriers that exist are quite obvious and consist of locked doors and barred windows. Less obvious is the fact that the walls of the cottages act as one side of the hallways and the other side consists of the barrier to the outside of the institution. As mentioned previously, the only way these hallways are used are as paths to other areas of the institution. They are identified by the name of streets in the city. The doors along the hallways are always locked and the person walking along them does not feel as though he has anyplace to go.

9. The only function of the hallways is to allow for the passage of people and keeping them protected from inclement weather. The hallways are not constructed to provide the clients with a sense of security or the feeling that viable community living is possible within them. No thought was given in the basic design to the impression the hallways make on the occupants and visitors. The primary concern of the architect was "the effect the individual unit will have in giving form to the building as seen from the outside. The relationship of individual units to one another and the provision of functionally useful and shared space at each level become secondary considerations" (Newman, 1972: 59).

10. While the instructor is at one end of the floor, youths may be at the other end on the bleachers, straining at the screens, hoping to weaken them so that escape may be possible later. Or boys may be able to slip into the hallways leading back to the chapel or to the shower room and take advantage of their disappearance from view.

11. The doors to the cottages are made of metal and are heavy. In the center of each door is a narrow vertical window, which, even if broken, is too narrow for all but the smallest youth to wriggle through. It should be noted, too, that the smallness of the window prohibits easy viewing either of what is going on in the hallway or, conversely, of what is happening in the cottage. Since defensible space requires visibility for the area to be protected, these windows do little to protect those in the halls.

12. Once the boy leaves the room, he is expected to move quickly to adjoining areas, treating the transition space as something to be passed through quickly.

13. The texture of the floor and walls remains the same regardless of where the boys go in the institution and the cottages. No special lamps, name plates, or other signs of occupancy are found. Also nothing breaks up the hallways to define them in even a limited fashion as belonging to one or another of the cottages.

14. The boys enter this facility with a lack of understanding of many of the social amenities which make genuine community living possible. Nothing may be found which gives them an idea of how that type of living may be achieved. Too, the only tradition found is that of institutional and staff rules, and the rules of the strong; there is nothing of the kind of rules found in normal community living. Everything the boys experience in relation to their institutional living is new and seldom corresponds with their experiences of the past.

# PART V

# CONCLUSIONS

*CHAPTER 15*

## CONCLUSIONS

**This is certainly not** the first, nor is it likely to be the last, in a long series of books, monographs, and articles which indict the juvenile correctional system as anti-therapeutic, anti-rehabilitative, and as exploitative and demeaning of keepers and kept alike. The juvenile correctional institution, not unlike every other type of total institution, is or can be far more cruel and inhumane than most outsiders ever imagine. The dynamic of a large juvenile correctional institution is not the inverse of the real, the outside world. In that both indigenous and imported patterns combine, the juvenile institution is a culmination of the worst features of a free society. If the concentration camp exaggerated the "sickness unto death" of Nazi Germany; a Siberian labor camp, the vicissitudes of life in the Soviet utopia; then the juvenile institution, the fortress prison, the mental hospital, the institute for the mentally defective, and the geriatric center define the current wisdom and conceptions of the management and control of deviant, dependent, and disruptive members in American life. Far from being a deviant social organization, the total institution, whatever its specific clientele of losers, reflects and embellishes the motifs of our era and the value priorities of the social system. If sociological concern with "nuts, sluts, and perverts," to borrow a handy phrase, seems extreme, it must be emphasized that insight and penetration into any social system can best be achieved at the margin. What we take for granted is much more significant than what we dispute. And what we now take as a given is a system of criminal justice and corrections which is all too often unjust and rarely corrective.

This book is concerned with a microcosmic view of the macro juvenile correctional system. We have tried to dissect, digest, organize, analyze, and understand the inner workings of what outwardly appears to be a fine, modern, humane, well-kept, well-staffed juvenile training school. Its residents are hard-core offenders who, because of their offenses or adjustment problems elsewhere in the system, are transferred or sent directly to this juvenile institution. We have been studying this training school since its formal dedication. It is close to the Ohio State University campus, and the various Ohio Youth Commission directors, their superintendents, and their chiefs of research and staff have been open and forthcoming, even eager, for Reckless and Dinitz and their students to examine and evaluate *every* facet of institutional life and to make policy and practice recommendations. In fairness, the latter, it should be noted, were more often disregarded than implemented through the years.

Various specific research interests prompted the present effort and make this book on inmate and staff exploitation unusually pertinent. First, we have been deeply involved in so-called "impact" studies for many years. These investigations have attempted to determine who, if anyone, benefits from incarceration, and which variables, among the many which can be assessed, determine the nature of institutional impact. Sociodemographic, juvenile history, psychological profile, psychiatric assessment and other systematically gathered data have all been used. They have been analyzed in conjunction with program participation information, staff evaluations, resident perceptions, peer assessment, and other subjective ratings as independent and intervening variables, singly and in clusters, and in how they influence positive or negative institutional impact. The sad fact emerging from these studies has been the absence of significant attitudinal and perceptual changes in the residents. Their self-concepts continue to stamp them as chronic losers and as candidates for further juvenile court appearances and criminal sanctions. Our consistent and disheartening array of negative results fully support the growing body of findings on the ineffectiveness of correctional treatment. It is now all too obvious that not even a dedicated staff, a low resident-staff ratio, an excellent physical plant, and a client-centered orientation are sufficient to offset prior experience and the general anti-therapeutic effects of coercive treatment.

In addition to impact research, careful and systematic studies have been conducted on institutional outcome. In one such investigation, 443 consecutive training school releases have been tracked to determine their community adjustment (Miller, 1971). Depending on the time period of follow-up, the recidivism rates of former residents increase with number of years after discharge—hardly a novel finding. Again, various independent variables were related to outcome without substantial predictive improvement or the identification of patterns of success and failure. This follow-up effort is now in its seventh year (the actual study began 14 years ago) and the known recidivism rates have been: at time of release from parole, 18 percent; 1.8 years after the last boy was released, 40 percent; 4 years after release, approximately 54 percent.

A third series of investigations focused on various aspects of stigma. For many years, the Training Institute of Central Ohio not only tagged each resident with an identification number but, based on the intake workup and prior personal and social problems, appended a suffix after his number when applicable. Two suffixes were commonly affixed. The first, an "R", signified that the resident was tough, aggressive and a real or potential management problem. (Often "Rs" were extremely *macho.*) The second, an "E" suffix, labelled the resident as a "kook" or, at the very least, as being in need of special mental health attention. Apart from the double stigma involved (adjudicated delinquent plus management problem and hyperaggressive or emotionally disturbed), a problem which long piqued our moral sensibilities and concern, the forty percent labelled "R" or "E" also suffered institutional and other disabilities. For example, no resident could be released until he was cleared of his suffix by a psychiatrist—a requirement which usually added at least three months to his institutional stay. In addition, followup research indicated that the "R" residents (not enough "Es" were available to reach any definitive conclusions) actually had *lower* recidivism rates than the general population of releasees (Miller, 1971). Thus, the training school provided a natural (noncontrived) setting for observing and evaluating the labelling process and its personal (self-concept), institutional (on staff, on interaction, on structure) and post-institutional consequences (community adjustment).

Indeed, the "R" and "E" suffixes provide one of the clearest vantage points from which to observe decision-making and the use of discretion by "team" professionals. Such labels imply a conception of dangerousness, maladaptation, character disorder, and potential disruptiveness which, once applied, cannot be erased from the minds of the recipients, staff, or peers even when the labels are expunged from the case folders. Sadly, one can never again be free of the additional stigma once the label has been attached. There are many ex-"R" or ex-"E" juveniles and adults around; there are no ex-ex-"Rs" or "Es" however.

The fourth issue which prompted this understanding was the acute problem of runaways. Although the actual number of escapees was and is small, the location of the institution, near the heart of the city, an unfavorable local press calling for ever greater security, and an understandably squeamish staff, especially in the central office, made it mandatory that the escapee problem be solved. This raised the inevitable question, "Why do some of these institution-wise boys, knowing the consequences [considerable additional time to serve] and often with little time left to serve, attempt to run?" In investigating this phenomenon, it became obvious that institutional exploitation and victimization made escaping the only feasible alternative available for these escape-prone youths. In many ways, the study of the runaway problem was the direct precipitator of this study on institutional exploitation and victimization and its consequences.

The juvenile training schools, even the largest ones, are unique, housing the as yet young losers in life. Their internal structure and organization has never ceased to arouse sociological interest. From Clemmer and Sykes to Heffernan and Gialombardo, the penal institution has been dissected like a cadaver in a morgue. No organ, no angle, no aspect has defied scrutiny and commentary. The net result of these analyses has been a literature which has hardened attitudes toward the institution as a snake pit; as a demonic invention conceived with the best of intentions but which, like so many other innovations grounded in the blind zeal of reformers, turn out to be as bad as or worse than the practices they replace. The pendulum has swung to the point that modern reformers—both lay and professional—would demolish the institution stone by stone. There is, of course, justifiable criticism of a system in which, as one prison physician testified in 1975, only a very few of the many thousands of inmates he examined had not been physically cut, beaten, stabbed, raped, or otherwise brutalized by other inmates and by staff. There is justifiable criticism of a social creation which makes people more maladaptive—or certainly no less so—after serving time than before their incarceration. There is justifiable criticism of the futility of what passes for treatment, of the tremendous discretion exercised by the few keepers and correlative powerlessness, rage and despair of the kept, of the emergence of counter cultures, and of the brutalization and hardening of all but a small minority of personnel and inmates.

Finally, there is justifiable criticism of a system which engenders the formation of the contraband gangs, sex gangs, drug gangs, and machine gun gangs that are found in our adult penal institutions. These gangs have made many institutions so dangerous they are closed to outside visitors. Juvenile facilities may not have all these features at present, but if the youths adopt them, as they do so many other adult behaviors, the future is indeed bleak.

But despite these well-documented criticisms and poignant personal accounts of life behind all too many of the walls, the population in our juvenile and adult penal institutions bottomed out several years ago and is again on a steep upward rise. Far from fading away, the correctional facility thrives and expands, an ever-present reminder of the failure of ideas and the muddled thinking about effective substitutes.

## RECAPITULATION AND DISCUSSION

In focusing on the exploitation matrix as a singularly important phenomenon in institutional life, we used every conceivable technique available to us. One of us had been a wing director, youth leader, and social worker at the institution and, in these capacities, was constantly involved with every facet of its administration and daily activities. He had complete access to staff and inmate records and reports, and somehow, despite his position and power, was defined as one of the "good" guys in the institution by most segments of the training school community. A former minister, long distance runner (he honed his skill and lowered his cross-country time chasing runaways), and counter culturalist, he had credentials to suit nearly every element in the training school. His former position and the trust and rapport he had earned facilitated our obtaining cooperation in the more objective methods used in the study. He also was able to conduct lengthy, detailed, and no-holds-barred talks with staff at all levels. Considering the substance of these talks, it is doubtful that anyone who inspired less than total confidence could have elicited these observations.

Apart from participant observation, involvement in the institution, lengthy interviews, and direct observations of interaction among the residents, we also utilized other techniques to complete the picture. These included the construction and the administration of a schedule for each cottage containing each boy's name in that cottage in alphabetical order. This schedule asked all youth leaders and social workers to rate each resident in the cottage on an exploitation continuum dealing with everything from food, commissary items, cigarettes, and packages from home to sexual activity. This schedule was supplemented by interviews with residents, these being by far the least reliable of our techniques.

In addition, every resident was administered a test battery consisting of the following specific tests:

(1) The Gough Adjective Checklist
(2) The Machover Draw-a-Figure Test
(3) The Jesness Personality Inventory

These psychological tests were administered in each cottage to all the residents. The Machover drawings were scored by Professor Franco Ferracuti at the University of Rome without any knowledge of the exploitation status of any respondent. The other psychological tests were scored routinely and again without knowledge of or reference to the exploitation-victimization status of the respondent.

Finally, data were collected on each youth's criminal history, sociodemographic characteristics, physical attribute, age, diagnosis, "R" or "E" status, other psychological test scores, institutional adjustment, and other more or less standard case folder information. We were very nearly inundated with scores, profiles, histories, assessments, interview tapes, incident reports, and just plain sociodemographic data. The processing of all this material to construct a faithful moasic, translate observations, and convey the sense of life and reality that is the training school was our most difficult task. How does one describe an interactional encounter in which one of the participants is deemed so unclean (having been made that way by those who perceived him so negatively) that he cannot work in any capacity in the food service facility? How does one describe the making and undoing of a newcomer? Or the creation of a heavy? Or the adjustments of staff and residents to the use of force, leverage—even blackmail—as an integral part of everyday life? How does one penetrate the system and elaborate the "it goes without saying" standards, norms, and patterns? Finally, how is one to integrate, synthesize, and portray the organization and structure of the training school and at the same time incorporate the needs, feelings, fears, and hopes of the several hundred people who live and work within its confines? The social scientist can describe and analyze; the novelist can portray and depict. Compared to the latter, the former seems sterile. Compared to the former, the latter seems idiosyncratic.

And so, using the tools at our command, we tried to both describe and quantify the inner workings of institutional life and the very real actors in the unfolding and changing drama. Our findings suggest that exploitation and victimization, like the deprivation of freedom and the other pains of punishment, are inherent aspects of institutional life. At least ninety percent of all the residents can be located at some point on the exploitation-victimization dimension. There are few eyewitnesses to the dynamics of what we have referred to as the exploitation matrix. To put it another way, exploiting or being victimized or doing both in different interactions is one of the "problems of living" as a delinquent ward of the state. To survive, one must make some kind of adaptation to being used or using others. In extreme cases, suicide, drugs, or an escape attempt are the only plausible solutions.

Exploitation-victimization arises out of interaction and, as such, is a complex phenomenon to study. In institutions, it is buttressed by norms and values and is supported by tacit staff approval. Indeed, staff is frequently involved, usually on the exploitation rather than the victimization end. However, to "keep the peace" and maintain some kind of control, the cottage staff, in particular, may use the exploiters to maintain law, order, and tranquility. Staff becomes, consciously or through drift, in the Matza sense, a party to the elaborate social system of exploitation.

There are considerable cottage and ecological variations within the training school which modify the ways the exploitation system works. In a cottage of relative newcomers, the older hands have prime targets. Add a strong, capable, and caring cadre of institution-wise cottage parents and the situation may alter drastically. Thus, while institutional and resident and even staff values support the exploitation system as normal and natural—even beneficial— the actual dynamics depend on a great many other variables, including the sociodemographic, leadership style, release policies, and openness of the institution to the community (home leave and visiting policies).

A few specific findings should be highlighted, although, to a degree, they have been subsumed in our more general discussion. These results include:

1. Most victimizations, within no less than outside the institution, involve the appropriation of property. Personal events are far less common. The rarest of all is sexual molestation, an area which has been explored in the criminological literature wholly out of proportion to its known prevalence. Nevertheless, this most demeaning and lurid of all forms of inmate victimization is a good index of the nature and quality of life in any penal setting. It tells us a great deal about the overall exploitation patterns, the organization, and the leadership of a juvenile correctional facility that is normally hidden from even the most perceptive of observers.

2. With regard, then, to sexual assaults on unwilling inmates, the results suggest that:

   (a) whites are victimized by blacks out of all proportion to the relative number of each;
   (b) after the whites, the weaker blacks are the next most frequently abused group;

(c) lower-class youths prey on the far less defensible and institution-wise middle- or lower-middle-class residents;

(d) as regards mental status, victimization describes a U-shaped curve. The more normal (on psychological tests) the resident, the greater the likelihood of being exploited; similarly, the mildly disturbed are also preyed upon more often than chance would dictate;

(e) normal or sick, black or white, lower- or lower-middle-class, prison-ized or newcomer, the sexually violated are accorded a pariah status by both inmates and staff—a status not dissimilar from that of a female rape victim, except for its much greater intensity and ines-capability in the confines of a closed social setting. It is extremely difficult to grasp the meaning of such a status for the incumbent. To be an outsider among outsiders, stigmatized among the labelled, is an irony which begs a novelist's touch.

3. Not only are inmates exploited in a definable pattern, but for organizational reasons, among others, staff members are also victimized in the various games that inmates play. In Chapter 11 we described some of these games, including physical, psycho-logical, theological, therapeutic, and educational cons. We indi-cated that the residents generally can run games more easily on the middle-class staff oriented to rehabilitation than with the hard-nosed types, who but for the grace of God, would themselves have been incarcerated. The closed social system and the front office pressure for peace and quiet give the non-treatment-oriented, lower-class staff the upper hand in these daily transactions. Tough inmates, though, can sometimes control staff regardless of the social class of the staff.

4. Like the residents, staff range from the exploiters to the victimized and are found at various intermediate points along the spectrum. One thing is certain—good intentions are no match for knowing and using the pressure points in the system to one's advantage. This is a fundamental principle understood by staff bent on exploitation.

5. At the sublest level, inmates signal or cue each other, and the personnel as well, concerning their accessibility. These cues are then tested in ritualistic and sometimes even in chance encounters. The results of this testing leads to the sorting of the inmates into the various exploitation-victimization categories as well as defining their social roles and status in the inmate social structure. Except for a few residents on either end of the spectrum, this testing and

jockeying is continuous, since the intake-release cycle compels persistent re-evaluation of self to others.

6. Resident victimization is facilitated by the diagnostic processing and labels, psychiatric and institutional, affixed to the residents' dossiers and to them as people. As noted above, the organization protects itself from the pressures of the community by labelling some residents with an "R" suffix (dangerous), or an "E" suffix (emotionally disturbed). Other jackets contain such diagnoses as character disorder, sociopath, chronically antisocial, and similar notations. Some residents are, therefore, already confirmed in their toughness, and their preying on weaker inmates is merely an extension of their disorder. In the argot of the school, no one is going to "mess him over"—not even the staff. Other groups are categorically available for "messing over" and institutional and personal expectations, in this regard, are rarely unfulfilled. This is a concrete illustration of the self-fulfilling prophecy; of the effectiveness of stigma in promoting exploitation and a pecking order within the institution.

7. We have already called attention to the enormous suffering and trauma inherent in the exploitation system. Under extreme circumstances, running away, attempts at suicide and resorting to drugs are the only remedies available—and these are invariably counter-productive. There is no strategy which is adaptive and surely none which is therapeutic or rehabilitative.

8. The literature, even predating Clemmer, is full of descriptions and references to inmate social types and the inmate code. Some of these social types have been given fancy names—the square john, the right guy, the jive butch—and their roles and symbiotic relationships carefully detailed. The overarching point is that each type or subtype is bound by and to a consensually derived inmate code which is functional for all in that it stands in total opposition to institutional values and norms.

This study suggests most emphatically that the inmate code is *not* functional for all or even most residents. It is obviously detrimental for the weak and beleaguered and works mostly to the advantage of the strong and aggressive. The inmate code, like the criminal code, favors the top dogs in the system. There is, in fact, no simple justice in the inmate social system—and undoubtedly far less justice and humanity than in the larger social system.

9. Similarly, the staff code, written and unwritten, militates against effective rehabilitation. Worse, it sets the parameters for but does not preclude staff exploitation of inmates.

The staff code inevitably tends to place a premium on stability, not change; on holding the fort, not storming the ramparts; on avoiding trouble, not making it. Like the residents, staff want to do easy time. To achieve this goal, staff create a gulf between themselves and the residents and use the latter to control the cottages, grounds, activities, and the integrity of the institution. A few inmate toughs and their henchmen can do this job for the staff. In return, these "heavies," to use the training school argot, are granted certain personal privileges as well as considerable leeway in their "management" policies—a cruel system, perhaps, but wholly rational in the context in which it exists. Add only the special needs of some of the self-selected staff members, and all the ingredients exist for the maintenance of the exploitation system. All who can are allowed to prey on those who cannot; even the latter may find a few on whom they, too, can prey.

10. In recent years, solo "gorillas" and exploiters, as well as their victims, have come to reflect less their individual problems and needs than the social unrest of our times. While gangs inside the walls have always existed, the current situation is qualitatively different in at least one significant respect: Predators and victims and those between now represent the fruit of group conflict in the streets. The former are frequently black, as noted, and the latter white. It is permissible, we think, to talk of the exploitation-victimization spectrum in social groups rather than in the physical, psychological, experimental terms of the past.

Since the staff is overwhelmingly black, the dynamics of the system are very different than is the case at an Attica or other adult maximum security penal setting in which staff is usually rural whites, and inmates ghetto blacks, Chicanos, and American Indians. The staff code, predicated on traditional distinctions, is inadequate and ineffective at the juvenile institution studied. The special problems faced by a black cottage staff member are not very unusual, but they do create new dynamics of institutional life. The same problems of dissonance in enforcing traditional criminal justice statutes bedevil the black policeman in an urban ghetto and, to a lesser degree, the black truant officer in a black school. This dissonance has been studied in the policeman but the marginal role and status of the black correctional officer has yet to be researched and its consequences elaborated.

The staff code governs the extent to which black or white officers and overseers can exploit youths under their supervision. Unless these unwritten standards are narrowed, residents will be victimized not only by their peers but by those on the staff who are in a position to exercise their will on their charges.

In contrast, effective, involved staff are the major deterrents to the jungle-like atmosphere with its so well disguised cosmetic effect of beautiful buildings, well-kept grounds, well-dressed residents, and private school ambience. Like much else in this world, the appearance of the institution belies its reality. The appearance conveys an excellent impression to strangers and visitors. Perhaps its therapeutic or rehabilitative effect would not improve markedly if the disparity between appearance and reality decreased through greater staff accountability and better administrative monitoring and practices.

Throughout this research investigation, various paradoxes in institutional life, organization, and management, and particularly in the exploitation-victimization spectrum, became increasingly evident. These paradoxes affect the operation of the juvenile correctional institution to the point that they demand satisfactory resolution by the correctional community. It is for this reason, and in furtherance of correctional reform, that we conclude this volume by calling attention to just a very few of the many paradoxes currently characteristic of the training school in the urban, highly industrial states, and very likely, throughout the country.

1. Sociological theories of deviance have imprinted upon us the perspective that deviants are produced by social processing; that the agencies of social control and not the behavior (which may be transitory and nonrecurrent) stabilize the deviance and create the negative societal responses to those so labelled. Tannenbaum, Becker, Cicourel, Scheff, to name a few major proponents of the labelling perspective, have implicitly or explicitly indicted the system for creating the stigma and then acting on the stigma as the reality. Goffman and Garfinkel have talked eloquently (and correctly) of spoiled identity and ceremonies of degradation. Indeed,

there are few who would dispute the principles and consequences stipulated by the labelling school.

The training school receives the worst of the labelled—the losers, the unwanted, the outsiders. These young men consider themselves to be among the toughest, most masculine and virile of their counterparts and they have the societal credentials to prove it. Yet in much the same way that they themselves were processed, they create, import, and maintain a system which is as brutalizing as the one through which they passed. If anything, the internal environment and the organization and interaction at TICO are less fair, less just, less humane, and less decent than the worst aspects of the criminal justice system on the outside. Brute force, manipulation, institutional sophistication carry the day, and set the standards which ultimately prevail. Remove the staff, and a feudal structure will emerge which will make the dark ages seem very enlightened. In viewing the prospects, one almost is pushed to the Hobbesian position; surely there is little to be said for the Enlightenment thinkers with regard to the nature of the human character.

To reiterate, socially and often seriously and irreversibly defined juvenile pariahs on the outside inflict considerable brutality on the inside. One can argue the explanation of this paradox—institutions cause this brutalization, or brutal men eventually create a brutal institution, or both. But the fact remains that some of the cottages are worse than the streets; that some of the strong in the streets become the meek in the institution; that the juvenile correctional institution is a misnomer, as is the industrial school, the training school, the adjustment center. All are euphemisms. No matter how pleasant the place may seem, very little correction, training, or adjustment occurs—or can, in fact, occur under present circumstances and social policies.

2. In the same paradoxical sense that many of the dangerous, tough delinquents (so labelled by the courts) become the meek and doubly or triply stigmatized, through a process of transformation which we have tried to understand and report, institutional life also presents another major paradox. This deals with the inversion of black-white relationships.

On the outside, whites are almost inevitably in superordinate roles and blacks in the inferior ones. "Black is beautiful" is a great slogan. But from toys to heroes, housing, jobs, health, morbidity, relative income, or any other hard or soft measure, the world is white. Black and white alike adjust as best they can to their fate, painful and degrading or privileged as it may be.

Inside the cottages and corridors, however, the values and norms, privileges and high statuses, preferred roles and inmate power reside in the black and not the white community. Interestingly—and as we have indicated before—neither community has adapted to this role and status reversal; neither knows quite how to relate to the other or to their mutual dissonance problems. Add to this situation both a cottage and treatment staff which is overwhelmingly black, and desperately eager to eliminate all vestiges of racism (in this case, the underdog status of the whites who constitute nearly but not quite half the residents) and the irony of the predicament is evident.

To a sensitive visitor, the blackness of the institution—the food, the music, the argot, the body gesture communication—all derive from the ghetto culture which predominates. Probing more deeply, as we have tried to do, compels the conclusion that power and status, in fact, reside in blackness. Almost no resident leader is white; the best a white can hope for is a lower-echelon power position. Most often, the whites are at the very bottom of the social order, a most unaccustomed position for both black and white.

In calling attention to this paradox, we have tried to examine in the body of this monograph not only the subtleties of the interaction but the consequences of this role reversal. It is an area well worth additional exploration, since there are few comparable instances in which the overdog-underdog roles are so obviously inverted, at the same time amenable to organizational and interpersonal analyses.

3. The last of the principal paradoxes lies in the "focal concerns" area, as Walter B. Miller has called it (1958). Nowhere are the "focal concerns" that Miller enunciated as characteristic of the juvenile gang—trouble, toughness, smartness, excitement, fate, autonomy—more evident than in institutional life. Rather than resocializing adjudicated and often personally very difficult delinquents to other values which are less likely to lead to recidivism and adult crime, the institution reinforces what Albert Cohen had

called "the inversion of middle-class norms." Successful institutional adaptation mandates conformity to lower-class standards (and even that is no certain protection against being "messed over"); such conformity paradoxically impedes and may preclude achieving material and status goals after release.

Another aspect of this paradox is that, instead of modeling themselves after other professional staff, the professional staff is subverted and adopts the style and values of the residents. We described this problem in the section on staff victimization and want to add only that as long as personnel are in the institution, they must react and respond in resident terms. The turf belongs to the inmates and it is lower-class, loser turf at that.

Little wonder then that from the far left to the far right on the political spectrum, there is consensus that, in John Conrad's phrase, "We should never have promised a hospital." Lipton, Martinson and Wilks have shattered by painstaking research a public myth and professional delusion that rehabilitation of offenders through institutional programs is an achievable goal (1975). Others, especially the offenders, have never needed to have this conclusion demonstrated.

And so, the ultimate paradox lies in the discrepancy between the rhetoric of juvenile corrections and the possibility and reality of its implementation. There are those who, like Jerome Miller, call for the dissolution of all juvenile institutions now (for all the reasons enumerated in this treatise). There are others who insist that, no matter how brutal the institution, incarceration is preferable to the alternative of deinstitutionalization because society deserves protection. Still others call for a justice model, a few for punishment and retribution, and the rest for whatever correctional practices will prevent and deter the potential offender.

If this research has taught us anything, it is the wisdom contained in two disparate but appropriate and slightly modified quotations:

Man is a wolf to man.

No pain equals an injury inflicted under pretense
of just punishment (or rehabilitation).

# BIBLIOGRAPHY

Allen, Harry and Clifford E. Simonsen
  1975    *Corrections in America: An Introduction* (Beverly Hills: Glencoe Press).
Atchley, Robert C. and M. Patrick McCabe
  1968    "Socialization in Correctional Communities: A Replication," American
          Sociological Review 33 (October), 774-785.
Axelrad, Sidney
  1952    "Negro and White Male Institutionalized Delinquents," American Journal
          of Sociology 57 (May), 569-574.

Bakal, Yitzhak
  1973    *Closing Correctional Institutions* (Lexington, Mass.: D.C. Heath).
Barker, Gordon H. W. and W. Thomas Adams
  1959    "The Social Structure of a Correctional Institution," Journal of Criminal
          Law, Criminology and Police Science 49 (January-February), 416-422.
Bartollas, Clemens
  1973    *Runaways at Training Institution. Central Ohio,* (unpublished Ph.D. dis-
          sertation. The Ohio State University).
Bartollas, Clemens, Stuart J. Miller and Simon Dinitz
  1974a   "Becoming a Scapegoat: A Study of a Deviant Career," Sociological
          Symposium 11 (Spring), 74-89.
Bartollas, Clemens, Stuart J. Miller and Simon Dinitz
  1974b   "The Informal Code: A Gatekeeper to Treatment in a Juvenile Institu-
          tion," Published by the Program for the Study of Crime and Delinquency
          of the Ohio State University and used in its annual report to the Admin-
          istration of Justice Division, Ohio Department of Economic and Com-
          munity Development (June).
Bartollas, Clemens, Stuart J. Miller and Simon Dinitz
  1974c   "The Inmate Who Profits," Unpublished paper presented to the American
          Society of Criminology (Chicago).
Bartollas, Clemens, Stuart J. Miller and Simon Dinitz
  1975a   "Staff Exploitation of Inmates: The Paradox of Institutional Control,"
          Viano and Drapkin, editors, *Exploiters and Exploited: The Dynamics of
          Victimization* (Lexington, Mass.: D. C. Heath).
Bartollas, Clemens, Stuart J. Miller and Simon Dinitz
  1975b   "The Informal Code in a Juvenile Institution: Guidelines for the Strong,"
          Journal of Southern Criminal Justice (Summer), 33-52.
Bartollas, Clemens, Stuart J. Miller and Simon Dinitz

1975c      "The Booty Bandit: A Social Role in a Juvenile Institution, Journal of
           Homosexuality (in press).
Bartollas, Clemens
    1975a      "Sisyphus in a Juvenile Institution," Social Work (in press).
Bartollas, Clemens
    1975b      "Runaways at the Training Institution, Central Ohio," Canadian Journal of
               Criminology and Corrections 17 (July), 221-235.
Bartollas, Clemens
    1975c      "Unmanageable and Unshareable Problems and How They Contribute to
               Runaway Behavior," Sociological Research Symposium IV (Richmond:
               Virginia Commonwealth University, 1975).
Bartollas, Clemens, Stuart J. Miller and Simon Dinitz
    1976a      "The White Victim in a Black Institution," Riedel and Vales, editors,
               *Treating the Offender: Problems and Issues* (New York: Praeger Publishers,
               1976).
Bartollas, Clemens, Stuart J. Miller and Simon Dinitz
    1976b      "The Exploitation Matrix in a Juvenile Institution," International Journal
               of Criminology and Penology (in press).
Becker, Howard S.
    1963       *The Outsiders* (New York: Free Press).
Berk, Bernard B.
    1966       "Organizational Goals and Inmate Organization," American Journal of
               Sociology 71 (March),   522-534.
Berne, Eric
    1964       *Games People Play* (New York: Grove Press).
Berne, Eric
    1972       *What Do You Say After You Say Hello* (New York: Grove Press).
Blau, Peter M.
    1967       *Exchange and Power in Social Life* (New York: John Wiley).
Blau, Peter M. and W. Richard Scott
    1962       *Formal Organizations* (San Francisco: Chandler).
Bluestone, Harvey, Edward P. O'Malley and Sydney Connell
    1966       "Homosexuality in Prison," Journal of Social Therapy 12(1), 13-24.
Bronfenbrenner, Vrie
    1958       "Socialization and Social Class Through Time and Space," Maccoby, New-
               comb, and Hartley, editors, *Readings in Social Psychology* (New York:
               Holt, Rinehart & Winston).
Bruyn, Severyn T.
    1966       *The Human Perspective in Sociology* (Englewood Cliffs, N.J.: Prentice-
               Hall).
Burns, Henry, Jr.
    1969       "A Miniature Totalitarian State: Maximum Security Prison," Canadian
               Journal of Corrections 9 (July), 153-164.

Carroll, James L.
    1970       "Status Within Prison: Toward an Operational Definition," Correctional
               Psychologists 4 (September-October), 49-56.
Carter, Robert M., Richard A. McGee and Kim Nelson

1975    *Corrections in America* (Philadelphia: J. B. Lippincott).

1967    *The Challenge of Crime in a Free Society* (Washington, D.C.: Government Printing Office).

1968    "The Determinants of Normative Patterns in Correctional Institutions," Christie, editor, *Scandinavian Studies in Criminology* (Oslo: Oslo University Press).

Clemmer, Donald

1958    *The Prison Community* (New York: Holt, Rinehart & Winston).

Cloward, Richard et al.

1960    Theoretical Studies in Social Organization of the Prison (New York: Social Science Research Council).

Cohen, Albert K.

1955    *Delinquent Boys: The Culture of the Gang* (New York: Free Press).

Cressey, Donald R., ed.

1966    *The Prison: Studies in Institutional Organization and Change* (New York: Holt, Rinehart & Winston).

Cressey, Donald R. and Withold Krassowski

1957    "Inmate Organization and Anomie in American Prisons and Soviet Labor Camps," *Social Problems* (Winter), 217-230.

Davis, Alan J.

1968    "Sexual Assaults in the Philadelphia Prison System and Sheriff's Vans," Trans-action 6 (December), 9-17.

Deutsch, Albert

1950    *Our Rejected Children* (Boston: Little, Brown).

Dinitz, Simon, Stuart J. Miller and Clemens Bartollas

1974    "Inmate Exploitation: A Study on the Juvenile Victim," Viano and Drapkin, editors, *Exploiters and Exploited: The Dynamics of Victimization* (Lexington, Mass.: D. C. Heath).

Ellenberger, Henri

1954    "Relations psychologiques entre le criminal et al victime," Review internationale de criminologie et de police technique 2 (April-June).

Empey, LaMar T. and George E. Newland

1968    "Staff-Inmate Collaboration," Journal of Research in Crime and Delinquency 5 (January), 1-17.

Etzioni, Amitai

1964    *Modern Organizations* (Englewood Cliffs, N.J.: Prentice-Hall).

Etzioni, Amitai, ed.

1961    *A Comparative Analysis of Complex Organizations* (New York: Free Press).

Fisher, Sethard

1961    "Social Organization in a Correctional Residence," Pacific Sociological Review 4 (Fall,) 87-93.

Fry, Margery

1951    *Arms of the Law* (London: Gollancz Press).

Gagon, John H. and William Simon
  1968    "The Social Meaning of Prison Homosexuality," Federal Probation 32
          (March), 23-29.
Garabedian, Peter G.
  1962    "Legitimate and Illegitimate Opportunities in the Prison Community,"
          Sociological Inquiry 32 (Spring), 172-184.
Garabedian, Peter G.
  1963    "Social Roles and Processes of Socialization in the Prison Community,"
          Social Problems 11 (Fall), 139-152.
Garfinkel, Harold
  1956    "Conditions of Successful Degradation Ceremonies," American Journal of
          Sociology 61 (March), 420-424.
Giallombardo, Rose
  1966    *Society of Women: A Study of a Woman's Prison* (New York: John Wiley).
Giallombardo, Rose
  1974    *The Social World of Imprisoned Girls* (New York: John Wiley).
Gibbs, Jack P.
  1966    "Conceptions of Deviant Behavior: The Old and the New," Pacific Socio-
          logical Review 9 (Spring), 9-14.
Glaser, B. G. and A. L. Strauss
  1967    *The Discovery of Grounded Theory: Strategies for Qualitative Research*
          (Chicago: Aldine).
Glasser, William
  1965    *Reality Therapy: A New Approach to Psychiatry* (New York: Harper &
          Row).
Goffman, Erving
  1961    *Asylums* (Garden City, N.Y.: Doubleday Anchor).
Goffman, Erving
  1959    *The Presentation of Self in Everyday Life* (Garden City, N.Y.: Doubleday
          Anchor).
Goffman, Erving
  1967    "Characteristics of Total Institutions," Dinitz, Dynes, and Clarke, editors,
          *Deviance: Studies in the Process of Stigmatization and Societal Reaction*
          (New York: Oxford University Press), 472-485.
Gough, Harrison and Alfred B. Heilbrun
  1965    "The Adjective Checklist Manual," Palo Alto, Calif.: Consulting Psychol-
          ogists' Press.
Gouldner, Alvin
  1954    *Pattern of Industrial Bureaucracy* (New York: Free Press).
Greco, Marshall C. and James C. Wright
  1944    "The Correctional Institution in the Etiology of Chronic Homosexuality,"
          American Journal of Orthopsychiatry 14: 304-305.
Grosser, George P.
  1958    "The Role of Informal Inmate Groups in Change of Values," Children 5
          (January-February), 25-29.
Grusky, Oscar
  1958-   "Role Conflict in Organization: A Study of Prison Camp Officials,"
  1959    Administrative Science Quarterly 3 (January-March), 452-472.

Grusky, Oscar
  1959-    "Organization Goals and the Behavior of Informal Leaders," American
  1960      Journal of Sociology 62 (July), 59-67.
Grusky, Oscar
  1964      "Guided Steps," Columbus: Ohio Youth Commission.

Hage, Jerald and Michael Aiken
  1970      *Social Change in Complex Organizations* (New York: Random House).
Halleck, Seymour L. and Marvin Hersko
  1962      "Homosexual Behavior in a Correctional Institution for Adolescent Girls,"
            American Journal of Orthopsychiatry 32 (October), 911-927.
Hayner, Norman S.
  1943      "Washington State Correctional Institutions as Communities," Social
            Forces 21 (March), 316-322.
Haynes, F. E.
  1948      "The Sociological Study of the Prison Community," Journal of Criminal
            Law and Criminology 39 (November-December), 432-440.
Hazelrigg, Lawrence E.
  1967      "An Examination of the Accuracy and Relevance of Staff's Perceptions of
            the Inmate in the Correctional Institution," Criminal Law, Criminology
            and Police Science 58 (June).
Hammer, Max
  1965      "Homosexuality in a Woman's Prison," Journal of Social Therapy 11
            (May), 168-169.
Heffernan, Esther
  1972      *Making It in Prison: The Square, The Cool, and Life* (New York: Wiley-
            Interscience Press).
Hood, R. G.
  1967      "Research on the Effectiveness of Punishments and Treatments," Collected
            Studies in Criminological Research I (Strasburg: Council of Europe).
Huffman, Arthur V.
  1961      "Problems Precipitated by Homosexual Approaches on Youthful First
            Offenders," Journal of Social Therapy 7 (3-4), 170-181.

Irwin, John
  1970      *The Felon* (Englewood Cliffs, N.J.: Prentice-Hall).
Irwin, John and Donald R. Cressey
  1962      "Thieves, Convicts and the Inmate Culture," Social Problems 10 (Fall),
            142-155.

Jesness, Carl F.
  1965      "Manual for the Jesness Inventory," Palo Alto, Calif.: Consulting Psychol-
            ogists' Press.
Jesness, Carl F.
  1965      "The Fricot Ranch Study," Sacramento: State of Calif., Department of the
            Youth Authority.
Johnson, Daniel
  1968      "Designation of R-Suffix," Columbus: Ohio Youth Commission Directive,
            March, Chapter E-3.

Johnson, Elmer H.
  1961    "Sociology of Confinement: Assimilation and the Prison 'Rat,' " Journal
          of Criminal Law, Criminology and Police Science 51 (January-February),
          528-533.
Junker, Buford J.
  1960    *Field Work: An Introduction to the Social Sciences* (Chicago: University of
          Chicago Press).


Konopka, Gisela
  1962    "Institutional Treatment of Emotionally Disturbed Children," Crime and
          Delinquency 8 (January), 52-57.
Kosofsky, Sidney and Albert Ellis
  1958    "Illegal Communication Among Institutionalized Female Delinquents,"
          Journal of Social Psychology 48 (August), 155-160.


Lefton, Mark and W. R. Rosengren
  1966    "Organizations and Clients: Lateral and Longitudinal Dimensions," Ameri-
          can Sociological Review 31 (December), 802-810.
Lemert, Edwin M.
  1951    *Social Pathology* (New York: McGraw-Hill).
Lipton, Douglas, Robert Martinson and Judith Wilkes
  1975    *The Effectiveness of Correctional Measures: A Survey of Treatment Evalu-
          ation Studies* (New York: Praeger Publishers).
Lofland, John
  1969    *Deviance and Identity* (Englewood Cliffs, N.J.: Prentice-Hall).


McCleery, Richard
  1960    "Communication Patterns as Bases of System of Authority and Power,"
          Cloward, Cressey, Grossner, McCleery, Ohlin, Sykes, and Messinger,
          editors, *Theoretical Studies in Social Organization of the Prison* (New
          York: Social Science Research Council), 56-61.
McCleery, Richard
  1961    "Policy Change in Prison Management," Etzioni, editor, *Complex Organi-
          zation: A Sociological Reader* (New York: Holt, Rinehart & Winston),
          376-400.
McCorkle, Lloyd, Albert Elias and F. Lovell Bixby
  1968    *The Highfields Story* (New York: Holt, Rinehart & Winston).
McCorkle, Lloyd and Richard Korn
  1954    "Resocialization Within Walls," Annals of the American Academy of
          Political and Social Science 293 (May), 88-98.
McCorkle, Lloyd W.
  1956    "Social Structure in a Prison," Welfare Reporter 8 (December), 5-15.
Machover, Karen
  1949    *Personality Projection in the Drawing of the Human Figure* (Springfield,
          Ill.: Charles C Thomas).
Mathiesen, Thomas
  1971    *Across the Boundaries of Organization* (Berkeley: Glendessary Press).

Matza, David
  1969    *Becoming Deviant* (Englewood Cliffs, N.J.: Prentice-Hall).
Matza, David
  1964    *Delinquency and Drift* (New York: John Wiley).
Mazur, Alan
  1973    "A Cross-Species Comparison of Status in Small Established Groups,"
          American Sociological Review 38 (October), 513-530.
Mendelsohn, B.
  1963    "The Origin of Victimology," Excerpta Criminologica 3 (May-June),
          239-241.
Miller, Stuart J.
  1971    "Post-Institutional Adjustment of 443 Consecutive TICO Releases," (un-
          published Ph.D. dissertation, The Ohio State University).
Miller, Stuart J. and Simon Dinitz
  1973    "Measuring Institutional Impact: A Follow-up," Criminology 11 (Nov-
          ember), 417-426.
Miller, Stuart J. and Simon Dinitz
  1974    "Measuring Perceptions of Organizational Change," Journal of Research in
          Crime and Delinquency 11 (2) (July), 180-194.
Miller, Stuart J., Clemens Bartollas, James Roberts and Simon Dinitz
  1974    "The 'Heavy' and Social Control," Sociological Research Symposium IV
          (Richmond: Virginia Commonwealth University).
Miller, Stuart J., Clemens Bartollas, Donald Jenifer, Edward Redd and Simon Dinitz
  1975    "Games Inmates Play: Notes on Staff Victimization," Viano and Drapkin,
          editors, *Exploiters and Exploited: The Dynamics of Victimization* (Lexing-
          ton, Mass.: D. C. Heath).
Miller, Walter B.
  1958    "Lower Class Culture as a Generating Milieu of Gang Delinquency,"
          Journal of Social Issues 3 (14): 5-19.
Moos, Robert
  1968    "The Assessment of the Social Climates of Correctional Institutions,"
          Journal of Research in Crime and Delinquency 5 (July), 174-188.
Moos, Robert
  1970    "Differential Effects of the Social Climates of Correctional Institutions,"
          Journal of Research in Crime and Delinquency 7 (January), 71-82.
Morris, Terrence, Pauline Morris and Barbara Beily
  1961    "It's the Prisoners Who Run this Prison," Prison Service Review 3
          (January), 3-11.
Mosier, Craig Harlan
  1972    *Delinquents' Perceptions of Institutional Impact,* unpublished Ph.D. dis-
          sertation.
Mouledous, Joseph C.
  1963    "Organizational Goals and Structure Change: A Study of the Organization
          of a Prison Social System," Social Forces 41 (March), 283-290.

Neese, Robert
  1959    *Prison Exposures* (Philadelphia: Chilton)
Newman, Oscar
  1972    *Defensible Space* (New York: Macmillan).

Ohlin, Lloyd E.
    1968     "The Reduction of Role Conflict in Institutional Staff," Children 5 (Feb-
             ruary-March), 65-69.
Ohlin, Lloyd E. and William C. Lawrence
    1959     "Social Interaction Among Clients as a Treatment Problem," Social Work 4
             (April), 3-14.
    1968     "OYC–The Way Forward with the Ohio Youth Commission," Columbus:
             Columbus Blank Book Company.


Perrow, Charles
    1963     "Reality Shock: A New Orientation Confronts the Custody-Treatment
             Dilemma," Social Problems 10 (Spring), 374-382.
Polsky, Howard
    1959     "Changing Delinquent Subcultures: A Social Psychological Approach,"
             Social Work 4 (October), 3-16.
Polsky, Howard
    1962     *Cottage Six–The Social System of Delinquent Boys in Residential Treat-
             ment* (New York: Russell Sage Foundation).
Polsky, Howard and Daniel S. Claster
    1968     *The Dynamics of Residential Treatment* (Chapel Hill: University of North
             Carolina Press).
    1974     "Profile of OYC Institutional Population and Youth Leader Staff," Colum-
             bus: Ohio Youth Commission (mimeo).


Robinson, James and Gerald Smith
    1969     "The Effectiveness of Correctional Programs," Crime and Delinquency
             (January), 67-80.
Rose, Arnold M. and George H. Weber
    n.d.      "Change in Attitudes Among Delinquent Boys Committed to Open and
             Closed Institutions," Journal of Criminal Law, Criminology and Police
             Science 52 (July-August), 166-177.
Rose, Gordon
    1959     "Status and Groupings in a Borstal," British Journal of Delinquency 9
             (April), 258-273.
Roth, Loren J.
    1971     "Territoriality and Homosexuality in a Male Prison Population," American
             Journal of Orthopsychiatry 41 (April), 510-513.
Rothman, David J.
    1971     *The Discovery of the Asylum* (Boston: Little, Brown).
Rushing, William A.
    1966     "Organizational Rules and Surveillance: Propositions in Comparative
             Organizational Analysis," Administrative Science Quarterly 10 (March),
             423-443.
Rutherford, Andrew
    1974     "The Dissolution of the Training Schools in Massachusetts," Columbus,
             Ohio: Academy for Contemporary Problems).

Schafer, Stephen
  1968    *The Victim and His Criminal* (New York: Random House).
Schrag, Clarence
  1944    "Social Types in a Prison Community," M. A. thesis.
Schrag, Clarence
  1954    "Leadership Among Prison Inmates," American Sociological Review 19
          (February), 37-42.
Schultz, Leroy G.
  1968    "The Victim-Offender Relationship," Crime and Delinquency 14 (April),
          135-141.
Schulze, Susanne
  1951    *Creative Group Living in a Children's Institution* (New York: Association
          Press).
Schur, Edwin M.
  1971    *Labeling Deviant Behavior* (New York: Harper & Row).
Selltiz, Claire, Marie Jahoda, Morton Deutsch and Stuart Cook
  1961    *Research Methods in Social Relations* (New York: Holt, Rinehart & Win-
          ston).
Sigler, Robert T.
  1969    "A Study of Informal Peer Group Leaders," unpublished M. A. thesis.
Smith, N. Corrine
  1974    "Ohio Youth Commission: State of Ohio," Columbus: Bureau of Com-
          munications, Ohio Youth Commission.
Street, David, Robert D. Vinter and Charles Perrow
  1966    *Organization for Treatment: A Comparative Study of Institutions for
          Delinquents* (New York: Free Press).
Street, David
  1965    "The Inmate Group in Custodial and Treatment Settings," American
          Sociological Review 30 (February), 40-55.
Sykes, Gresham
  1966    "Men, Merchant, and Toughs, A Study of Reactions to Imprisonment,"
          Social Problems (October), 130-138.
Sykes, Gresham
  1958    *Society of Captives* (Princeton University Press).
Sykes, Gresham and Sheldon L. Messinger
  1960    "The Inmate Social System," Cloward et al., editors, *Theoretical Studies in
          Social Organization in the Prison* (New York: Social Science Research
          Council).
  1967    *Task Force Report: Juvenile Delinquency and Youth Crime* (Washington,
          D. C.: Government Printing Office).


Taylor, A. J. W.
  1965    "The Significance of 'Darls' or 'Special Relationships' for Borstal Girls,"
          British Journal of Criminology 5 (October), 406-419.
Thomas, Charles W.
  1970    "Toward a More Inclusive Model of the Inmate Contraculture," Crimi-
          nology 8 (November), 251-262.

Thomas, Charles W. and Samuel C. Foster
  1972    "Prisonization in the Inmate Contraculture," Social Problems 20 (Fall),
          299-339.
Thomas, Charles W. and Samuel C. Foster
  1973    "The Importation Model Perspective on Inmate Social Roles," Sociological
          Quarterly 14 (Spring), 226-234.
Thomas Piri
  1967    *Down These Mean Streets* (New York: Alfred A. Knopf).
Tittle, Charles R.
  1972    *Society of Subordinates* (Bloomington: Indiana University Press).
Tittle, Charles R.
  1964    "Social Organization of Prisoners: An Empirical Test," Social Forces 43
          (December), 216-221.
Tittle, Charles R.
  1969    "Inmate Organization: Sex Differentiation and the Influence of Criminal
          Subcultures," American Sociological Review 34 (August), 492-505.
Toigo, Romulo
  1962    "Illegitimate and Legitimate Cultures in a Training School for Girls,"
          Proceedings of the Rip Van Winkle Clinic, 13.
Troyer, Joseph G. and Dean E. Frease
  1975    "Attitude Change in a Western Canadian Penitentiary," Canadian Journal
          of Criminology and Corrections 17 (July), 250-262.

Vaz, Edmund W.
  1971    "Explorations in the Institutionalization of Juvenile Delinquency," Journal
          of Criminal Law, Criminology and Police Science 62 (December), 532-542.
Vinter, Robert D. and Morris Janowitz
  1959    "Effective Institutions for Juvenile Offenders: A Research Statement,"
          Social Service Review 33 (June), 118-131.
Vinter, Robert D. and Roger Lind
  1958    *Staff Relationships and Attitudes in a Juvenile Correctional Institution*
          (Ann Arbor: School of Social Work).
Von Hentig, Hans
  1948    *The Criminal and His Victim* (New Haven: Yale University Press).

Wallerstein, James S. and Clement J. Wylie
  1947    "Our Law-abiding Law Breakers," Probation (April), 107-112.
Ward, David A. and Gene G. Kassebaum
  1965    *Women's Prison: Sex and Social Structure* (Chicago: Aldine).
Warren, Marguerite Q.
  1967    "The Community Treatment Project: History and Prospects," Yefsky,
          editor, Law Enforcement, Science and Technology (Washington: Thomp-
          son Book Company).
Wellford, Charles
  1967    "Factors Associated with the Adoption of the Inmate Code," Journal of
          Criminal Law, Criminology and Police Science 58 (June), 197-203.
Wheeler, Stanton
  1961    "Socialization in Correctional Communities," American Sociological
          Review 26 (October), 697-712.

Williams, Robin
  1970     *American Society: A Sociological Interpretation* (New York: Alfred A.
           Knopf).
Williams, Vergil L. and Mary Fish
  1974     *Convicts, Codes, and Contraband: The Prison Life of Men and Women*
           (Cambridge, Mass.: Ballinger).
Wilson, John M. and Jon D. Snodgrass
  1969     "The Prison Code in a Therapeutic Community," Journal of Criminal Law,
           Criminology and Police Science 60 (4), 472-478.


Young, Frank W.
  1970     "Reactive Subsystems," American Sociological Review 35 (April),
           297-307.


Zald, Mayer N.
  1960     "The Correctional Institution for Juvenile Offenders: An Analysis of
           Organization 'Character,' " Social Problems 8 (Summer), 57-67.
Zald, Mayer N.
  1962a    "Power Balance and Staff Conflict in Correctional Institutions," Admin-
           istrative Science Review 6 (June), 22-49.
Zald, Mayer N.
  1962b    "Organizational Control Structures in Five Correctional Institutions,"
           American Journal of Sociology 1968 (November), 335-345.
Zald, Mayer N.
  1963     "Comparative Analysis and Measurement of Organizational Goals: The
           Case of Correctional Institutions for Delinquents," Sociological Quarterly
           4 (Summer), 206-230.
Zingraff, Matthew T.
  1973     "Conflicting Processes of Socialization among Juveniles in the Prison
           Community," Georgia Journal of Corrections 2 (August), 63-70.

## APPENDIX A

### ADDITIONAL POPULATION CHARACTERISTICS
### OF YOUTHS ADJUDICATED TO THE
### OHIO YOUTH COMMISSION [*]

TOTAL NUMBER OF MALES
| | |
|---|---|
| Institutions | 1917 |
| Aftercare | 2132 |

TOTAL NUMBER OF FEMALES
| | |
|---|---|
| Institutions | 499 |
| Aftercare | 675 |

COMMITMENT OFFENSE CATEGORY
| | |
|---|---|
| Crime against Person | 18.9% |
| Crime against Property | 31.7% |
| Other Felonies & Gross Misdemeanors | 20.2% |
| Minor Misdemeanors & Status Offenses | 21.4% |
| Parole Violation/No Data | 7.8% |

LIVED WITH:
| | |
|---|---|
| Both Parents | 33.3% |
| Mother Alone | 34.5% |
| Father Alone | 5.0% |
| Step Parent/Parents | 15.4% |
| Relative | 5.4% |
| Non-Relative | 6.0% |
| No Data | 0.3% |

NUMBER OF SIBLINGS
| | |
|---|---|
| None | 2.9% |
| 1-2 | 23.6% |
| 3-4 | 31.7% |
| 5-9 | 36.2% |
| 10 or more | 2.3% |
| No Data | 3.4% |

FATHER'S OCCUPATION
| | |
|---|---|
| Professional/Managerial | 7.3% |
| White Collar | 4.7% |
| Agriculture | 1.2% |
| Blue Collar/Skilled | 18.8% |
| Blue Collar/Semi-Unskilled | 52.6% |
| Not Employed | 15.4% |

*From a mimeographed Ohio Youth Commission paper entitled "Profile of O Y C Institutional Population and Youth Leader Staff."

## APPENDIX B

### Data Collection Form for Staff Rankings of Youths and the Boys' Personal Characteristics

This study concerns troublesome boys in this institution. We are especially interested in finding out whether each of the students in your cottage is likely to be taken advantage of or "messed over". You will notice that the first four columns contain general statements concerning the likelihood of being victimized and the last seven are specific ways that students may be used. Please check (✓) all columns that apply to the specific student named. All answers are confidential and will not be available to either administrators, boys, or anyone other than researchers. Thank you.

STUDENT

| | LIKELIHOOD OF STUDENT EXPLOITATION | | | | | IF EXPLOITED, IS LIKELY TO BE USED AS FOLLOWS: | | | | | | |
|---|---|---|---|---|---|---|---|---|---|---|---|---|
| | Likely to exploit others | Likely not to be exploited | Likely to be exploited occasionally | Likely to be exploited often | Clothing: socks, pants, etc. | Food, canteen, desserts, etc. | Ciga- rettes | Sex: Mas- turbate Others | Sex: Anal Sodomy | Sex: Oral Sodomy | Other |
| | | | | | | | | | | | |

FOR RESEARCHERS' USE ONLY: DO NOT FILL IN THESE SPACES

| Cottage | D.O.B. | Age at Admission | Special Designa- tion: R&E | Number of Previous Commitments | Committing County | Race | Weight | Height | IQ | Number of Previous Offenses | Offense lead- ing to this Commitment |
|---|---|---|---|---|---|---|---|---|---|---|---|
| | | | | | | | | | | | |

STUDENT

| | LIKELIHOOD OF STUDENT EXPLOITATION | | | | | IF EXPLOITED, IS LIKELY TO BE USED AS FOLLOWS: | | | | | | |
|---|---|---|---|---|---|---|---|---|---|---|---|---|
| | Likely to exploit others | Likely not to be exploited | Likely to be exploited occasionally | Likely to be exploited often | Clothing: socks, pants, etc. | Food, canteen, desserts, etc. | Ciga- rettes | Sex: Mas- turbate Others | Sex: Anal Sodomy | Sex: Oral Sodomy | Other |
| | | | | | | | | | | | |

FOR RESEARCHERS' USE ONLY: DO NOT FILL IN THESE SPACES

| Cottage | D.O.B. | Age at Admission | Special Designa- tion: R&E | Number of Previous Commitments | Committing County | Race | Weight | Height | IQ | Number of Previous Offenses | Offense lead- ing to this Commitment |
|---|---|---|---|---|---|---|---|---|---|---|---|
| | | | | | | | | | | | |

APPENDIX C

SCHEMATIC BREAKDOWN OF THE OHIO YOUTH COMMISSION
CORRECTIONS AND COMMUNITY SERVICE DIVISIONS

| Corrections | | | Community Service | | |
|---|---|---|---|---|---|
| Assistant Deputy Director | | | Assistant Deputy Director | | |
| | Program Coordinator | Education Adm. | Community Dev. | Probation Dev. | Juvenile Placement (Regional Offices) |
| | | Education Service Unit | Education | Community Volunteers | Akron |
| | | | Employment | | Athens |
| Camps | Diagnostic Center | Institutions | Recreation | | Cincinnati |
| | | | Law Enforcement | | Cleveland |
| Maumee | | Fairfield | | | Columbus |
| Mohican | | Scioto Village | | | Dayton |
| | | Cuyahoga Hills | | | Toledo |
| | | Training Institution, Central Ohio (TICO) | | | |
| | | Riverview Training Center | | | |
| | | Indian River | | | |
| | | Child Study Center | | | |
| | | Training Center for Youths | | | |
| | | Buckeye Youth Center | | | |

APPENDIX D

FOCUSED QUESTIONS
FOR STAFF INTERVIEWS

Prior to interviewing, several selected staff members were informed as to the project's intent. At the first interview, the interviewer reaffirmed our interest in the troublesome boys in the cottages. More specifically, he stated that we were primarily interested in those boys who were "messed over" or who "messed over" others. Following are samples of some of the questions asked which enabled the researchers to explore in depth the nature of life in the cottages. As the staff raised unexpected issues and contributed new insights, these new directions were explored accordingly.

1. What goes on in a cottage concerning exploitation? How much exploitation goes on?

2. How would you describe a cottage's hierarchy of exploitation? Of prestige?

3. How much of what goes on is consensual?

4. What do prestige and power hinge on? How are they expressed?

5. What happens when a totally naive boy enters the institution? Can you tell what is going to happen? How? What is the process by which a boy is tested?

6. What characteristics of the kid lead to his being exploited?

7. What constitutes strength? Weakness?

8. Boys seem to remain in a stable status for awhile and then go in one direction or another. Can you describe the boy, for example, who is tipping toward being exploited? Not being exploited?

9. What makes the difference whether a boy who is exploited is exploited on food, clothing or sex?

10. Can you describe the relationship between the boy who is about to be exploited and the exploiter? What does the exploited feel about the exploiter?

11. What keeps a boy from becoming involved? What are the pitfalls the boys
    fall into?

12. What happens when a boy stops being exploited? How does it come about?
    What changes can you see in him? What happens to him in his relations
    with others? Can you describe the interaction?

13. How would you describe the typical exploited boy? The boy who exploits
    but is not exploited? The boys who are neither exploiters nor exploited?
    The boys who exploit and are exploited? The boys who don't exploit and
    and occasionally exploited?

14. What role do the following play in exploitation? Race, height, weight,
    looks.

 15. How do the boys respond to a kid once he has been exploited?

16. How does a boy who tips over to being exploited act before and after
    being exploited? What do they do about the act? How do they feel?
    Do they try to strike back at the exploiter? In the institution?
    Do they show much resentment? That is, what about their self-control?
    Do boys try to hide the fact of their exploitation?

17. What can you say about the idea of the exploited being the tough guy
    on the outside and the exploited on the inside?

18. To what extent are these exploited boys exploited because they are:

    a) Guilty of something and wanting to be punished?

    b) Just simply too weak and immature to protect themselves?

    c) Tempt others because they are seductive in their actions?

    d) Simply desire the attention of others? Do you consider this exploitation?
       Do they do it to be part of the group? Do they like it? How much, in
       other words, is it consensual?

    e) Do they have something against others and the relationship develops
       into exploitation?

    f) To what extent are they exploited because their exploitation is a
       challenge to others?

    g) Does their reputation preceed them? i.e., from other institutions?

    h) Are there any boys who are simply beaten, without being exploited?

19. Do these boys who are exploited, exploit others? How often does this

happen? Can you give some examples? What types of crimes do they commit, i.e., what types of trouble do they get into? Do they ever try to do the same thing to others as they have had done to them? Are they successful?

20. When a boy comes into the institution, what is said to him? How is it said?

21. Do guys ever borrow things from peers? Do you want them to? What do you say? Do they do it anyway? What can you do about it?

23. Do the kids gang up on others? Why? For what? What do they say? Do?

24. Is there anyone who is messed over all the time? Why? What about those who let others mess over them?

25. Suppose a white and black come into the cottage. Is there a difference? What happens to each one? How? Who says what?

26. Who are the toughest guys in there, blacks or whites? What makes them tough or weak?

27. Suppose that there are several boys who are possible victims. How would one be chosen over another?

## GOUGH ADJECTIVE CHECKLIST AND DEFINITIONS

Prior to administering the Gough Adjective Checklist (Gough and Heilbrun, 1965) simple definitions were made up for each of the adjectives. Then, when boys did not know the meaning of certain words, the definitions were read to them. Following are the 300 adjectives and the meanings developed by the researchers. *

1.  absent minded - forget things often

2.  active - always on the go, always looking for something to do

3.  adaptable - can change to meet new situations as they arise

4.  adventurous - like to do new things, daring

5.  affected - fake, artificial, trys to impress people falsely

6.  affectionate - warm toward others and show it

7.  aggressive - go after things you want

8.  alert - aware of what is going on around you

9.  aloof - hold yourself apart from others and happenings around you

10. ambitious - have high goals, want to get ahead

11. anxious - uneasy, worried as though expecting something to happen

12. apathetic - don't give a damm, don't care

13. appreciative - you show you like it when somebody does something for you

14. argumentative - when somebody says something you usually disagree

15. arrogant - you strut around and let people know how good you are

16. artistic - you are creative, like to draw or work with things

17. assertive - you are straight-forward, you say what you think

18. attractive - you are considered good looking by others

19. autocratic - you won't let anyone else help you run things, you have to do it all yourself

20. awkward - fall over things, drop things, stumble, not coordinated

21. bitter - you have bad feelings about something, act like you're in a bad mood

22. blustery - you are boastful, you brag a little

23. boastful - brag alot, even about little things

24. bossy - always ordering people around, telling them what to do

25. calm - keep cool, never get excited

26. capable - can do things

27. careless - not careful, make stupid mistakes

28. cautious - careful, plans things out, don't just jump into things

29. changeable - change your mind easily, do one thing one time, another another

30. <u>charming</u> - smooth, good talker, can flatter people easily

31. <u>cheerful</u> - gay, happy, of a pleasant nature

32. <u>civilized</u> - can settle things without fighting

33. <u>clear thinking</u> - use your head well

34. <u>clever</u> - smart, cool, can get around things and do things others can't

35. <u>coarse</u> - rough guy, run over people

36. <u>cold</u> - turn people off, don't let them get too close

37. <u>commonplace</u> - just an average person, don't stand out

38. <u>complaining</u> - a griper, feel that things are always going wrong

39. <u>complicated</u> - have a lot of depth, many different feelings

40. <u>conceited</u> - better than most others

41. <u>confident</u> - know that you are O.K., that what you do is right

42. <u>confused</u> - can't get things straight, don't know what you are supposed to do

43. <u>conscientious</u> - do what other people expect you to do, what you are supposed to do

44. <u>conservative</u> - not very flashy, don't show off like others

45. <u>considerate</u> - concerned with other people, help them out

46. <u>contented</u> - happy with things the way they are

47. <u>conventional</u> - don't do far out things, pretty much middle of the road

48. <u>cool</u> - don't blow up, calm

49. <u>cooperative</u> - help others do things, try to work with others

50. <u>courageous</u> - unafraid, willing to speak out and do things bravely

51. <u>cowardly</u> - afraid to speak out and do things

52. <u>cruel</u> - like to see other people and things hurt

53. <u>curious</u> - always asking questions, looking into things

54. <u>cynical</u> - think others do things for their own good, that they don't really care, question everything

55. <u>daring</u> - will jump in when others hold back

56. <u>deceitful</u> - you say things that aren't so

57. <u>defensive</u> - you keep watching to make sure people don't put you on the spot

58. <u>deliberate</u> - do things with a definite purpose, proceed carefully

59. <u>demanding</u> - expect a lot from others

60. <u>dependable</u> - others can rely on you

61. <u>dependent</u> - rely on others a lot

62. <u>despondent</u> - depressed, sad don't think things will work out well

63. <u>determined</u> - can't be put off, go ahead with what you want

64. <u>dignified</u> - noble, VIP distinguished

65. <u>discreet</u> - keep personal things to yourself, don't talk about them

66. <u>disorderly</u> - not very neat, your things are "messed up" often

67. <u>dissatisfied</u> - don't like the way things are going

68. <u>distractible</u> - your mind wanders easily, others can get you to stop what you are doing

69. <u>distrustful</u> - you don't trust other people

70. <u>dominant</u> - you can get others to do what you want them to do

71. <u>dreamy</u> - you like to sit around and think about things alot

72. <u>dull</u> - you're not much fun to be around, you don't do much

73. <u>easy going</u> - you let things go along as they are, you don't push things

74. <u>effeminate</u> - weak, unmanly, can be pushed around by others

75. <u>efficient</u> - don't waste time or money

76. <u>egoistical</u> - you're the best, you think very highly of yourself

77. <u>emotional</u> - you are very sensitive, lose your cool easily

78. <u>energetic</u> - always ready to go, always ready to do something

79. <u>enterprising</u> - can find new ways of doing things

80. <u>enthusiastic</u> - enjoy doing things, like to get going on them right away

81. <u>evasive</u> - don't give exactly the right answer, you talk around it

82. <u>excitable</u> - you get excited easily, nervous

83. <u>fair-minded</u> - you want others to get what they rightly deserve

84. <u>fault-finding</u> - always finding something wrong with things

85. <u>fearful</u> - afraid something is going to happen

86. <u>feminine</u> - you are a very gentle person, very emotional

87. <u>fickle</u> - can't be satisfied easily, change your mind often

88. <u>flirtatious</u> - you give people you like the "come on"

89. <u>foolish</u> - do things you shouldn't, reckless

90. <u>forceful</u> - state your position strongly, you push your way

91. <u>foresighted</u> - can look ahead, see things in advance

92. <u>forgetful</u> - can't remember things

93. <u>forgiving</u> - don't hold things against people, can forget

94. <u>formal</u> - not casual, stiff, dressed up too much

95. <u>frank</u> - speak out say what you think

96. <u>friendly</u> - get along well with others, you like other people

97. frivolous - do things that aren't really important

98. fussy - complaining alot about little things

99. generous - willing to give up things to others

100. gentle - not rough with others, you take it easy with them

101. gloomy - always expecting the worst and acting like it

102. good-looking - physically appealing to others

103. good-natured - take things well, don't get angry easy

104. greedy - try to get all you can for yourself, want more

105. handsome - good-looking, rugged good looks

106. hard-headed - stick to your own ideas, don't change your mind, usually right

107. hard-hearted - can say no, even when others want something

108. hasty - always hurried, in a rush

109. headstrong - go ahead with your ideas, even though you may be wrong

110. healthy - no problems physically

111. helpful - willing to pitch in

112. high strung - get nervous easily

113. honest - tell the truth

114. hostile - angry toward others, against them

115. humorous - able to crack jokes and keep things light

116. hurried - rushed, trying to get things done

117. idealistic - have high ideals and goals, expect things to be good

118. imaginative - have new ideas, figure out new ways of doing things

119. immature - need to grow up some yet

120. impatient - in a hurry for things to get done

121. impulsive - do things without thinking, have to do them

122. independent - rely on yourself

123. indifferent - don't care about things, don't care which direction things go

124. individualistic - do things by yourself

125. industrious - hard working, always keeping after things

126. infantile - childlike sometimes, don't act grown up

127. informal - casual, easygoing

128. ingenious - clever, smart

129. inhibited - reserved, hold yourself back, don't let yourself go

130. <u>initiative</u> - do things without someone pushing you, a self starter

131. <u>insightful</u> - know the real reasons why you and others do things

132. <u>intelligent</u> - bright, smart, able to figure things out

133. <u>interests narrow</u> - only a few things which you really like to do

134. <u>interests wide</u> - many things you really like to do

135. <u>intolerant</u> - get upset easily at things other people do

136. <u>inventive</u> - can come up with new ways of doing things

137. <u>irresponsible</u> - can't be relied upon, don't carry through with things

138. <u>irritable</u> - snap at people when they do something

139. <u>jolly</u> - like to laugh and enjoy things

140. <u>kind</u> - very considerate and warm toward others

141. <u>lazy</u> - hard for you to get going, don't like to work that much

142. <u>leisurely</u> - take it easy, not hurried,

143. <u>logical</u> - can think things through accurately

144. <u>loud</u> - noisy

145. <u>loyal</u> - stand by your friends

146. <u>mannerly</u> - polite, courteous

147. <u>masculine</u> - strong, tough, can stand up for yourself

148. <u>mature</u> - act like an adult

149. <u>meek</u> - quiet, timid, can be pushed around

150. <u>methodical</u> - accurate, careful, "do things by the numbers"

151. <u>mild</u> - gentle, easy, calm, considerate

152. <u>mischievous</u> - pull pranks or tricks on others

153. <u>moderate</u> - middle of the road, don't go to extreme

154. <u>modest</u> - don't bragg, don't blow your own horn

155. <u>moody</u> - gloomy, let things upset you often

156. <u>nagging</u> - keep on other people's backs so they'll do things

157. <u>natural</u> - act just the way you are, don't put anything on

158. <u>nervous</u> - high-strung, jittery

159. <u>noisy</u> - loud

160. <u>obliging</u> - gladly do what others want

161. <u>obnoxious</u> - turn people off

162. <u>opinionated</u> - you know you're right

163. <u>opportunistic</u> - quick to take advantage of things

164. <u>optimistic</u> - look on the good side of things, usually think things will turn out O.K.

165. <u>organized</u> - you have everything under control, thought out

166. <u>original</u> - you do things differently than most

167. <u>outgoing</u> - free and easy with others, enjoy talking with others

168. <u>outspoken</u> - you say things even though you know others may disagree

169. <u>painstaking</u> - very careful with what you do, pay attention to details

170. <u>patient</u> - you don't get in a hurry, can let things develop as they will

171. <u>peaceable</u> - don't like fighting, would rather not get involved in an argument

172. <u>peculiar</u> - sort of different, not like most people

173. <u>persevering</u> - don't give up, keep plugging away

174. <u>persistent</u> - keep after things

175. <u>pessimistic</u> - don't think that things will work out

176. <u>planful</u> - plan things out, always look things over carefully

177. <u>pleasant</u> - pleasing, nice to have around

178. <u>pleasure-seeking</u> - try to find things to do that feel good

179. <u>poised</u> - ready and confident

180. <u>polished</u> - smooth, good manners, know what to say

181. <u>practical</u> - do things wisely, usefully

182. <u>praising</u> - compliment others quickly

183. <u>precise</u> - exact, as near perfect as possible

184. <u>prejudiced</u> - don't like certain types of people

185. <u>preoccupied</u> - you aren't aware of what's going on around you because you're thinking of something else

186. <u>progressive</u> - ahead of the people around you in ideas

187. <u>prudish</u> - somewhat strict in terms of sex

188. <u>quarrelsome</u> - argue over just about everything

189. <u>queer</u> - strange, unusual

190. <u>quick</u> - sharp, fast to catch on

191. <u>quiet</u> - keep to yourself, don't say much

192. <u>quitting</u> - when things get tough there is no sense in going on

193. <u>rational</u> - think things through, figure them out, keep your cool

194. <u>rattlebrained</u> - can't keep things straight, get things mixed up

195. <u>realistic</u> - don't expect things that can't happen

196. <u>reasonable</u> - will listen to others and try to cooperate whenever possible

197. <u>rebellious</u> - like to mess everything up, throw people out

198. <u>reckless</u> - not careful, do things hastily

199. <u>reflective</u> - like to sit down and think things through

200. <u>relaxed</u> - not up tight, take things easy

201. <u>reliable</u> - can be counted on

202. <u>resentful</u> - don't **like things** that have been done to you

203. <u>reserved</u> - hold back, don't jump into things

204. <u>resourceful</u> - can find things you need to get things done

205. <u>responsible</u> - do the things you are expected to do

206. <u>restless</u> - can't sit still, have to keep going

207. <u>retiring</u> - withdraw from others, reserved, shy

208. <u>rigid</u> - unyielding, don't bend

209. <u>robust</u> - strong and healthy, strongly built

210. <u>rude</u> - cut people down

211. <u>sarcastic</u> - make harsh and bitter remarks about others

212. <u>self-centered</u> - think mainly of yourself

213. <u>self-confident</u> - know you can do whatever you try

214. <u>self-controlled</u> - keep ahold of yourself

215. <u>self-denying</u> - can put off things you want until later

216. <u>self-pitying</u> - feel sorry for yourself

217. <u>self-punishing</u> - down on yourself, blame yourself for things

218. <u>self-seeking</u> - try to get things for yourself, get ahead

219. <u>selfish</u> - won't give up your things to others

220. <u>sensitive</u> - very aware of the feelings of others, your feelings are hurt easily

221. <u>sentimental</u> - things touch you, you get choked up easily

222. <u>serious</u> - don't laugh at things much

223. <u>severe</u> - harsh, serious, causing distress because of extreme conditions

224. <u>sexy</u> - turn people on sexually

225. <u>shallow</u> - not many interests, half-learned

226. <u>sharp-witted</u> - quick, good comments

227. <u>shiftless</u> - good for nothing

228. <u>show-off</u> - like to do things that make people look at you

229. <u>shrewd</u> - clever, smart, know how to get things

230. shy - don't like to meet people or be the center of attention

231. silent - quiet, don't say much

232. simple - not very complicated, easy to understand

233. sincere - believe and mean what you say

234. slipshod - shoddy, sloppy, not well done

235. slow - not very quick, lag behind

236. sly - tricky, sneaky, do things in a clever manner

237. smug - self satisfied, proudly pleased with what you have done

238. snobbish - superior, sort of look down on others because they're inferior

239. sociable - friendly, accessible, enjoy getting along well with others

240. softhearted - tender hearted, kind toward others, help them

241. sophisticated - practical, wise in the ways of the world

242. spendthrift - really go through your money

243. spineless - don't stand up for yourself

244. spontaneous - do things on the spur of the moment

245. spunky - not afraid to jump in, hang in there

246. stable - don't get upset, stay strong, a steadying influence

247. steady - firm, solid, don't waver

248. stern - strict, don't let people change

249. stingy - don't like to spend your money, give up things

250. stolid - not easily moved or stirred mentally, don't show emotion

251. strong - can carry others through their problems

252. stubborn - bull-headed, keep pushing your own ideas, do things your own way

253. submissive - let people push you around, you are a doormat

254. suggestible - you influence easily, change your mind

255. sulky - pouting, stay away by yourself over in a corner

256. superstitious - believe that certain things cause bad luck

257. suspicious - you think people are after you in some way

258. sympathetic - you have feelings for others, understand their feelings

259. tactful - you know how to say things to smooth them over

260. tactless - you say what you think, sometimes hurting people

261. talkative - you express yourself continuously, keep on talking, never shut up

262. <u>temperamental</u> - you get upset over little things, get moody and angry

263. <u>tense</u> - up tight, ready to blow up

264. <u>thankless</u> - you don't thank people for helping you

265. <u>thorough</u> - you complete your jobs carefully

266. <u>thoughtful</u> - you think of others, do things for them

267. <u>thrifty</u> - watch your money carefully, don't spend it on foolish things

268. <u>timid</u> - don't like to be the center of attention, fearful of others

269. <u>tolerant</u> - accept others who are different, can put up with others

270. <u>touchy</u> - very sensitive about some things, get upset over them

271. <u>tough</u> - nobody messes with you, you're a man

272. <u>trusting</u> - you believe what people tell you

273. <u>unaffected</u> - a real person, don't try to impress people

274. <u>unambitious</u> - not driving hard to get ahead, really don't care

275. <u>unassuming</u> - modest, simple, don't put on a show

276. <u>unconventional</u> - do things differently, not the same as other people

277. <u>undependable</u> - can't be relied upon, people can't count on you

278. <u>understanding</u> - you know why people do things, don't get upset at them

279. <u>unemotional</u> - keep cool, don't cry, show anger, etc.

280. <u>unexcitable</u> - stay calm, don't get nervous or upset

281. <u>unfriendly</u> - don't really like people, try to keep them away

282. <u>uninhibited</u> - not afraid to make a fool of yourself

283. <u>unintelligent</u> - not too bright, a little slow

284. <u>unkind</u> - cruel, will hurt  others or say bad things to them

285. <u>unrealistic</u> - want things that can't happen, that aren't practical

286. <u>unscrupulous</u> - sneaky, try to take unfair advantage of others

287. <u>unselfish</u> - willing to give up your things to others willingly

288. <u>unstable</u> - emotional, lose your cool, all upset inside

289. <u>vindictive</u> - would like to get even with people

290. <u>versatile</u> - can do many things, talented

291. <u>warm</u> - like to show affection toward others

292. <u>wary</u> - try to be careful, don't trust people too far

293. <u>weak</u> - don't stand up for yourself

294. <u>whiny</u> - complain a lot

295. <u>wholesome</u> - a good solid person

296. <u>wise</u> - smart, intelligent, know how to do things

297. <u>withdrawn</u> - stay away from others, by yourself

298. <u>witty</u> - bright and funny, crack alot of jokes

299. <u>worrying</u> - concerned that things aren't going to go right

300. <u>zany</u> - crazy, do strange and wild things

*Adjectives reprinted by permission of Consulting Psychologists' Press.


APPENDIX  F

RULES TO BE FOLLOWED BY BOYS IN ONE COTTAGE

PINE COTTAGE RULES


1. Students not permitted behind double doors without permission.

2. One student in bathroom at one time.

3. No smoking past double doors.

4. No smoking in rooms.

5. Students must wear proper dress to school and church.

6. Students not permitted in another's room.

7. Fighting and horseplay not allowed.

8. Profanity not allowed.

9. Student's rooms must be kept clean and orderly.

10. Students must respect all staff at all times.

11. Students must address staff as Mr.

12. Details are to be done without being reminded.

13. Students must maintain a good attitude in school.

14. Students are to keep hygiene together--showers, shaves, etc.

15. Students must respect state property.

16. Students must wear proper dress in dining area.

17. Students caught stealing will be punished.

18. Possession of contraband not allowed, such as weapons, drugs, matches, lighters, glass jars or bottles, alcohol, obscene material, black and white, heavy grease, etc.

19. Overnight restrictions from school will result in weekend restrictions.

20. Pre-Release students getting more than two restrictions per month from the school area will have a disciplinary meeting held on him for removal of Red Badge.

21. Any type of restrictions will not be permitted to have radios in rooms.

APPENDIX  G

VARIABLES DIFFERENTIATING RUNAWAYS
FROM NON-RUNAWAYS*

| VARIABLE | SIGNIFICANCE LEVEL |
|---|---|
| 1. Race | .01 |
| 2. Drugs and Alcohol Abuse | .01 |
| 3. "R" and "E" suffix | .05 |
| 4. Runaway pattern in other institutions | .001 |
| 5. Months at O Y C institutions | .02 |
| 6. Home Visits | .001 |
| 7. Disciplinary meetings | .05 |
| 8. Homosexual behavior | .05 |
| 9. Completed year in school | .01 |
| 10. Average grade in school | .01 |
| 11. Outcome on parole | .001 |

*Statistical tests used included chi-square and analysis of variance.

APPENDIX  H

OFFENSE CLASSIFICATION BY
SERIOUS, MODERATE, OR SLIGHT

The materials in this section have been adapted from a previous study
by Reckless and Dinitz.  The original classification by these authors is
listed and then followed by other offenses and descriptions of offenses
unique to this study and classified by this author.

SERIOUS OFFENSES:  Police contacts rated as serious by the Reckless

Classification.  This rating includes any offense normally considered

a Felony or Part I crime.

Reckless Classification

Aggravated assault                      Molesting
Armed robbery                           Murder
Arson                                   Purse snatching
Assault and battery                     Receiving and concealing
                                          stolen property
Assault with a deadly weapon            Theft from the mail
Auto theft                              Unarmed robbery
Breaking and entering                   Vandalism
Burglary                                Sodomy
Escape from custody                     Embezzlement
Felonious assault                       Rape
Forgery, fraud                          Grand larceny
Hit and run                             Housebreaking
Influencing a minor

Specific offense description in institutional sample also classified as serious.

Attempted rape                          Breaking into coke machine
Attempted assault                       Vending machine theft
Molesting younger sisters               Parking meter theft
Oral sodomy                             Injury to person
Assault with knife                      Unlawful entering and stealing
Driving stolen car                      Physical assault on girl
High speed auto chase                   Assaultive behavior
Assault police officer                  Bastardy
Chase man with knife                    Chase boys with loaded shotgun
Assault on teacher                      Sexual & assaultous behavior
Striking school teacher                 Boat theft
Theft from person                       Unlawful entry
Cutting episode                         Helping girl get gun--who com-
                                          mitted suicide
Threaten neighbors, throw knife
  at father (incorrigible)

MODERATE OFFENSES:  Police contacts rated as moderate by Reckless Classifica-

tion.  This rating includes any offense which does not clearly fit into

the Serious or Slight offense category.

Reckless Classification

| | |
|---|---|
| Any serious offense attempted or investigated | Attempted arson |
| Carrying a concealed weapon | Obscene literature |
| Impersonating a police officer or a member of the armed forces | Glue sniffing |
| Malicious destruction of property | Gasoline |
| Petit larceny | Shoplifting |
| Riding in a stolen car | Resisting arrest |
| Starting a careless fire | Illicit sex with consent |
| Car tampering or stripping | |

Specific offense descriptions in institutional sample also classified as moderate.

| | |
|---|---|
| Attempted arson | Soliciting for prostitute |
| Theft | Shoplifting |
| Stealing | Attempted suicide |
| Bicycle theft | Auto trespass |
| Auto larceny | Auto looting |
| Riding in stolen car | Sniffing gasoline, glue |
| Borrowing car without permission | Extortion |
| Abduction for immoral purposes | Extortion from children |
| Drunkenness, strike police | Homosexuality |
| Rock throwing episode | Sex offense with young girl |
| Harboring 2-14 year old girls (runaway) | Sex with sister, with 11 year old |
| | Borrow motorbike without permission |

SLIGHT OFFENSES:  Police contacts rated as slight by Reckless Classification.

These offenses are usually considered as minor misdemeanors or Part 2

crimes.

| | |
|---|---|
| Curfew violation | Discharging firearms in city limits, BB gun |
| Disorderly conduct | |
| Fighting | False fire alarm, false report |
| Improper language | Incorrigibility |
| Intoxication | Possession of fireworks |
| Pointing firearms | Menacing threats |
| Obstructing justice | Suspicious person |
| Throwing missiles | Truancy from home |
| Swimming in an unguarded area | Violating probation |
| Trespassing | Delinquency |
| Truancy from school | Riding double on a bicycle |
| Gambling | Misrepresentation of minor status |
| Indecent exposure | Unlawful assembly |
| Failure to appear in court | |
| Shooting pool | |

Specific offense description in institutional sample also classified as slight.

| | |
|---|---|
| Parole violation | Threat to kill mother |
| Sex offense | Threat to kill teacher |
| Exhibitionism | Minor sex offense |
| Window peeping | Overt sex behavior |
| Immorality | Note requesting sex |
| Gave incorrect age for driver's license | |

APPENDIX I

RANK ORDERING OF GOUGH ADJECTIVE
CHECKLIST BY SPECIAL DESIGNATION

| Scales | R | E | NONE | BOTH |
|---|---|---|---|---|
| Defensiveness | 3 | 2 | 4 | 1 |
| Self-confidence | 3 | 2 | 4 | 1 |
| Self-control | 4 | 3 | 2 | 1 |
| Lability | 4 | 3 | 2 | 1 |
| Personal Adjustment | 3 | 1 | 4 | 2 |
| Achievement | 3 | 1 | 4 | 2 |
| Dominance | 3 | 1 | 4 | 2 |
| Endurance | 3 | 1 | 4 | 2 |
| Order | 3 | 1 | 4 | 2 |
| Intraception | 3 | 2 | 4 | 1 |
| Nurturance | 3 | 1 | 4 | 2 |
| Affiliation | 3 | 2 | 4 | 1 |
| Heterosexuality | 3 | 2 | 4 | 1 |
| Exhibition | 3 | 4 | 1 | 2 |
| Autonomy | 2 | 3 | 1 | 4 |
| Aggression | 2 | 4 | 3 | 1 |
| Change | 2 | 4 | 3 | 1 |
| Succorance | 2 | 4 | 3 | 1 |
| Abasement | 2 | 4 | 3 | 1 |
| Deference | 4 | 2 | 3 | 1 |
| Counsel Readiness | 2 | 3 | 1 | 4 |

## APPENDIX J

### TYPOLOGY BY OTHER DEMOGRAPHIC, CRIMINAL HISTORY AND EXPLOITATION DATA

#### TABLE 1

#### TYPOLOGY BY RACE

|                | Blacks | Whites | Total |
|----------------|--------|--------|-------|
| Exploiters     | 19     | 9      | 28    |
| Give & Takes   | 32     | 18     | 50    |
| Independents   | 7      | 8      | 15    |
| Sometimes Boys | 12     | 19     | 31    |
| Victims        | 6      | 19     | 25    |
| TOTAL          | 76     | 73     | 149   |

Degrees of Freedom 4        $x^2 = 15.8448$        $P = .01$

#### TABLE 2

#### TYPOLOGY BY I.Q.

| TYPOLOGY       | MEAN  | STANDARD DEVIATION | N   |
|----------------|-------|--------------------|-----|
| Exploiters     | 88.75 | 10.50              | 28  |
| Give and Takes | 86.36 | 11.84              | 50  |
| Independents   | 94.33 | 12.86              | 15  |
| Sometimes Boys | 92.32 | 11.85              | 31  |
| Victims        | 93.16 | 14.50              | 25  |
|                | 89.99 | 12.44              | 149 |

Between degrees of freedom 4          $F = 2.3556$

Within degrees of freedom 144          $P = NS$

TYPOLOGY BY OTHER DEMOGRAPHIC,
CRIMINAL HISTORY AND EXPLOITATION DATA

TABLE 3

TYPOLOGY BY SERIOUSNESS OF OFFENSE
LEADING TO PRESENT COMMITMENT

|  | A Exploiters | B Give&Takes | C Independents | D Sometimes Boys | E Victims | N |
|---|---|---|---|---|---|---|
| Serious | 17 | 33 | 9 | 19 | 13 | 96 |
| Moderate | 4 | 7 | 2 | 8 | 2 | 23 |
| Slight | 3 | 8 | 3 | 4 | 1 | 19 |
|  | 28 | 49 | 15 | 31 | 24 | 147 |

TABLE 4

TYPOLOGY BY SPECIAL DESIGNATION

|  | A Exploiters | B Give&Takes | C Independents | D Sometimes Boys | E Victims | N | % |
|---|---|---|---|---|---|---|---|
| R | 15 | 22 | 8 | 16 | 14 | 75 | 50.3 |
| E | 1 | 12 | 2 | 4 | 2 | 23 | 15.4 |
| NONE | 11 | 13 | 5 | 9 | 7 | 45 | 30.2 |
| BOTH | 1 | 3 | 0 | 2 | 0 | 6 | 4.0 |
|  | 28 | 50 | 15 | 31 | 25 | 149 | 100% |

APPENDIX K

TABLE ___1___

GOUGH ADJECTIVE CHECKLIST AND
DOES BOY EXPLOIT SEXUALLY

|  | NO N=124 | YES N=25 | TOTAL MEAN | F | P |
|---|---|---|---|---|---|
| Defensiveness | 24.071 | 23.174 | 23.919 | 0.0981 | NS |
| Self-confidence | 36.696 | 36.087 | 36.593 | 0.0860 | NS |
| Self-control | 30.393 | 30.391 | 30.393 | 0.0007 | NS |
| Lability | 38.286 | 38.826 | 38.378 | 0.0447 | NS |
| Personal Adj. | 20.036 | 19.783 | 19.993 | 0.0093 | NS |
| Achievement | 21.848 | 22.304 | 21.926 | 0.0464 | NS |
| Dominance | 20.268 | 20.391 | 20.289 | 0.0044 | NS |
| Endurance | 26.946 | 26.435 | 26.859 | 0.0561 | NS |
| Order | 29.902 | 29.391 | 29.815 | 0.0431 | NS |
| Intraception | 13.152 | 13.261 | 13.170 | 0.0011 | NS |
| Nurturance | 11.571 | 11.043 | 11.481 | 0.0291 | NS |
| Affiliation | 21.125 | 20.522 | 2Г.022 | 0.0325 | NS |
| Heterosexuality | 23.241 | 23.304 | 23.252 | 0.0011 | NS |
| Exhibition | 50.714 | 49.957 | 50.585 | 0.2323 | NS |
| Autonomy | 59.455 | 58.000 | 59.207 | 0.4050 | NS |
| Aggression | 69.920 | 69.783 | 69.896 | 0.0034 | NS |
| Change | 36.036 | 37.304 | 36.252 | 0.5482 | NS |
| Succorance | 70.893 | 71.870 | 71.059 | 0.3501 | NS |
| Abasement | 59.795 | 62.174 | 60.200 | 2.4240 | NS |
| Deference | 35.313 | 37.000 | 35.600 | 0.5735 | NS |
| Couns. Readiness | 70.571 | 71.261 | 70.689 | 0.1829 | NS |

Between degrees of freedom    1

Within degrees of freedom    133

TABLE    2

GOUGH ADJECTIVE CHECKLIST
BY HOW LEANED ON

| GOUGH SCALES | NOT AT ALL N = 39 | ITEMS N=81 | SEX N=15 | TOTAL MEAN | F | P |
|---|---|---|---|---|---|---|
| Defensiveness | 22.949 | 22.802 | 32.467 | 23.919 | 4.1426 | .05 |
| Self-confidence | 35.615 | 35.926 | 42.733 | 36.593 | 4.1076 | .05 |
| Self-control | 28.385 | 30.309 | 36.067 | 30.393 | 2.9682 | NS |
| Lability | 39.385 | 37.099 | 42.667 | 38.378 | 1.8337 | NS |
| Personal Adj. | 18.974 | 18.901 | 28.533 | 19.993 | 4.9382 | .01 |
| Achievement | 20.256 | 20.975 | 31.400 | 21.926 | 10.1691 | .01 |
| Dominance | 19.154 | 19.185 | 29.200 | 20.289 | 10.8551 | .01 |
| Endurance | 25.744 | 25.790 | 35.533 | 26.859 | 7.8553 | .01 |
| Order | 28.000 | 28.914 | 39.400 | 29.815 | 7.4542 | .01 |
| Intraception | 11.128 | 12.235 | 23.533 | 13.170 | 4.5912 | .05 |
| Nurturance | 10.333 | 10.519 | 19.667 | 11.481 | 3.2202 | .05 |
| Affiliation | 19.538 | 20.062 | 30.067 | 21.022 | 3.3768 | .05 |
| Heterosexuality | 24.436 | 21.444 | 29.933 | 23.252 | 4.0515 | .05 |
| Exhibition | 51.333 | 50.284 | 50.267 | 50.585 | 0.3221 | NS |
| Autonomy | 61.538 | 59.012 | 54.200 | 59.207 | 3.0651 | NS |
| Aggression | 70.538 | 70.568 | 64.600 | 69.896 | 1.8939 | NS |
| Change | 36.615 | 36.259 | 35.267 | 36.252 | 0.1746 | NS |
| Succorance | 72.333 | 71.506 | 65.333 | 71.059 | 5.9103 | .01 |
| Abasement | 60.641 | 60.753 | 56.067 | 60.200 | 3.3151 | .05 |
| Deference | 34.385 | 35.370 | 40.000 | 35.600 | 1.8865 | NS |
| Couns. Readiness | 72.128 | 71.198 | 64.200 | 70.689 | 8.2509 | .01 |

Between degrees of freedom    2

Within degrees of freedom   132

TABLE  3

MEAN OF EXPLOITATION CHECKS
BY RACE

| RACE | MEAN | N |
|------|------|---|
| Black | 2.829 | 76 |
| White | 5.164 | 73 |

Between degrees of freedom 1          F = 11.6581      P = .01

Within degrees of freedom 147


TABLE  4

MEAN OF EXPLOITATION CHECKS
BY SERIOUSNESS OF OFFENSES LEADING
TO PRESENT COMMITMENT

| SERIOUSNESS OF OFFENSE | MEAN | N |
|------------------------|------|---|
| Serious | 4.05 | 96 |
| Moderate | 3.57 | 23 |
| Slight | 3.42 | 19 |

TABLE   5

MEAN OF EXPLOITATION CHECKS
BY HOW LEANED ON

| HOW LEANED ON | MEAN | N |
|---|---|---|
| Not at all | 0.00 | 42 |
| Items | 4.35 | 91 |
| Sex | 12.25 | 16 |

APPENDIX L

TOTAL NUMBER OF EXPLOITATION CHECKS
BY DEMOGRAPHIC, PHYSICAL, AND
CRIMINAL HISTORY DATA

TABLE   1

MEAN OF EXPLOITATION CHECKS
BY SPECIAL DESIGNATION

| DESIGNATION | MEAN | N |
|---|---|---|
| R | 4.200 | 75 |
| E | 5.000 | 23 |
| NONE | 3.133 | 45 |
| BOTH | 3.500 | 6 |
|  | 3.9732 | 149 |

Between degrees of freedom 3      F = 1.0943      P = NS

Within degrees of freedom 145

TABLE   2

MEAN OF EXPLOITATION CHECKS
BY COTTAGE

| COTTAGES | MEAN | N |
|----------|------|---|
| Cottage A | 3.952 | 21 |
| Cottage B | 1.375 | 16 |
| Cottage C | 3.643 | 14 |
| Cottage D | 3.583 | 17 |
| Cottage E | 3.450 | 20 |
| Cottage F | 7.235 | 17 |
| Cottage G | 3.500 | 24 |
| Cottage H | 4.950 | 20 |
| | 3.9732 | 149 |

Between degrees of freedom  7          $F = 2.6645$
Within degrees of freedom 141         $P = .01$


APPENDIX M


TABLE   1

TYPOLOGY BY MACHOVER
ON SEXUAL IDENTIFICATION

| | MALE | FEMALE | UNDECIDED |
|--|------|--------|-----------|
| EXPLOITERS | 14 | 2 | 9 |
| GIVE & TAKES | 21 | 4 | 17 |
| INDEPENDENTS | 10 | 1 | 2 |
| SOMETIMES BOYS | 12 | 2 | 10 |
| VICTIMS | 12 | 4 | 6 |

TABLE   2

RANK ORDERING OF MACHOVER SCALES

| | | | | |
|---|---|---|---|---|
| Aggression | 5 | 2 | 4 | 3 | 1 |
| Inferiority | 3 | 1 | 5 | 2 | 4 |
| Maladjustment | 5 | 3 | 4 | 1 | 2 |
| Anxiety | 4 | 3 | 5 | 1 | 2 |

TABLE   3

RACE BY GOUGH ADJECTIVE CHECKLIST

| SCALE | RACE | | F | P |
| | BLACK | WHITE | | |
|---|---|---|---|---|
| Defensiveness | 24.855 | 22.939 | 0.7931 | NS |
| Self-confidence | 36.290 | 36.909 | 0.1580 | NS |
| Self-control | 31.174 | 29.576 | 0.7754 | NS |
| Lability | 38.768 | 37.970 | 0.1723 | NS |
| Personal Adjustment | 20.928 | 19.015 | 0.9347 | NS |
| Achievement | 21.435 | 22.439 | 0.3973 | NS |
| Dominance | 19.609 | 21.000 | 0.9228 | NS |
| Endurance | 27.507 | 26.182 | 0.6647 | NS |
| Order | 30.130 | 29.485 | 0.1219 | NS |
| Intraception | 14.159 | 12.136 | 0.6507 | NS |
| Nurturance | 12.783 | 10.121 | 1.3196 | NS |

| | | | |
|---|---|---|---|
| Affiliation | 22.087 | 19.909 | 0.7508 | NS |
| Heterosexuality | 23.072 | 23.439 | 0.0358 | NS |
| Exhibition | 50.391 | 50.788 | 0.1143 | NS |
| Autonomy | 59.333 | 59.076 | 0.0237 | NS |
| Aggression | 68.739 | 71.106 | 1.5003 | NS |
| Charge | 36.681 | 35.803 | 0.4643 | NS |
| Succorance | 71.072 | 71.045 | 0.0096 | NS |
| Abasement | 61.246 | 59.106 | 3.4951 | NS |
| Deference | 35.681 | 35.515 | 0.0111 | NS |
| Counsel. Readiness | 71.391 | 69.955 | 1.4195 | NS |

Between degrees of freedom      1
Within degrees of freedom     134                    N = 135


APPENDIX N

RACE BY DEMOGRAPHIC, PHYSICAL AND CRIMINAL
HISTORY DATA, AND GOUGH ADJECTIVE
CHECKLIST


TABLE 1

I.Q. BY RACE

| RACE | N | I.Q. | STANDARD DEVIATION |
|---|---|---|---|
| Black | 76 | 85.868 | 10.201 |
| White | 73 | 94.288 | 13.145 |

Between degrees of freedom    1          F = 19.1693

Within degrees of freedom   147          P =    .01

TABLE 2

RACE BY DEMOGRAPHIC, PHYSICAL
AND CRIMINAL HISTORY DATA

| RACE | AGE AT AD-MISSION | WEIGHT | HEIGHT | NO. OF PRE-VIOUS COM-MITMENTS | NO. OF PRE-VIOUS OFFENSES |
|------|-------------------|--------|--------|-------------------------------|---------------------------|
| Black | 16.803 | 151.842 | 68.158 | 1.408 | 4.34 |
| White | 17.014 | 153.151 | 67.918 | 1.534 | 4.90 |
| F = | 1.8975 | 0.0585 | 0.3557 | 0.3357 | 1.3995 |

Between degrees of freedom    1

Within degrees of freedom   147

# INDEX OF NAMES

# INDEX OF SUBJECTS

NOTES

# NOTES